War Time Preaching and Teaching

War Time Preaching and Teaching

By

Jeffrey Jon Richards

War Time Preaching and Teaching, by Jeffrey Jon Richards

This book first published 2009

Cambridge Scholars Publishing

12 Back Chapman Street, Newcastle upon Tyne, NE6 2XX, UK

British Library Cataloguing in Publication Data
A catalogue record for this book is available from the British Library

Copyright © 2009 by Jeffrey Jon Richards

All rights for this book reserved. No part of this book may be reproduced, stored in a retrieval system, or transmitted, in any form or by any means, electronic, mechanical, photocopying, recording or otherwise, without the prior permission of the copyright owner.

ISBN (10): 1-4438-1255-2, ISBN (13): 978-1-4438-1255-9

Dedicated to two wonderful daughters

**Lauren Meredith Richards Rosenfarb
and
Emily Katherine Richards**

TABLE OF CONTENTS

Preface ix

Introduction 1
   A. Traditional Views of Bultmann and Bonhoeffer
   B. Towards an Interpretation of the Relationship of Bultmann
      and Bonhoeffer

Chapter One 25
Rudolf Bultmann's Hermeneutics and His Sermons
   A. Introduction
   B. Hermeneutical Methodology
   C. Sermonic Exposition
   D. Hermeneutics and Preaching: Conclusion

Chapter Two 121
Dietrich Bonhoeffer's Practical Exegesis and His Hermeneutics
   A. Introduction
   B. Bonhoeffer's Method
   C. Reconstruction of Bonhoeffer's Hermeneutical Principles
   D. View of the Prison Letters and the Hermeneutical Program
      Formulated within the Prison Cell

Chapter Three 195
Comparison
   A. Introduction
   B. Bultmann
   C. Bonhoeffer
   D. Bultmann and Bonhoeffer: Summary

Bibliography 217

Index 223

PREFACE

Both Bultmann and Bonhoeffer have interested me for many years, and eventually the prospect of writing concerning their method of interpreting and presenting the Scriptures nurtured and became an adventure. Both theologians are somewhat misunderstood, and it seems they are either totally accepted or rejected, depending in many instances upon one's personal understanding of the method of biblical interpretation. This work attempts to objectively view their methods and how they expressed their research in their writings, preaching and teaching. Both concluded that the presenting of the Gospel in a relevant manner is the ultimate message for humankind today.

Bultmann and Bonhoeffer both lived during a most challenging period of world history, and they proclaimed the Gospel in a captivating manner. Certainly the times in which we live today call for those who possess a similar commitment.

INTRODUCTION

A. Traditional Views of Bonhoeffer and Bultmann

The typical caricature of Dietrich Bonhoeffer seemingly is either that of a splendid theologian who had a gift for coining revolutionary theological phrases or one who was able to write clear and concise letters during devastating air raids while being held prisoner by the Nazis. Many American theologians have attempted to make Bonhoeffer the source of some of the more non-orthodox theologies of the 1960s. In some instances, he seems to be almost impervious to theological classification since theologians of varied persuasions quote his words and cite his life experiences. Many American theologians, especially during the decade of the 1960s, quoted several phrases which he wrote, such as "world come of age" or "religionless Christianity." However, one aspect of this theologian's contribution which is greatly minimized is his understanding of hermeneutics and its relationship to homiletics.

Having lived only to age thirty-nine, one can only speculate what else he might have accomplished had he lived a longer life. In many measures, he lived a life of privilege as his father was a well-known psychiatrist, and all indications are that he was raised in a loving family. His father, Karl Bonhoeffer, was stern but approachable. His mother, Paula, was a caring if not somewhat doting mother to her eight children. Dietrich was strong physically as a child. His family did not encourage him to study theology, and some members thought that the life of a pastor would leave him endlessly bored.

Bonhoeffer did not live in a theological desert; in fact, the converse was the situation. He came under the influence of Germany's leading theologians, and he was heir to many diverse theological currents peculiar to Europe between World War II. Much of the theology Bonhoeffer acquired, he reworked; thus, it bore his personality, features, and thought. However, one can always see upon closer inspection the vestige of his mentors such as Barth, Harnack, Heidegger, Seeberg, and Schlatter.[1]

---

[1] Eberhard Bethge, *Dietrich Bonhoeffer: A Biography* (Minneapolis: Fortress Press, 2000), 53-54, 116. Though Bonhoeffer disagreed with Schlatter over the latter's support of National Socialism, Bohoeffer held Schlatter in high esteem, and

How should one sift through the thoughts and influences of Bonhoeffer? In Germany the literature concerning Bonhoeffer comprises basically two schools. The first is that of Gerhard Ebeling and his endeavor to search through the implications of the *Letters and Papers from Prison*. The second, usually credited to Eberhard Bethge, sees Christology as the *Leitmotiv*. In America there seemingly is a division between those who see Bonhoeffer's work as ecclesiological and others who believe the theme of discipleship is more prevalent.[2] Of course, there are innumerable approaches and themes which have not been utilized. This work will explore the connection between Bultmann's and Bonhoeffer's hermeneutical and homiletical systems.

The primary supposition of this book is that for Bultmann exegesis leads to preaching and for Bonhoeffer preaching leads to exegesis. Each had a vital concern for authentic communication.

Rudolf Bultmann died in the summer of 1976, a short period of time after the death of Martin Heidegger.[3] The result of his teaching at Marburg for thirty years and extensive work after his retirement assured the continuing impact of his scholarship.

Bultmann was born at Wiefelstede, Oldenburg, on August 20, 1884. He was a student at Marburg and like Bonhoeffer, he studied at both Tübingen and Berlin. He held teaching positions at both Breslau and Giessen before returning to Marburg as a professor of New Testament in 1921. Retiring in 1951, Bultmann had already gained international attention as a scholar. He gave the Shaffer Lectures at Yale in 1951 and the Gifford Lectures in Edinburgh University in 1955.

---

he seemingly was the only professor from his time of studies in Tübingen who had a lasting impression on him. Bultmann also studied with Schlatter during his three terms as a student at Tübingen. Bethge specifically states that Bonhoeffer identified with the scholarship that he read in Bultmann. Cf. Martin Evang, *Rudolf Bultmann in seiner Frühzeit* (Tübingen, J. C. B. Mohr (Paul Siebeck, 1988), 8-21. Evang lists all the courses which Bultmann studied as a student in Tübingen, Berlin and Marburg Universities.
[2] Dallas M. Roark, *Dietrich Bonhoeffer* (Waco: Word Books, 1972). 28-9.
[3] Some claim the actual date of "the beginning of the end" came in 1954 with Ernst Käsemann's critique, "Das Problem des historischen Jesus," *Zeitschrift für Theologie und Kirche* 51 (1954) : 125 ff. Cf. Schubert Ogden, "The Significance of Rudolf Bultmann for Contemporary Theology" in *The Theology of Rudolf Bultmann*, ed., Charles W. Kegley (New York: Harper and Row, 1966), 117-26.

His father, Arthur Bultmann, was an Evangelical-Lutheran pastor.[4] His maternal grandfather was a pastor in the pietistic tradition, while his paternal grandfather was a missionary to Africa. Rudolf married in 1916, and he had two daughters.

Bultmann, claimed that his theology had no relationship to the chaos produced by World War I:

> So I do not believe that the war has influenced my theology.... My view is that if anyone is looking for the genesis of our theology he will find that internal discussion with the theologies of our teachers play an incomparably greater role than the impact of the war or reading Dostoevsky.[5]

Bultmann is greatly indebted to one of his teachers, Wilhelm Herrmann. But it was Heidegger who primarily influenced Bultmann.[6]

Bultmann was a very systematic and scientific theologian and New Testament scholar who in a sense saw himself as a modern-day Luther who strongly disagreed with nineteenth-century liberalism. His desire was to revive the Lutheran doctrine of *sola fides,* and Bultmann believed this emphasis to be the means to presenting the New Testament in order to present a message of meaning for modern humankind. Günther Bornkamm believes that "Bultmann cannot accept any 'objective' revelatory realm of being that can be recognized, established, and understood in and by itself prior to its relation to faith."[7]

Bultmann consistently held to the same theological position for over half a century, though there are some who claim he did not.[8] Roberts claims:

---

[4] Roger Johnson, ed., "Introduction", *Rudolf Bultmann: Interpreting Faith for the Modern Era.* Collins Liturgical Press, San Francisco, 1987), 9.

[5] Walter Schmidthals, *An Introduction to the Theology of Rudolf Bultmann,* Trans. John Bowden (Minneapolis: Augsburg Publishing House, 1968), 9-10.

[6] Eberhard Bethge, *Dietrich Bonhoeffer: A Biography.* (Minneapolis: Fortress Press, 2000), 132-133. Bethge uses the phrase "accident of locality" to refer to Bultmann and Heidegger in Marburg. Bultmann was heavily dependent upon Heidegger's philosophy and though Bonhoeffer criticized Bultmann for what he believed was overdependence on Heidegger, Bonhoeffer quoted extensively the latter in his *Act and Being.*

[7] Gunther Bornkamm, "The Theology of Rudolf Bultmann," in *The Theology of Rudolf Bultmann,* ed., C. W. Kegley (New York: Harper and Row, 1966), 16.

[8] Roberts, states: "... as far as I can tell, Bultmann has not changed his mind on any issue of importance since the early 1920's." Robert C. Roberts, *Rudolf Bultmann's Theology: A Critical Interpretation* (Grand Rapids: Wm. B. Eerdman's Publishing Co., 1976), 9.

"We cannot avoid the impression that this work is an extraordinary unity, exhibiting the touch of a master German thinker who knows how to hold his every thought in place by the power of a single idea."[9]

B. Towards an Interpretation of the Relationship of Bultmann and Bonhoeffer

1. Synthesis

Is it possible to correlate Bultmann's and Bonhoeffer's thought? The "Bultmannian synthesis" as expressed by Gerhard Ebeling and Ronald Gregor Smith continues to be an interpretation of Bonhoeffer's theological contribution. Woelfel cogently writes:

> Central to the Bultmann-inspired outlook on Bonhoeffer is the two-fold assumption that Bultmann has from the beginning fully and explicitly shared Bonhoeffer's intense concern for the communication of the gospel to modern secular man, and furthermore that Bonhoeffer's "dereligionizing" of biblical concepts and Bultmann's demythologizing of the New Testament are much closer together, both in intention and in execution, than Bonhoeffer imagined.[10]

Essentially Woelfel is stating this attempt for a synthesis between Bultmann and Bonhoeffer encompasses the areas of hermeneutics and homiletics. Bethge gives another understanding of the connection between Bultmann and Bonhoeffer:

> The interest of the existential interpretation lies clearly with the individual, which encourages a sterility toward the kinds of questions that transcend the individual. Because of this it has been noted that there is a connection between Bultmann's theology and the pietistic world that Bonhoeffer termed "religious."[11]

---

[9] Roberts, *Rudolf Bultmann's Theology: A Critical Interpretation*, 21.
[10] James W. Woelfel, *Bonhoeffer's Theology* (Nashville: Abington Press, 1970), 295-296.
[11] Bethge *Dietrich Bonhoeffer: A Biography* (Minneapolis: Fortress Press, 2000), 875. Cf. John deGruchy, *Introduction to Dietrich Bonhoeffer: Witness to Jesus Christ*. (Minneapolis: Fortress Press, 1988), 38. According to de Gruchy, Bonhoeffer sees religion as a genuine hindrance to genuine dependence upon Christ.

2. Difference

It is possible to compare Bultmann and Bonhoeffer in many facets of theology. This book has alluded to Woelfel's reference to a "Bultmannian syntheis." However, there are some who believe that one should not see a great similarity between these two theologians:

> Bultmann calls for an "existential" interpretation, Bonhoeffer a "nonreligious" one; but it is by no means self-evident that the two theologians mean the same thing. Bultmann thinks in the anthropological terms of man's self-understanding, Bonhoeffer in the "theanthropological" terms of the new reality eternally uniting God and the world in Jesus Christ. For Bultmann "demythologizing" involves the academic question of hermeneutics, namely, the question of interpreting the Bible by means of "existentials" of Heidegger's existentialist philosophy in order to disclose the biblical understanding of human existence. On the other hand, Bonhoeffer's "dereligionizing" is concerned not only with the hermeneutical question, but with the question of existence of the church itself . . . . For Bonhoeffer, Bultmann's interpretation is too introspective and individualistic, and thus too religious.[12]

Dumas expresses many interesting insights into the thought of Bultmann and Bonhoeffer. He claims that Bultmann is more intellectual; Bonhoeffer conversely is a person of action in both a spiritual and political sense. Bultmann emphasizes the free gift of salvation, whereas Bonhoeffer is more interested in the problem of worldly responsibility.[13] Dumas claims: "Just as Bultmann put demythologization at the service of existential interpretation, Bonhoeffer puts the 'nonreligious interpretation of Christianity' at the service of his theological method, which is to speak of God in the midst of man's everyday life in the world."[14]

However, Dumas believes there is a fundamental difference in the two. Bultmann operates within the structure of transcendental Kantianism; thus, miracles are excluded. Bonhoeffer, though, operates within an incarnational Hegelianism which emphasizes the value of the miraculous.[15]

Perhaps Palmer offers a helpful insight:

---

[12] John D. Godsey, *The Theology of Dietrich Bonhoeffer* (Philadelphia: The Westminster Press, 1958), 278-79.
[13] Andre Dumas, *Dietrich Bonhoeffer: Theologian of Reality*, trans. Robert McAfee Brown (New York: The Macmillan Co., 1968), 18-19.
[14] Ibid., 35.
[15] Ibid., 246-49.

Bonhoeffer differs from Bultmann in holding that mythology is not the problem, and existentialism is not the answer. Where Bultmann wants to replace biblical ("mythological") categories with better (existential) ones, Bonhoeffer seeks to replace traditional Christian ("religious") categories with more biblical ones. Nonreligious interpretation is more radical than demythologizing in the sense that it forswears reliance on metaphysics and inwardness, and focuses instead on God's identification with the world in Christ, culminating in the cross.[16]

3. Common Situation: Post-Liberal Theology

Like Bultmann, Bonhoeffer was a child of the German liberal heritage. His professors, however, represented a variety of theological positions; some were more liberal than others. He was indebted to such profound theologians as Ernst Troeltsch, Karl Holl, Reinhold Seeberg, Adolf Schlatter and Adolf von Harnack. It would be possible to ferret through the thought of each one of these theological giants and point to similarities between each one and Bonhoeffer, but perhaps such a venture is impractical and unwarranted. Bonhoeffer's personal passion for individualism would possibly rebuff one for such an attempt. However, Woelfel is correct in remarking:

> The lasting influence of Adolf Harnack upon his young Berlin neighbor and university student Bonhoeffer was his passion for truth and his intellectual integrity. . . . The passion for truth and intellectual honesty which Bonhoeffer learned from Harnack appears again and again in his writings. All of Bonhoeffer's writings, discussing wide-ranging topics such as church and state, war and peace, history and philosophy, as well as purely theological and exegetical themes, display a painstaking careful concern to clarify precisely the issues involved and to offer concrete solutions based on explicit premises.[17]

While not resurrecting the doctrine of *sola fides* as did Bultmann, Bonhoeffer as the latter was greatly influenced by the Lutheran tradition. Woelfel states:

> Another formative influence in Bonhoeffer's theological development was his adherence to Lutheran Christianity. He was profoundly molded by the personality and thought of Luther himself, as well as by the theological emphases and ethos of the Lutheran tradition. Bonhoeffer must always be

---

[16] Russell W. Palmer, "Demythologization and Non-Religious Interpretation: A Comparison of Bultmann and Bonhoeffer," *The Iliff Review* 31 (Spring 1974): 15.
[17] Woelfel, *Bonhoeffer's Theology*, 20.

seen within this context, for it gave to his "religionless Christianity" some of its most distinctive, not to say paradoxical and puzzling, characteristics. Many of the riddles and seeming antinomies in Bonhoeffer's prison writings can be resolved only if he is seen to the very end as a Lutheran churchman.[18]

However, one disadvantage (some believe it to be an advantage) is that all of Bonhoeffer's writings have not been retained. The corpus of Bultmann's writings are more complete. There are problems and questions in Bonhoeffer's system which remain unanswered. Godsey states:

> What does Bonhoeffer have in mind when he speaks of "natural" piety and "unconscious Christianity," which he links with the differentiation that the old Lutheran dogmaticians made between *fides directa* and *fides reflexa*? These must all remain tantalizing questions for us, but perhaps this is not a misfortune. Indeed, perhaps one of the reasons why Bonhoeffer's theology is so fascinating and stimulating is because it was cut off in the midst of a great thrust of creativity, because we do *not* have all the answers![19]

Bonhoeffer refuses to be part of a "cookie cutter" mentality. Even though a protégé of Germany's greatest liberal tradition, one is always not cognizant of the fact that Bonhoeffer felt somewhat estranged from the great nineteenth-century theologians' thought and systems. Bethge sums up cogently Bonhoeffer's feelings:

> Despite his respect for the greatness of the nineteenth century and its church father, Schleiermacher, Bonhoeffer believed that this *a priori* obscured the Reformation. He viewed Seeberg and his friends with their anthropological and theological optimism, as incapable of understanding the collapse and crisis that followed the First World War, and thereby incapable of interpreting those events to his generation. For Seeberg and others, the collapse did not give birth to a fundamental reappraisal of ideas; for them, the war had merely been an unhappy episode.[20]

Bethge states that Bonhoeffer broke with Seeberg in 1933 over the issue of the Church struggle.[21]

Bonhoeffer, then, refuses to be placed in a nice, neat theological slot. One can hardly say that he was in sympathy with the German liberal tradition. However, it is not possible to say that he was a dialectical theologian, though he did have a high regard for Karl Barth. As Barth, he

---

[18] Ibid., 72.
[19] Godsey, *The Theology of Dietrich Bonhoeffer*, 279.
[20] Bethge, *Dietrich Bonhoeffer: A Biography*, 71.
[21] Ibid., 72.

too was vitally interested in the Reformation concept of revelation. However, revelation for Bonhoeffer was inextricably connected with ecclesiology. Actually, Bonhoeffer considered the dialectical method too abstract and one that placed too much attention upon the individual.[22] It cannot be justified to merely view Bonhoeffer as just another dissenting, radical, young theologian attempting to ignore theological tradition. However, it would not be correct to state that he was void of such a temperament. Godsey claims:

> How Bonhoeffer, as an exponent of the new theology, joins the battle against "liberalism" on the left and Roman Catholicism on the right, while at the same time criticizing the new movement from within, provides an unusual introduction to the main issues facing contemporary Protestant theology.[23]

4. Post-Liberal Theology After World War I: Bultmann's Post-Liberal Theology

The issue of how to proceed in theological studies, or theological method, is of primary concern for Bultmann. Kegley writes pertaining to this topic:

> In the central claims that a new way must be discovered for interpreting the Bible and communicating its message to contemporary man, namely, that of demythologizing and existential interpretation, two now clearly defined points of view have developed. Method is at issue of both.[24]

Bultmann's methodology manifests itself in the following twofold manner: first in demythologization (*Entmythologisierung*) of the biblical message and next in expressing the existential analysis (*Daseinanalyse*) of the gospel message.[25]

Bultmann realizes that premises (*Voraussetzungen*) are crucial in the manner in which one approaches the question of method in theology. Bultmann writes:

> A comprehension – an interpretation – is, it follows, constantly oriented to a particular formulation of a question, a particular "objective." But

---

[22] Godsey, *The Theology of Dietrich Bonhoeffer,* 14-15.
[23] Ibid., 15.
[24] Charles W. Kegley, Preface to *The Theology of Rudolf Bultmann,* ed., C. W. Kegley (New York: Harper and Row, 1966), XII.
[25] Thomas C. Oden, *Radical Obedience* (Philadelphia: Westminster Press, 1964), 47.

included in this, therefore, is the fact that it is never without its own presuppositions; or, to put it more precisely, that it is governed always by a prior understanding of the subject, in accordance with which it investigates the text. The formulation of a question, and an interpretation, is possible at all only on the basis of such a prior understanding.[26]

Bultmann believes that exegesis without presuppositions is not possible: ". . . We must say that there cannot be any such thing as presuppositionless exegesis."[27] He builds his system upon the premises of the historical method for the interpretation of the New Testament; he claims, "Indeed, exegesis as the interpretation of historical texts is a part of the science of history."[28] Bultmann holds to the position that an understanding of the use of grammar and the manner in which words are constructed is highly significant, and that ". . . every text speaks in the language of its time and of its historical setting."[29] He holds to the presupposition that Scripture is similar to documents of history; thus, one must approach the study of the New Testament in a similar manner.[30]

Everything in the world operates according to the law of cause and effect: "The historical method presupposes that it is possible . . . to understand the whole historical process as a closed unity."[31] Neo-Kantianism inherently excludes the possibility of the miraculous, and God is perceived in a *deus absconditus* manner. Bultmann grounds his theology in the scientific method, and the emphasis is placed upon science. He writes: "In any case, modern science does not believe that the course of nature can be interrupted or, so to speak, perforated by supernatural power."[32]

Bultmann believes that those who lived in the New Testament era were obviously unsophisticated in terms of a scientific understanding of the

---

[26] Rudolf Bultmann, *Essays Philosophical and Theological*, Trans. James C. Grieg (New York: The Macmillan Company, 1955), 239.
[27] Rudolf Bultmann, *Existence and Faith*, Trans. Schubert Ogden (London: Hodder and Stoughton, 1960), 289. Cf. Bultmann, "Ist Voraussetzunglose Exegese Möglich?" *Theologische Zeitschrift* 13 (1957), 409-17.
[28] Bultmann, *Existence and Faith*, 291.
[29] Ibid.
[30] Reason came to be seen as superior to faith which had been emphasized during the Medieval period. Instead of *fides quae creditor*, the emphasis was placed upon *sola ratione*. Johann Salomo Semler (1725-91), a Halle professor, is usually credited with being the initiator of the historical-critical method.
[31] Bultmann, *Existence and Faith*, 291.
[32] Rudolf Bultmann, *Jesus and Mythology* (New York: Charles Scribner's Sons, 1958), 15.

cosmos, and they would readily accept the concept of the miraculous; thus, it is not necessary for the modern-day person to accept accounts in the Bible of such things as literally resurrecting from the dead, walking on water, and believing in the devil and angels. To ask people today to accept such beliefs would require a *sacrificium intellectus*. The concept of myth is that ideas which are other worldly are presented in such a manner that they appear to be part of the known world.[33]

At this point Bonhoeffer disagrees with Bultmann:

> You can't as Bultmann supposes, separate God and miracle, but you must be able to interpret and proclaim both in a "nonreligious" sense. Bultmann's approach is fundamentally still a liberal one (i.e. abridging the gospel), whereas I'm trying to think theologically.[34]

Though Bultmann holds that myth must be demythologized, he still claims that the mythological elements are needed and must not be abandoned. Edwin M. Good's explanation is helpful:

> Therefore, the angels, demons, miracles, and so forth which play such a significant role in the worldview of the New Testament, must be interpreted in terms of their contribution to the New Testament's understanding of human existence.[35]

Though the biblical view of the world is not to be accepted literally, the mythological elements therein give understanding concerning the human experience.

Bultmann believes that the Scriptures ". . . must be translated, and translation is the task of historical science."[36] Bultmann, then, attempts to remove that which he believes is unnecessary through the hermeneutical process of demythologization in order to discover the true existential meaning which is encased in the unscientific *Weltanschauung* in Scripture.[37]

---

[33] Rudolf Bultmann, "New Testament and Mythology," in *Kerygma and Myth*, ed., H.W. Bartsch, trans. R.H. Fuller (New York: Harper and Row, 1961), 10.
[34] Dietrich Bonhoeffer, *Letters and Papers from Prison*, ed. Eberhard Bethge (New York: Macmillan Publishing Co, Inc., 1978), 285.
[35] Edwin M. Good, "The Meaning of Demythologization," in *The Theology of Rudolf Bultmann*, ed., C. W. Kegley (New York: Harper and Row, 1966), 26.
[36] Bultmann, *Existence and Faith*, 292.
[37] Form criticism claims to be able to distinguish between individualized styles of writing in the Gospels. Cf. Rudolf Bultmann, *Die Geschichte der synoptischen Tradition* (Göttingen: Vandenhoeck & Ruprecht, 1921).

The issue of history was of primary concern for Bultmann.[38] In particular, he is interested in how history relates to the ultimate goal of *Daseinanalyse*. There is a connection between the interpreter of Scripture and the biblical text. Bultmann explains:

> ... the subject matter with which the text is concerned also concerns us and is a problem for us. If we approach history alive with our own problems, then it really begins to speak to us. Through discussion the past becomes alive, and in learning to know history we learn to know our present; historical knowledge is at the same time knowledge of ourselves.[39]

Bultmann considers the concept of *Vorverständnis* (preunderstanding) of the interpreter to be highly significant. He states, "Man has a *Vorverständnis* of all things, because 'deep down' he is all things, including God."[40]

Bultmann writes: "For the facts of the past become historical phenomena only as they become meaningful to a subject who stands within history and participates in it, i.e., as they speak—which they can do only to a subject who understands them."[41] Bultmann distinguished between "existential" and "existentialist." The word *existentielle* alludes to an individual's involvement with an issue at a deeply personal level, as Bultmann states, one "... participates in it with his whole existence."[42]

Wilhelm Dilthey and Neo-Hegelian thought impacted Bultmann's view of history, and he accepted the view of the distinction between *Geschichte* and *Historie*.[43] The challenges of how to interpret history he believes can be overcome by placing the emphasis upon encountering, which is inherently found within the concept of *Existentielle*. Bultmann believes, "The presupposition for understanding is the interpreter's

---

[38] "Rudolf Bultmann's Philosophy of History," in *The Theology of Rudolf Bultmann*, 51.

[39] Bultmann, *Existence and Faith*, 294.

[40] Andre Malet, *The Thought of Rudolf Bultmann*, trans. Richard Strachan (New York: Doubleday & Co., 1971), 15.

[41] Bultmann, *Essays Philosophical and Theological*, 254.

[42] Bultmann, *Existence and Faith*, 294. Cf. Roger A. Johnson, *Introduction to Rudolf Bultmann: Interpreting Faith for the Modern Era*. (Collins, San Francisco, 1987), 22. Johnson describes Bultmann's distinction between "existential" and "existentialist." The former relates to an human being experiencing his/her own existence and making choices which have significance for the future, while the latter alludes to a particular method of interpreting existence.

[43] Rudolf Bultmann, *History and Eschatology* (New York: Harper and Row Publishers, 1962), 110-137.

relationship in his life to the subject, which is directly or indirectly expressed in the text."[44]

In Bultmann's understanding, ". . . historical knowledge is never closed or definitive knowledge."[45] There is no fixed manner in which to understand the Bible since the Bible confronts one in his/her personal life situation. Bultmann says, "The *existentiell* decision out of which the interpretation ermerges cannot be passed on, but must always be realized anew."[46] Thus, to Bultmann, simply viewing and interpreting Scripture merely according to an historical view is insufficient because "always anew it will tell him who he, man, is and who God is, and he will always have to express this word in a new conceptuality."[47] Bultmann adds: "To each historical phenomenon belongs its future, a future in which alone it will appear as that which it really is . . . . For ultimately it will show itself in its very essence only when history has reached its end."[48] The following, then, are Bultmann's premises for the exegesis of biblical texts: 1. the historical-critical method is the foundation for historical research; 2. the universe is closed and operates according to cause and effect; 3. preunderstanding (*Vorverständnis*) assures that there will be an *existentielle* decision on the part of the individual; and 4. there is an incessant openness to the future since a mere historical understanding of the scriptural text is insufficient.

Malet claims that inherent within existentialist philosophy, *Dasein*, or *being*, is ultimately an expression of what is termed *ec-sistance*, which can be translated as ". . . to stand forth from oneself . . . ."[49] Thus, the person in his/her essence, the "I", can choose either for authenticity or non-authenticity. To live authentically, one must not choose the temporal, or that which is associated with the world, for to do so would be to choose the opposite of authenticity. Schubert Ogden believes:

> To be a man is to be continually confronted with the decision. . . whether to "lose" oneself in the past constituted by one's inner and outer world or rather to become the new future self that it is always being offered one to become.[50]

---

[44] Ibid., 123.
[45] Bultmann, *Existence and Faith*, 294.
[46] Ibid., 296.
[47] Ibid.
[48] Bultmann, *History and Eschatology*, 120.
[49] Malet, *The Thought of Rudolf Bultmann*, 5.
[50] Schubert Ogden, Introduction to *Existence and Faith,* by Rudolf Bultmann, 16.

Johnson claims that Bultmann's theology is based upon a fusion between Marburg Neo-Kantianism and Lutheran anthropology.[51]

It is doubtful if Bultmann would agree that there is a dualistic division in his theology. But interestingly, he states that when he reads the Scriptures he finds

> .... a curious contradiction which runs right through the New Testament. Sometimes we are told that human life is determined by cosmic forces, at others we are challenged to a decision. Side by side with the Pauline indicative stands the Pauline imperative. In short, man is sometimes regarded as a cosmic being, sometimes as an independent "I" for whom decision is a matter of life or death.[52]

Thus, Bultmann believes that since there is oppositional thought found in Scripture, it is justifiable to go beyond the Bible to enlist the enablement of existentialist philosophy which will help one to understand more fully the New Testament. Bultmann writes:

> Our task ... is to discover the hermeneutical principle by which we can understand what is said in the Bible .... In other words, the question of the "right" philosophy arises .... Our question is simply which philosophy today offers the most adequate perspective and conceptions for understanding human existence.[53]

5. Post-Liberal Theology during World War: Bonhoeffer's Post-Liberal Theology

Bonhoeffer's preoccupation with religion was intense, and one of his most famous phrases is "religionless Christianity,"[54] In 1944 he wrote: "I am gradually working on my way to the non-religious interpretation of biblical concepts."[55] To understand Bonhoeffer's concern with this issue, one must understand how he defines the word "religion." Bethge suggests that Bonhoeffer's interpretation of the word encompasses the following elements: metaphysics, individualism, partiality, privilege, *deus ex machina*, tutelage, guardianship and dispensability.[56] Perhaps these factors

---

[51] Roger A. Johnson, *The Origins of Demythologization*, (Leiden: E. J. Brill, 1974), 86.
[52] Rudolf Bultmann, "New Testament and Mythology," in *Kerygma and Myth*, ed. H.W. Bartsch, Trans. R.H. Fuller (New York: Harper and Row, 1961), 11-12.
[53] Bultmann, *Jesus Christ and Mythology*, 54-55.
[54] Bethge, *Dietrich Bonhoeffer*, pp. 871-79.
[55] Bonhoeffer, *Letters and Papers from Prison*, 359.
[56] Bethge, *Dietrich Bonhoeffer*, 872-878.

can be summarized by stating that religion has become egocentric, "I" centered instead of "other" orientated. However, Dumas sees its as meaning "pretense."[57]

Bethge comments upon these self-centered features of religion:

> We may ask whether such characteristics must necessarily be features of "religion." Bonhoeffer considered them to be actually present, and believed that religion, with these characteristics, had become a western phenomenon, thus limiting the challenge and the nature of Jesus to a very specific direction. But this direction leads us into dead ends and should be abandoned [58]

How does this relate to his concept of "religionless Christianity"? Bethge claims that this is not a good English translation and the phrase has done some injustice to Bonhoeffer. In Coventry Cathedral on October 30, 1967, Bethge claimed: "The isolated use and handing down of the famous term, 'religionless Christianity' has made Bonhoeffer the champion of an undialectical shallow modernism which obscures all that he wanted to tell us of the living God."[59] What then is "religionless Christianity"? According to Godsey, it encompasses the following elements: (1) the abolishing of ecclesiastical self-interest and clerical arrogance; (2) preaching is not sufficient, the Church must also live the Gospel; (3) the Church must become the instrument for proclaiming the Gospel; however, it must employ nonreligious language; (4) the Church must regain her own peculiar life.[60] Perhaps these points by Godsey can be summarized by stating that the Church needs to be active in the world but still retain her own identification. There must be *Gemeinschaft* among the community of believers, but the *Verkündigung* of the Gospel must also take place in the world. The *Predigtwort* is not only for the *ekklesia* but also for the *Welt*.

Bonhoeffer's concept of religion, which is encapsulated in the phrase "non-religious Christianity," came to be somewhat of a departure from his earlier understanding of the word. In *Akt und Sein*, his inaugural address of 1931, Bonhoeffer seemingly understood "religion" in a different manner as compared with his later years.

---

[57] Dumas, *Dietrich Bonhoeffer: Theologian of Reality*, 207.
[58] Bethge, *Dietrich Bonhoeffer*, 873.
[59] Mary Bosanquet, *The Life and Death of Dietrich Bonhoeffer*, 279, quoted in Clyde Fant, *Bonhoeffer: Worldly Preaching* (Nashville: Thomas Nelson Inc., 1975), 78.
[60] Godsey, *The Theology of Dietrich Bonhoeffer*, 273.

What reason can learn from itself (thus Hegel) is revelation, and so God is incarnated in consciousness. Through living refelexion on itself, the I understands itself from itself. It directly relates to itself, hence to God, in reflexion. It follows that religion is here equivalent to revelation.[61]

He seemingly previously saw religion as *Offenbarung*; thus, his understanding was similar to that of Karl Barth's. Fant, however, believes that he saw religion as a synonym for faith.[62]

Another key phrase in Bonhoeffer's thought is that of "world come of age." He does not have in mind with this phrase an evolutionary scheme or even the idea of concern for this world as opposed to the eternal. Connected with this phrase is that of "this-worldliness."

By this-worldliness I mean living unreservedly in life's duties, problems, successes and failures, experiences and perplexities. In so doing we throw ourselves completely into the arms of God, taking seriously, not our own sufferings, but those of God in the world – watching with Christ in Gethsemane.[63]

A phrase that is somewhat more mysterious in its meaning is that of "secret discipline." Bonhoeffer writes: "There are degrees of knowledge and degrees of significance; that means that a secret discipline must be restored whereby the mysteries of the Christian faith are protected from profanation." [64] What is the meaning of *Arkandiziplin*? Paul Lehman claims that this term is one of the more obscure of Bonhoeffer's. Fant suggests that the origin of the phrase comes from the early Christian practice of separating preaching from the Lord's Supper. Only a select group could participate in the latter.[65] William Hamilton and William Lillie understand "secret discipline" as alluding to Bonhoeffer's desire that the Church become hidden in her worship.[66] Dumas understands Bonhoeffer's desire for a "secret discipline" by citing three reasons as follows: (1) either because men cannot understand the language of faith; (2) or because prayer, suffering, and the sacraments are a more significant means of expressing the presence of God in the world than preaching; (3) or finally because Bonhoeffer does not feel the time is ripe for a language

---

[61] Dietrich Bonhoeffer, *Act and Being,* Trans. Bernard Noble (New York: Harper and Row, 41.
[62] Fant, *Worldly Preaching*, 76.
[63] Bonhoeffer, *Letters and Papers from Prison*, 370.
[64] Ibid., 286.
[65] Fant *Worldly Preaching*, 94.
[66] Ibid., 95.

purged of its religious and pious overtones.[67] Certainly the first two could not be what Bonhoeffer wished to convey since they would be the antithesis of his view of being involved in the world. Therefore, the third explanation seems more appropriate.

We have seen, then, Bonhoeffer is more concerned with eradicating the religious overtones which have encumbered the Church and even the interpretation of the Gospel. But does he say anything about actual exegesis? In *Christ the Center* he states:

> In the exegesis of Scripture we find ourselves on very uncertain ground. So we may never stick to the point, but must move over the whole of the Bible, from one place to another, just as a man can only cross a river covered in ice floes if he does not remain standing on one particular floe but jumps from one to another.[68]

It is somewhat uncertain exactly what Bonhoeffer means here, but clearly Bonhoeffer did not see exegesis as the only key for unlocking the true meaning of Scripture. Many times in his writings, Bonhoeffer will quote a verse and not give any interpretation of it. He comments that Jesus' sayings can only be interpreted by Jesus himself.[69] Perhaps Marty's observation has some truth to it:

> Bonhoeffer imposed his own views on Scripture; he seemed impatient with historical research; after he gained his credentials as a boring writer of academic dissertations, he deserted arcane theology; he was an intuitive if not the most profound or seminal systematic thinker.[70]

Whether or not he imposed his views on Scripture could be a matter of debate. However, it is a fact that he was not enthused with the historical-critical method. He constantly speaks against any demythologizing:

> It is neither possible nor right for us to try to get behind the Word of Scripture to the events as they actually occurred. Rather, the whole of Scriptures summons us to follow Jesus. We must not do violence to the

---

[67] Dumas, *Dietrich Bonhoeffer: Theologian of Reality*, 212.
[68] Dietrich Bonhoeffer, *Christ the Center*, Trans. John Bowden (New York: Harper and Row, 1966), 76.
[69] Dietrich Bonhoeffer, *Ethics,* ed. Eberhard Bethge, trans. Neville H. Smith (New York: Macmillan Publishing Co., 1978), 69.
[70] *nweal*, 93 (October 2, 1970): 27-8.

Scriptures by interpreting them in terms of an abstract principle, even if that principle be a doctrine of grace.[71]

Perhaps a key to understanding Bonhoeffer's hermeneutical system is seeing his understanding of Scripture as Christocentric. Harrelson writes:

> The christocentric interpretation of the Old Testament appears in Bonhoeffer's sermons as well, ... In the lecture on re-presentation he goes farther and offers a defense of the allegorical interpretation of Scripture, under certain limitations. Explicit logical and grammatical meanings of a word or verse many not exhaust its meaning. The word may contain other perspectives of meaning also. When symbolic or allegorical meanings are not found, however, they must point to Christ alone, and they must hold fast to the text itself.[72]

Perhaps all that can be said with certainty is that Bonhoeffer considered Scripture to be the Word of God. He does not explain intricate details or theories of inspiration. The message is centered in Christ. Paul Ballard claims: "All Bonhoeffer's thought is fundamentally Christological."[73] Bonhoeffer writes: "We want to meet Christ in his Word. We go to the text curious to hear what he wants us to know and give us through his word."[74] If Bonhoeffer was not explicit concerning hermeneutics and exegesis, he was certain of the effects of the Word: "It (Word) does only one thing: it calls us to faith and obedience to the truth once recognized in Jesus Christ."[75]

6. The Disparate Character of the Works of Bultmann and Bonhoeffer – and the Concentration of the Relation of Hermeneutics to Homiletics

It was alluded to previously that Bonhoeffer's works are somewhat fragmentary; thus, in studying Bonhoeffer one can have the impression

---

[71] Dietrich Bonhoeffer, *The Cost of Discipleship*, trans. R.H. Fuller (New York: Simon & Schuster, 1995), 84.
[72] Walter Harrelson, "Bonhoeffer and the Bible," in *The Place of Bonhoeffer*, ed. Martin Marty (New York: Association Press, 1964), 118.
[73] Paul Ballard, Worship in a Secular World: Bonhoeffer's Secret Discipline," *Princeton Seminary Bulletin* 68 (Autumn 1975): 28.
[74] Dietrich Bonhoeffer, *The Way to Freedom*, ed. E.H. Robertson, trans. E.H. Robertson and John Bowden (New York: Harper and Row, 1977), 58.
[75] Ibid., 177.

that he is piecing his thoughts together. Phillips cogently states concerning this problem:

> A look at the production of Bonhoeffer's eighteen years as a theologian reveals the unsystematic character of his thinking. The biographical aspects of his career often affected his theological work, and it is a basic assumption on the part of many of his interpreters that the history of the time through which and in which Bonhoeffer lived is an important factor to be considered in the assessment of his thought.[76]

However, through his works one is able to come to some definite conclusions concerning the hermeneutical system of Dietrich Bonhoeffer.

Unlike Bultmann, Bonhoeffer was not a scientific exegete. He was not concerned with obtaining the "kernal" of the message by the process of demythologization. Why was this? Because to Bonhoeffer demythologization had not gone far enough. According to him, those elements which Bultmann terms mythology, i. e. resurrection, etc., are to be understood literally. However, Bonhoeffer wishes to rid Christianity of religion and in a sense this relates to Bultmann's reductionism. "But for Bonhoeffer it is not the mythological concepts that are problematic, but the 'religious' ones."[77]

Phillips states an interesting comment about the method and procedure of Bonhoeffer:

> Scientific exegesis with the aim of disclosing the original form of a text or uncovering the historical setting of a particular passage was just not Bonhoeffer's concern. His question, by passing textual criticism (and leaving for us the problem of the relationship between this and what he wished to do), was how to hear and obey the Word of God. He feared losing sight of this problem in textual and critical theorizing. . . . His meditation upon and obedience to the Word of scripture was, therefore, not a side issue in Bonhoeffer's theology, but close to its center.[78]

Bonhoeffer, even though a protégé of professors who espoused the historical-critical method of interpretation, did not believe that this method to be of vital importance for a procedure of scriptural interpretation.

> From the very beginning of his interest in the problem of Scriptural interpretation, he was intensely involved with the question of how one

---

[76] John A. Phillips, *Christ for Us in the Theology of Dietrich Bonhoeffer* (New York: Harper and Row Publishers, 1967), 19-20.
[77] Godsey, *The Theology of Dietrich Bonhoeffer,* 253.
[78] Phillips, *Christ for Us in the Theology of Dietrich Bonhoeffer,* 85.

relates oneself to scripture; how scripture became actual and concrete in life. "Scientific" exegetical thinking should grow from this basis, not vice versa. His thoughts on scripture were thus taken up along with his meditations on questions concerning ethics and proclamation.[79]

One almost obtains the impression that for Bonhoeffer the Word could not be meaningful through the critical method.

> Bonhoeffer now speaks of the Bible as, in the first place, the devotional center of the Christian life of faith. At the same time, he clearly recognizes that the two approaches to the Scriptures, a "devotional" and a "theological" approach, cannot finally be allowed. Critical work had become meaningless for his devotional life—"breaking the ground" of the Bible was now utterly beside the point. He therefore found it necessary to admit his willingness to suspend certain critical reservations in order to confront a Bible whose every part is theologically trustworthy and whose integrity and unity is unquestioned.[80]

While Bonhoeffer accepted Scripture as the Word of God, it is doubtful if he held to what contemporary evangelical theologians term "verbal-plenary inspiration," meaning that God gave human agents the very words of the Bible. Bonhoeffer claims concerning Genesis 1:6-10: "The idea of verbal inspiration will not do. The writer of the first chapter of Genesis is behaving in a very human way."[81] Bonhoeffer seemingly is more interested in ridding the Christian world of troublesome concepts than performing exacting exegesis and word studies upon the Scriptures. According to Dumas, Bultmann operates within the structure of transcendental Kantianism; thus, there is a lack of objectivizing the Old Testament. However, Bonhoeffer operates within an incarnational Hegelianism which emphasizes the value of the Old Testament.[82] But it seems that Bonhoeffer in regard to obtaining the original understanding of Scripture has more in common with Barth than with Bultmann. Both Barth and Bonhoeffer would not capitulate the mythological world or the language of the Bible.[83] Why would Bonhoeffer not accept Bultmann's method?

---

[79] Ibid., 89.
[80] Ibid., 92.
[81] Dietrich Bonhoeffer, *Creation and Fall,* trans. John C. Fletcher (New York: Macmillan Publishing Co., 1978), 29.
[82] Dumas, *Dietrich Bonhoeffer: Theologian of Reality,* 246-47.
[83] Phillips, *Christ for Us in the Theology of Dietrich Bonhoeffer,* 220.

Demythologization, while it is part of the process of differentiation and assessment, has failed fully to reflect the concern of a non-religious interpretation not only because it frequently confuses interpretation with substitution, but also to the extent to which it has found comfort in the religious apriori of existentialism.[84]

Two interpreters of Bonhoeffer, Ronald Gregor Smith and Gerhard Ebeling, contend that Bonhoeffer is closer to Bultmann than any other contemporary theologian.[85] Their similarities and contrasts have already been discussed. Possibly the most striking comparison between the two is their view of Scripture. Like Bultmann, Bonhoeffer does not mean that the Bible is a consistent whole, historically or theologically. There are some portions of Scripture which have "degrees of significance."[86] This premise seemingly is peculiar to both Bultmann and Bonhoeffer.

Both also place a heavy emphasis upon the individual interpreter. Bonhoeffer claims: "Thus the interpreter makes the claim to be able to distinguish the Word of God and the word of man in Holy Scripture. He himself knows where is the Word of God and where is the word of man. So, for example, the theology of Paul is the word of man, the so-called religion of Jesus is divine."[87]

He claims:

> The doctrine of sin and justification are temporal and past, the struggle for the good and pure is eternal . . . . With this the key to the exposition of the Scripture is put into our hand. Just as in secular writing we can distinguish the genuine words of the author from the spurious additions, so now in the Bible we can distinguish the Word of God from the word of man and can separate the one from the other.[88]

7. Hermeneutics and Homiletics

What is preaching for Bonhoeffer and upon what is it based? These and similar questions will be explored. Bethge writes of Bonhoeffer:

> Bonhoeffer loved to preach. When a relative discovered that she might have only months to live, he wrote, "What would I do if I learned that in

---

[84] Ibid., 220
[85] Woelfel, *Bonhoeffer's Theology*, 113.
[86] Ibid., 108.
[87] Dietrich Bonhoeffer, *No Rusty Swords*, ed. E. H. Roberston (New York: William Collins Sons & Co., 1977), 308-9.
[88] Ibid., 309.

four to six months my life would reach its end? I believe that I would try to teach theology as I once did and to preach often."[89]

However, there seemingly is no unanimity concerning Bonhoeffer and his role as a preacher. Fant states:

> Bonhoeffer's work does not limit itself to the realm of any single group of specialists. Therefore, to the theological specialist Bonhoeffer is too much the preacher and to the preacher Bonhoeffer is too much the theologian. For the theologian, the preacher is always technically too imprecise and humanly too specific; while to the ecclesiastical practitioner, the theologian is too troublesome because he watches everything too closely and often critically.[90]

Perhaps it is not possible to conclude whether Bonhoeffer preferred preaching over teaching; however, there is no denying that he felt a deep commitment to the pulpit.

What are Bultmann's thoughts concerning preaching? He claims that the message preached is God's Word.

> If we ask for plain convincing reasons why God speaks actually here, in the Bible, then we have not understood what God's sovereignty means. For it is due to his sovereign will, that he has spoken and speaks here. The Bible does not approach us at all like other books. . . . It claims from the outset to be God's Word. . . . The Church's preaching, founded on the Scriptures, passes on the word of the Scriptures. It says: God speaks to you here! In his majesty he has chosen this place! We cannot question whether this place is the right one. We must listen to the call that summons us.[91]

Bultmann believes that God speaks to humanity in the preaching of the Word.[92] He speaks of the existential present of Christian preaching and faith.[93] Bultmann places the emphasis upon the preaching and reception of the kerygma by stating the following: "The faith of Easter is just this – faith in the word of preaching."[94]

---

[89] Eberhard Bethge, ed., *Gesammelten Schriften*, 7, quoted in Clyde Fant, *Bonhoeffer: Worldly Preaching*, 4.
[90] Fant, *Bonhoeffer: Worldly Preaching*, 5.
[91] Bultmann, *Existence and Faith*, 168.
[92] George E. Ladd, "What Does Bultmann Understand by the Acts of God?" *Journal of the Evangelical Theological Society* 5 (summer 1962): 91.
[93] Carl E. Braaten, "A Critical Introduction," in *Kerygma and History,* eds. and trans. Carl E. Braaten and Roy A. Harrisville (Nashville: Abingdon Press, 1962), 15.
[94] Bultmann, "New Testament and Mythology," in *Kerygma and Myth,* ed., H.W. Bartsch, 41.

Bonhoeffer, however does not speak of a closed world system; therefore, there is more of an emphasis upon a relationship with Christ.

> The preacher, as one who addresses the communion, must "know" what he preaches: Jesus Christ was crucified (I Cor. 2:2). He has full power to announce the gospel to the hearer, for forgiving sins in preaching and sacrament. There may be no uncertainty here, no not-knowing: all must be made plain from the Word of God who has bound himself in revelation, for in the preaching which produces faith Christ causes himself to be declared the "subject" of the spoken words.[95]

Bonhoeffer apparently holds to the Reformation principle of preaching as the *deus loquens*, the Word of God is actually proclaimed by the preacher.

Bonhoeffer's preaching tends to be orientated toward more of a social gospel message than Bultmann's preaching. For Bonhoeffer:

> The Bible recognizes no difference of principle between preaching for unbelievers and preaching for believers. The Bible teaches that the proclamation and activity of the congregation take place in responsibility for the world. This responsibility can never be disregarded, for God loved the world and desires that all men shall be helped.[96]

Bonhoeffer believes that the Church must speak to the world; the Gospel must be presented in such a manner that the world will comprehend it. Bethge claims for Bonhoeffer preaching in a "world come of age" has the following elements: (1) it must avoid the approach of *deus ex machina*; (2) it must be involved with the world and even seek advice from such; (3) the preacher need not use only the language of Zion; (4) the preacher must realize his life speaks more loudly than his words; and (5) the preacher accepts limitations.[97]

Bonhoeffer implemented his preaching philosophy in the seminary at Finkenwalde. He believed that one of the most important means of developing in the art of homiletics was through listening to sermons. He claimed even the poorest of sermons contained the Word of God. Always he kept before him the challenge not to make the Word relevant but merely to testify to it. An important question which the preacher must ask himself is: "What is the text saying directly to me?" It is not necessary for the preacher to discover new ideas or extraordinary experiences in his meditation, but he should allow the Word to dwell within.

---

[95] Bonhoeffer, *Act and Being*, 142.
[96] Bonhoeffer, *Ethics,* 317-18.
[97] Eberhard Bethge, ed., *Dietrich Bonhoeffer*, 789, quoted in Fant, *Bonhoeffer: Worldly Preaching,* 105.

Bonhoeffer thought of himself as an homiletician. His thought is replete with novel concepts of preaching. He suggests that the real birthplace of a sermon is not in the study but in the pulpit. He is adverse to any mannerisms which might call attention to the preacher instead of to the message. Emotionalism must be absent from the message.

Bonhoeffer's theological presuppositions express themselves in the manner in which he approaches and interprets the Word. According to Fant, Bonhoeffer's preaching is grounded in the Word. The *Predigtwort* originates in the incarnation of Christ.[98] The preacher is merely a vehicle (*Handlanger*) according to Bonhoeffer. The preacher allows himself/herself to be used in order that the Word might come to the congregation. Bonhoeffer believes:

> The most concrete part of preaching is not the application I give, but the Holy Spirit himself, who speaks through the text of the Bible. Even the clearest application, the most distinct appeal to the congregation, is irrelevant so long as the Holy Spirit himself does not create the *concretissimum,* the present.[99]

Again Bonhoeffer claims: "The Word moves on its own accord, and all the preacher has to do is to assist that movement and try to put no obstacle in its path. The Word comes forth to take men to itself."[100]

Constantly Bonhoeffer distinguishes between the human and divine message. "Preaching is not meant to be my word about God, however serious, however honorable, however faithful, but God's own Word. So there can be preaching only where there is divine commission."[101] However, Bonhoeffer seemingly does not limit the proclaiming of the Word merely to ordained clergy, rather, it can be proclaimed throughout the community.

> When one person is struck by the Word, he speaks it to others. God has willed that we should seek and find his living Word in the witness of a Brother, in the mouth of man. Therefore, the Christian needs another Christian who speaks God's Word to him.[102]

Bonhoeffer's method of preaching, then, makes use of exegesis. The preacher must allow himself/herself to be the vehicle for the message of God. Correct exegesis testifies to the living Christ. "The only method of

---

[98] Fant, *Bonhoeffer: Worldly Preaching*, 126.
[99] Bonhoeffer, *No Rusty Swords*, 315.
[100] Bonhoeffer, *The Cost of Discipleship*, 279-80.
[101] Bonhoeffer, *The Way to Freedom*, 186.
[102] Bonhoeffer, *Life Together*, 22-23.

presentation is therefore the exegesis of the content of the text as the witness of Christ, and such exegesis has the promise of the presence of Christ."[103] Again Bonhoeffer states: "So Christ is present in the church as the spoken Word, not as magic and not as art. He is present in the spoken Word of judgment and forgiveness."[104]

Bonhoeffer apparently does not see preaching as the culmination of the office of pastor. "If we are to be 'shepherds' of the community, as Christ was, that means more than saying that we are preachers."[105] In *Life Together* Bonhoeffer emphasizes the need for *koinonia* and that God's Word is not limited only to the ordained. "Therefore the Christian needs another Christian who speaks God's Word to him. He needs him again and again when he becomes uncertain and discouraged."[106] The congregation, the body of Christ, is "the society of authority."[107]

Bonhoeffer holds preaching in the highest esteem. His understanding of homiletics stems from his view of exegesis and his particular system of hermeneutics. Bonhoeffer witnesses to the living Christ, whereas Bultmann speaks of a faith in the "Word of preaching." For Bonhoeffer, the Word is a ship "loaded to its capacity." The preacher need not concern himself with a sparkling introduction or any other gimmick to obtain attention but must commit himself/herself directly to the preaching of the Word.

---

[103] Bonhoeffer, *No Rusty Swords,* 315.
[104] Bonhoeffer, *Christ the Center,* 53.
[105] Dietrich Bonhoeffer, *True Patriotism.* Trans. E.H. Robertson and John Bowden (New York: Harper and Row Publishers, 1973), 106.
[106] Bonhoeffer, *Life Together,* 23.
[107] Dietrich Bonhoeffer, *The Communion of Saints,* trans. William Collins and Sons (New York: Harper and Row Publishers, 1960), 165.

Chapter One

Rudolf Bultmann's Hermeneutics and His Sermons

A. Introduction

This section on Bultmann examines several of his significant works pertaining to hermeneutics. The intention is to give an explanation of the theoretical concepts of Bultmann's hermeneutics in relationship to his practical interpretation of Scripture as expressed in his preaching. It is not possible to fully comprehend his preaching unless one has an understanding of the foundation of his sermons—namely, his existential hermeneutic. One could mistakenly read his sermons and conclude in many of them that he is merely telling a simple story based upon Scripture, or that the message has perhaps only a minimal relationship to the lives of those who heard the messages. The depth of his exegetical skills sometimes is ignored or even denied by many conservative scholars who do not fully understand the basis of his hermeneutical foundation and how it is expressed in his sermons. There are five representative texts included in this section which Bultmann wrote giving insight into his hermeneutical methodology. These texts are arranged chronologically; that is, they proceed from 1925-1957.

Written in 1925, "The Problem of a Theological Exegesis of the New Testament" is critical of Idealism, Naturalism, and the History of Religions School. Bultmann believes that one must confront history in such a manner that one truly interacts with the text and not simply views it objectively. Only a truly existential hermeneutic will allow one to understand what is being said and then apply the message to one's particular life situation. One must confront the text asking questions and challenging what is being claimed; exegesis is always challenging since there is the ceaseless claim of the message upon one's life. The text must never be viewed in a detached, impersonal manner, but always with an awareness that the text is intimate and life-changing. The method which Bultmann advocates actually goes beyond that of merely a historical and/or exegetical analysis in that he is stating we must realize our present responsibility to the demands of the text.

Published in 1948, though given as a lecture seven years previously, "New Testament and Mythology" advocates a complete paradigm shift in how the New Testament is to be viewed and interpreted. The person of faith has the capacity to live a truly authentic life, and the New Testament's claim is that authentic existence has been accomplished in Christ whom we see by faith. There is much contained within the New Testament which must be demythologized since Jewish apocalypticism and Gnosticism have influenced the writers of the New Testament. The contemporary person must not be expected to accept the unverifiable mythological aspects of the New Testament—myth must not be discarded, but interpreted existentially. The mythological elements in the New Testament point toward the transcendent. Though Bultmann has a very high regard for philosophy, he believes that only the New Testament explains humanity's fallen condition and also the deliverance which Christ has provided. Bultmann places emphasis upon the event of Jesus' death upon the cross which along with the resurrection of Christ can be realized in the present.

"The Problem of Hermeneutics" Bultmann wrote in 1950 in order to give clarity to his program of an existentialist interpretation. He accentuates that everyone has presuppositions and that the interpretation is always guided by a pre-understanding of the text. It is commendable to understand the original intent of the author, but this understanding does not guarantee a complete interpretation. One must understand that a more precise interpretation occurs when both the writer and the interpreter have the same experience of the subject matter. One must attempt to get behind what objectively has been stated in order to have a more thorough understanding of the text. The questions which the interpreter asks are not haphazard as he has a pre-understanding of the material; however, he must be careful in order not to allow his pre-understanding to convince him that he already knows the results. To many it may seem to be foolish to state that one can have a pre-understanding of God; however, Bultmann believes that there is present in human beings an existential knowledge of God.

Bultmann gave lectures at various American universities in the fall of 1951, and he shared much of the material found in "Jesus Christ and Mythology." According to Bultmann, the central theme of Jesus' teaching is the subject of the kingdom of God, which kingdom is interpreted eschatologically. Eschatological preaching reminds one to live fully in the present while aware that the future is coming. Bultmann in this work is adamant that he is not attempting to eliminate various myths contained in the New Testament, but he is attempting to interpret them. Philosophical Idealism in Bultmann's opinion is not as comprehensive as is the method of existentialism which method is concerned solely with the human condition—especially as pertaining to the issue of human choice and individual responsibility. One must be willing to abandon every human security in order that he may find ultimate security in God.

Bultmann wrote "Is Exegesis without Presuppositions Possible?" in 1957. He explains that the concept of exegesis without presuppositions means that one must not manipulate what the results will be even though everyone possesses a particular worldview. There is a closedness in history; thus, the breaking in of the miraculous must not be emphasized. There is a sense in which the word of Scripture does not speak on a particular topic in a final manner since the interpretation always arises out of the experience of the person interpreting the Scripture. The methodology which is prevalent in the natural sciences, that of subject and object, has no such correspondence in an existentiell encounter with the Scriptures.

Bultmann certainly does have his detractors. There are some who claim that Bultmann's existential interpretation is based upon a meaningless inner subjectivity and not upon sound exegesis. To understand some of the criticism against Bultmann, there will be citing of various authors who are in disagreement with him.

Walter C. Kaiser claims that Bultmann applied form criticism to the New Testament in such a manner that his results were dubious. Kaiser believes: "Certainly the way Rudolf Bultmann applied form criticism to the New Testament made it a dubious and very ineffective tool without external controls."[1] While Kaiser has some positive comments regarding form criticism, he is especially critical of Bultmann's methodology.

Carson, Moo, and Morris discuss the issue of the historical Jesus. They believe that Bultmann ignored much of the supernatural in the New Testament and conclude concerning the analogy of peeling away the husk from the kermal, that "Rudolph Bultmann kept peeling until there was almost nothing left. His form-critical studies of the Gospels convinced him that we could know very little for sure about Jesus himself: the accounts have simply been reinterpreted too thoroughly by the early church."[2]

---

[1] Kaiser, Walter, *Toward an Exegetical Theology* (Grand Rapids: Baker Book House, 1985), 95.
[2] D.A. Carson, Douglas J. Moo and Leon Morris, *An Introduction to the New Testament* (Grand Rapids: Zondervan Publishing House, 1992), 51.

According to Greidanus, Bultmann's view of the closed continuum of historical events is not logical. Greidanus asserts that Bultmann's presupposition that past occurrences cannot be caused by the supernatural excludes a particular solution and therefore is unscientific.[3]

Some scholars even refer to Bultmann's method as "radical." R.C. Sproul, John Gerstner and Arthur Lindsley claim that Bultmann's view that revelation occurs expeditiously, *senkrecht von oben*, and not in a linear manner removes the possibility of revelation occurring in an objective fashion. They claim that Bultmann's view is too subjective.[4]

Smith's conclusion appears to be extreme. He claims, "It would seem that Bultmann's presuppositions . . . led only to a meaningless despair."[5] Frame states that Bultmann's presuppostional method is opposed to historic Christianity.[6]

Geisler seems to believe that Bultmann's method leads one to a quasi-atheism. He states, "On the left wing, Bultmann insisted that our life-transforming encounter with the Word of God yields no factual information whatever, and that the nature of true faith is to trust God, knowing that, in the strict sense, one knows nothing about Him at all."[7]

According to Conn, Bultmann has inverted the true center of the New Testament message. He asserts: "Bultmann not only does great injustice to

---

[3] Sidney Greidanus, *The Modern Preacher and the Ancient Text* (Grand Rapids: William B. Eerdmans Publishing Co., 1996), 33.
[4] R.C. Sproul, John Gerstner, and Arthur Lindsley, *Classical Apologetics* (Grand Rapids: Zondervan Publishing Co., 1984), 142.
[5] David L. Smith, *A Handbook of Contemporary Theology* (Baker Book House, 1998), 78.
[6] John Frame, *Apologetics to the Glory of God* (P&R Publishing, Phillipsburg, NJ: 1994), 130. Cf. John Frame, *The Doctrine of the Knowledge of God* (Phillipsburg, NJ: P&R Publishing, 1987), 317. Frame writes, "Bultmann, for example, denied that he was selling out to the "modern worldview." At times he even expressed his indifference on the question of whether that worldview is true. Rather, he said, he used the modern world view as a tool of communication to reach modern man with the gospel. In his view, he was not denying the gospel at all, for the gospel, as he understood it, is neutral on the question of worldview. Thus we can present the gospel in faithfulness to the Scriptures without affirming the existence of angels or the possibility of miracle. Now in my judgment, Bultmann's point is absurd. . . . He believed that he had not only a scientific warrant for believing as he did but a scriptural warrant, a theological warrant, as well. And for him, as a Christian theologian, the theological warrant was far more important. If (Bultmann tried to convince his readers) Scripture did not permit his construction, then he would not hold it merely to agree with the scientists."
[7] Nornan Geisler, *Inerrancy* (Grand Rapids: Zondervan Publishing Co., 1980), 205.

the God-centered character of Christianity. He also loses the only center by which man in his essence can be understood properly. The real purpose of the New Testament is to proclaim that the sovereign God has come, and He has come in Christ to restore man's proper nature as image of God. The heart of the New Testament remains not man but God."[8]

Toon has an interesting comment upon Bultmann's premise that modern man is somehow superior intellectually to those who lived in the first century. Toon is reacting against what he believes to be Bultmann's exaggerated claim that the modern person understands phenomena solely from a scientific framework. He somewhat sarcastically comments, "It seems not to have occurred to Bultmann that in certain respects modern man may be cognitively inferior to human beings in earlier periods of human civilization."[9]

Pinnock has some scathing words of criticism directed to Bultmann with his comments:

> Bultmann is guilty of twisting the Scriptures to bring them into line with his own extrabiblical presuppositions. He forces the kerygma to become what his secular worldview requires it to be. Certainly the kerygma is an existentially meaningful proclamation, but according to the New Testament this is because it is first factual and true independently. . . . The New Testament cannot be fairly interpreted in a purely existentialist manner. . . . Bultmann has come up with an existential salvage operation that lets one preach to modern humanity from certain limited features of the New Testament message.[10]

A not uncommon criticism against Bultmann is that his program of demythologization leads to a nebulous, internal self-understanding. Miller and Grenz state:

> . . . instead of defining the Christian proclamation in terms of what God has announced and accomplished "out there" in biblical history and, centrally, in the ministry, cross, and resurrection of Jesus Christ, Bultmann defined it in terms of what individuals experience in their own personal confrontation with existence . . . . all the high-flown talk about responsible and authentic existence does not really issue in anything concrete and real.

---

[8] Harvie M. Conn, *Contemporary World Theology* (Phillipsburg, NJ: P&R Publishing, 1974), 36.
[9] Peter Toon, *The End of Liberal Theology* (Wheaton, IL: Crossway Books, 1995), 192.
[10] Clark H. Pinnock, *Tracking the Maze* San Francisco: Harper & Row Publishers, 1990), 115.

What do responsibility, authenticity, openness to the future, and so on really mean?[11]

B. Hermeneutical Methodology

1. Bultmann's Hermeneutical Writings

a. Presuppositions

Bultmann's hermeneutical concern begins with two major issues: *Vorverständnis* and an openness to the meaning of man. He rejects both the allegorical interpretation and the extreme dogmatic prejudices. Bultmann gives insight by writing:

> The question of exegesis without presuppositions in the sense of unprejudiced exegesis must be distinguished from this same question in the other sense in which it can be raised. And in this second sense, we must say that there cannot be any such thing as a presuppositionless exegesis. That there is no such exegesis in fact, because every exegete is determined by his own individuality, in the sense of his special biases and habits, his gifts and his weaknesses, has no significance in principle. For in the sense of the word, it is precisely his "individuality" that the exegete ought to eliminate by educating himself to the kind of hearing that is interested in nothing other than the subject matter of which the text speaks. However, the one presupposition that cannot be dismissed is the historical method of interrogating the text. Indeed, exegesis as the interpretation of historical texts is a part of the science of history.[12]

Historical understanding presupposes an understanding of both the subject matter and persons in history. He also believes, "The historical method includes the presupposition that history is a unity in the sense of a closed continuum of effects in which individual events are connected by the succession of cause and effect . . . . and the historical method presupposes that it is possible . . . . to understand the whole historical process as a closed unity."[13]

---

[11] Ed. L. Miller and Stanley J. Grenz, *Introduction to Contemporary Theologies* Minneapolis: Fortress Press, 1998), 51-52.
[12] Rudolf Bultmann, "Is Exegesis without Presuppositions Possible?" in *Existence and Faith* (New York: The World Publishing Co., 1963), 290-91.
[13] Ibid., 291-92. Cf. Bultmann, "The Problem of Hermeneutics," in *Rudolf Bultmann: Interpreting the Faith for the Modern Era* (Collins Publishers, 1987), 154. Bultmann states that in order to understand history not as arbitrary occurrences, one must have a preunderstanding of the historical possibilities

The second major concern for Bultmann is that the interpreter of Scripture is to determine what the text has to say about meaning for the individual.

> Finally, the objective of interpretation can be given by an interest in history as the sphere of life in which human existence takes place, in which we acquire and develop our possibilities, and in which, by reflecting on these possibilities, we each come to an understanding of ourselves and our own possibilities. In other words, the objective can be given by the question about human existence as one's own existence.[14]

He also makes a keen observation that "interpretation does not come about simply because 'the individuality of the interpreter and that of the author do not stand over against one another as two incomparable facts' but because or insofar as both have the same relation to the subject matter under discussion or in question . . . they both stand in the same context of life."[15] The essential meaning of any piece of literature, then, is what it has to say about the person in his existential context. Edwin Good adds insight by stating:

> The ambiguity of our one word may be sufficient guarantee of our confusion. What Bultmann intends by it [existential] is that we be existentially concerned with the question of man in our approach to the text, and that the business of interpretation be carried out in existentialist terms. We must understand in order to interpret. And the interpretation must go on to be understandable, that is to convey the meaning of the text to the hearer or reader so that he too is summoned to decision in regard to the meaning of his own existence.[16]

Bultmann, then, places a heavy emphasis upon the human being's ability to relate the message of the New Testament to the *Sitz im Leben* of

---

wherein they possess their significance, thus, their character as historically important.
[14] Bultmann, "The Problem of Hermeneutics," in *Rudolf Bultmann: Interpreting the Faith for the Modern Era*, 151.
[15] Ibid., 142.
[16] Edwin M. Good, "The Meaning of Demythologization," in *The Theology of Rudolf Bultmann* (New York: Harper & Row Publishers, 1966), 24-25. Good alludes to *Existential* and *Existentiell* as "two confusing words." The former has to do with methods of existentialist philosophy and can perhaps be translated "existentialist." The latter means that which is involved in one's own existence and should be translated "existential." Others suggest that *existential* could be translated "ontological," and *existentiell* as the difference between being and philosophizing about being.

the modern hearers. His concern for contemporary persons to understand the New Testament message leads him to interpret it in a manner which is relevant.

Bultmann was heavily influenced by his mentors, the Religionsgeschichtliche Schule, and form criticism. A synopsis of his view of hermeneutics and myth will be helpful as this subject relates to his hermeneutical scriptures.

Within Bultmann's writings, the primary reason for emphasizing the mythological *Weltanschauung* of the Bible is the disparate scientific mentality of our own time. The world and even humans are interpreted by categories of inherent causality and historical analogy. To Bultmann, the Bible presents a simple cosmology—a three-storied universe with heaven above, hell below, and the earth in between. In this triadic environment are beneficent and evil angels who come to either help or harm human beings. These beings can even intervene within the social and psychological processes of human beings. God "sent" his only Son, a pre-existent being indwelling a human body, "to" earth for the primary reason of dying "for" humanity. Then he mysteriously arose from the dead and went back to heaven where he had been for all eternity. Someday in the future, he will return to earth and defeat all wickedness and bring about the new heavens and new earth.

The preaching and teaching of these beliefs have unnecessarily caused the intensification of the skandalon of the Gospel. Such a message cannot appeal to the modern person since it represents a pre-scientific mindset. With the advances in the understanding of the cosmos, the modern day individual cannot be expected to accept such a view of the world and human beings. In fact, according to Bultmann, Christian preaching does not need to expect the modern man to accept such a view. He asks a question and supplies an answer: "Can Christian preaching expect modern man to accept the mythical view of the world as true? To do so would be both senseless and impossible. It would be senseless because there is nothing specifically Christian in the mythical view of the world as such. It is simply the cosmology of a pre-scientific age."[17] He continues:

> Again it would be impossible, because no man can adopt a view of the world by his own volition—it is already determined for him by his place in history. Of course such a view is not absolutely unalterable, and the individual may even contribute to its change. But he can only do so when he is faced by a new set of facts so compelling as to make his previous

---

[17] Rudolf Bultmann, "New Testament and Mythology," in *Kerygma and Myth*, ed., Hans Werner Bartsch (New York: Harper & Row, 1961), 3.

view of the world untenable. He has then no alternative but to modify his view of the world or produce a new one. The discoveries of Copernicus and the atomic theory are instances of this, and so was romanticism with its discovery that the human subject is richer and more complex than enlightenment or idealism had allowed, and nationalism, with its new realization of the importance of history and the tradition of peoples.[18]

Bultmann locates the mythological construction and worldview of the Bible in Jewish apocalypticism and Greek Gnosticism. Bultmann states that when we preach the Gospel today, in a sense we have to ask our converts to accept such a cosmology. Of course, since he does not believe this cosmology, Bultmann says the only alternative is to engage in demythologizing all of these mythical elements.[19] Therefore, to Bultmann, the kerygma lies somewhat hidden, and only a particular method can extricate it. Dinkler believes that Bultmann attempts to ". . . advance in the same direction the liberal tradition of exegesis in order to overcome the theological limitations of pure reconstruction and to preserve the values of liberal criticism."[20]

However, Bultmann is quite critical of liberal theology in the nineteenth century. He does not discuss the origins of liberal theology from previous movements in past centuries such as the Enlightenment, the Renaissance, Rationalism, and Romanticism. He is critical of Harnack, who Bultmann claims has reduced the kerygma to some fundamental points of ethics and religion. Bultmann is concerned that preaching meets the modern person with a credible challenge. He asks: ". . . is it possible that Jesus' preaching of the Kingdom of God still has any importance for modern men and the preaching of the New Testament as a whole is still important for modern men? The preaching of the New Testament proclaims Jesus Christ, not only his preaching of the Kingdom of God but first of all his person, which was mythologized from the very beginnings of earliest Christianity."[21] To find a solution to this question is to ask about the issue of hermeneutics; it is an issue of understanding. Liberalism attempted to eliminate mythology and desired to retain the Bible's abiding truth of morality and religion. However, Bultmann believes that ". . . it [liberalism] is no longer the proclamation of the decisive act of God in

---

[18] Ibid., 3.
[19] Ibid.
[20] Erick Dinkler, "Existentialist Interpretation of the New Testament," *The Journal of Religion,* XXXII, No. 2 (April, 1952), 94.
[21] Bultmann, "Jesus Christ and Mythology," in *Rudolf Bultmann: Interpreting Faith for the Modern Era,* 292.

34   Chapter One

Christ."[22] Conversely, Bultmann believes that one could understand the myth by entering to the strata of self-understanding which created the mythological assertion and which is still buried within the myth.[23]

b. Myth

Though Bultmann understands the need to make the Gospel clear for the modern person, this is not the only reason for a deeper understanding of myth. It is an issue which is not possible to ignore. As a preacher and professor of the Word, he desires to make the kerygma tangible and clear to people who listen to him whether it be in a church or in a classroom. He states: "Mythology is the use of imagery to express the other worldly in terms of this side."[24] He continues: "Mythological thought regards the divine activity whether in nature or in history as an interference with the course of nature, history, or the life of the soul, a tearing of it asunder—a miracle, in fact."[25] Bultmann suggests yet another meaning of myth. His states that the ". . . myth is the report of an occurrence or an event in which supernatural powers or persons are at work; hence the fact that it is often defined simply as history of the gods."[26]

It appears that with the first explanation of myth, Bultmann is referring to the manner in which humans have a tendency to objectify language. Relating this to the Cartesian philosophical school, to "objectify" something is to place it ". . . within the subject—object correlation fundamental for all acts of theoretical cognition."[27] Bultmann appears to emphasize at this point more of the transcendence of God over His immanence. Bultmann stresses that God's revelation cannot be manipulated by human beings. Schubert Ogden believes essential to Bultmann's thought is the separation between transcendence and finitude.[28] This suggests that

> . . . . there is nothing that man is or has or done (and the same is true, of course, of the created order generally) that is directly divine or can be

---

[22] Bultmann, "New Testament and Mythology," in *Kerygma and Myth*, 13.
[23] Ibid., 12.
[24] Ibid., 10.
[25] Ibid., 197.
[26] Rudolf Bultmann, *Kerygma and Myth,* Vol. II, ed., H. W. Bartsch (Hamburg: Herbert Reich Evangelischer Verlag, 1952), 180, cited by Schubert Ogden, *Christ without Myth* (New York: Harper and Brothers, 1961), 24.
[27] Ogden, *Christ without Myth*, 25.
[28] Schubert Ogden, "Introduction," *Existence and Faith* (New York: The World Publishing Co., 1960), 14-17.

assigned divine function or significance. God infinitely transcends the world, and everything human and creaturely is only indirectly or paradoxically identified with him.[29]

This idea also implies that any "act" of God must be seen from a cause-effect connection, and only faith is able to see this. The *existentielle* situation connects the question of God and the question of my own existence. His second explanation pertains to his view that the universe is self-contained; thus, divine incursions cannot be documented. Bultmann explains, "To every other eye than the eye of faith the action of God is hidden. Only the natural happening is generally visible and ascertainable. In it is accomplished the hidden act of God."[30] The third understanding of myth is an extension of the first two. Here myth assumes the form of the "holy" and alternative history alongside the secular and profane stream of history. Bultmann has a difference of opinion concerning the Heilsgeschichte school, especially as reflected by Cullmann in his *Christ and Time*. To Bultmann, the concept of history extending from a "midpoint" into a primal beginning and into an eschatological end is not tenable.

Perhaps the major reason Bultmann supports for demythologization is that he believes this attempt already has been made in the New Testament itself. Some of the aspects of its mythology are contradictory, for example, the giving of the law by God and by angels. Another significant point is that man's existence is portrayed dualistically; he is presented as under the control of cosmic forces and also as responsible for his own decisions.[31] The New Testament itself demythologizes and invites this kind of criticism; John, for example, unified the Parousia and Pentecost into one event.[32] Bultmann explains:

> We are compelled to ask whether all this mythological language is not simply an attempt to express the meaning of the historical figure of Jesus and the events of his life; in other words, significance of these as a figure and event of salvation. If that be so, we can dispense with the objective form in which they are cast.[33]

Ladd states that there are three major summary facts about Bultmann's interpretation of New Testament theology. His second point is, "All ideas

---

[29] Ibid., 17.
[30] Bultmann, "Bultmann Replies to His Critics," in *Kerygma and Myth*, 197.
[31] Bultmann, "New Testament and Mythology," in *Kerygma and Myth*, 11-12.
[32] Ibid., 32-33.
[33] Ibid., 35.

of supernatural acts—real incarnation, virgin birth, miracles, bodily resurrection, etc.—are ipso facto unhistorical but mythological."[34] Macquarrie summarizes succinctly Bultmann's program of demythologization:

> Bultmann has been able to show how myths of creation, the fall, the last things, can be existentially interpreted, and when this is done, the block in communication is at least to some extent overcome. The myths can be shown to conceal within themselves a self-understanding which is just as relevant today as ever—a self-understanding in which we are made aware of the finitude and disorder of human existence that is always lived in the face of the end. The fact that Bultmann's method produces such a coherent and convincing picture is itself a remarkable testimony to the sound- ness of that method. He is surely right in stressing the existential orientation of religious language, and this needs to be stressed since the objectifying language of myth can easily obscure it from us.[35]

c. Representative Hermeneutical Writings

The study and discussion of hermeneutics[36] was a lifelong endeavor for Bultmann. What is the text saying to me at this moment and what is my response are constant questions with which he is concerned. There are five representative texts which give insight into his understanding of hermeneutics which are as follows: (1) "The Problem of a Theological Exegesis of the New Testament," (2) "New Testament and Mythology," (3) "The Problem of Hermeneutics," (4) "Jesus Christ and Mythology," and (5) "Is Exegesis without Presuppositions Possible?"

"The Problem of a Theological Exegesis of the New Testament" was presented as a public lecture at Marburg on February 1, 1921. After some revision, the lecture was given a few days later at Göttingen University during the time of Karl Barth's professorship. It was requested of Bultmann that he avoid any public discussion with Barth since an open rift between the two could weaken Barth's position at the university. Martin

---

[34] George Elden Ladd, *A Theology of the New Testament* (Grand Rapids: William B. Eerdmans Publishing Co., 1993), 11.
[35] John Macquarrie, *Christian Theology* (New York: Charles Scribner's Sons, 1977), 133.
[36] James M. Robinson, "Hermeneutics since Barth," in *New Frontiers in Theology*, eds. John M Robinson and John B. Cobb, Jr., (New York: Harper & Row, 1964), 1. Robinson claims the Greek noun *hermeneia* broadly means "interpretation" and that it could be applied to any general activity in order to bring the unclear to clarity. "It is in this way that one is to understand the constant application of *hermeneia* to the messages of the gods, in that they are by their very nature mysterious, obscure, and in need of clarification."

Heidegger as well as several students from Marburg went with Bultmann to Göttingen for the lecture. Bultmann's lecture displays the intersection of both existential philosophy and Dialectical Theology. "Das Problem einer theologischen Exegese des Neuen Testament" initially appeared in the journal of *Dialectial Theology, Zwischen den Zeiten* (1925). Two individuals, Louis DeGrazia and Keith R. Crim, translated the article into English and editor James M. Robinson published the material for *The Beginning of Dialectical Theology* in 1968. In this essay, Bultmann argues that there is no neutral exegesis. Textual interpretation is always connected with the exegete's interpretation of himself. Bultmann argues that unlike nature, we cannot distance ourselves from history; we stand in history, and how we interpret history is similarly how we interpret our own existence.

Bultmann begins by stating that Orthodox Lutheran exegesis views the Bible as containing a variety of doctrines which can enrich the life of the Christian. This method sees the Bible in a manner in which to help one's inner or spiritual life and also to give direction on how to live. However, with the rise of the Hegelian or Idealist school of philosophy, as represented by the Tübingen school, history is viewed more with an end or purpose; thus, history is seen as more teleologically induced. Ideas came to be seen as forces which compel historical movements. Concurrently another movement, Naturalism, views man as the recipient of forces of history, and history and humankind are causally determined. Causal factors are varied such as understanding the person biologically or psychologically. The latter, Bultmann believes, is especially seen in the exegesis of the history of religions school, and he is quite critical of this methodology since in his opinion, it leads to the possibility of some doctrines being obscured or reduced to mere experiences and moods. Bultmann is highly critical of all of the above methodologies since he believes that it is possible only to interpret according to one's own position, or by an existential interpretation. Historical and psychological exegesis primarily establish what has been thought or said at a particular time, but on the whole do not reflect on the meaning and especially the demands of what has been said.

To Bultmann, the real issue is that we confront history in such a manner that we realize its claims upon us. He believes that one should not merely ask about the content of a given historical situation but also its meaning for me personally and to what type of reality it will lead me. Historical exegesis merely asks: "What is said?" Bultmann says we must ask: "What is meant?" He claims that there actually is no such discipline as neutral exegesis and that we do not encounter nature as we do history. History displays how we interpret our own existence which Bultmann terms "problematic." He is against any type of exegesis which views the possibilities of human existence as closed or foreseeable. He suggests that we confront the text and be in relation with it just as we are in relationship with existing persons. This kind of approach will enable one to understand his existential possibilities. Such a relationship with the text will guard one from reconstructing the text to suit his own desires.

Interestingly, Bultmann observes that the essential presupposition of every exegete is awareness of the uncertainty of our existence and also the understanding that the free acts of our decisions are part of existence. He repeatedly states that he is not inventing any new method.

He believes that there is only revelation concealed in human words. God's Word is a hidden word spoken to human beings. In the New Testament we find words which pertain to man and God. He believes that it is important to transform the historical into present-day concepts. Bultmann states that there must be an attempt to discern the expression of the Spirit of Christ and mere human statements. He believes that there can be no such discipline as "pneumatic" exegesis, or an appeal to an inner light. Certainly exegesis is of vital importance for Bultmann, but what is important is to be able to grasp the significance of a particular passage, especially the Greek text, in the concrete contemporary situation. An existential interpretation is the foundation for all historical, philological, and historical interpretations.

Bultmann addressed the Society of Evangelical Theology on June 4, 1947, in Alpirsbach, Germany on the topic "New Testament and Mythology." Though the immediate result was intense debating in Germany, the work was not known in a wider sense until its publication in 1948 in *Kerygma und Mythos*. The effect of this essay was to incite controversy regarding demythologization for the next fifteen years. In this essay, Bultmann argues that human existence apart from faith is inauthentic existence. The life of faith is authentic existence. The ultimate meaning of the resurrection is that the cross is efficacious. Philosophy can describe authentic existence, but only God can make it possible; the message of the New Testament is that it has already been accomplished in Jesus Christ.

He begins by stating that the cosmology of the New Testament is characterized by myth. For Bultmann, myth is concerned with views of reality which are not in harmony with a scientific understanding of the cosmos. For example, Bultmann reasons that the account of Jesus' resurrection from the dead cannot refer to a fact rooted in reality since scientifically one cannot prove this event as historical

Bultmann believes that by eliminating certain features of the kerygma, i.e., the mythological, the kerygma is even more acceptable to the audience. For example, the doctrine of the Virgin Birth is not mentioned by either St. Paul or John, and if one does not accept the doctrine, it still does not impact the mythical quality of redemption. Myth is not to be interpreted anthropologically but existentially. The ultimate purpose of myth is to tell of a transcendent power which controls the cosmos and human beings. However, it takes effort to explain what myth is. Bultmann believes that such effort is necessary to explain to the Christian the perceived contradictions found in the New Testament.

He asks the question whether or not it is possible to interpret the kerygma apart from mythology; his answer is that only an existential interpretation offers the solution. He reminds the reader that this is not an easy task, and in his opinion it will take a generation of theologians to accomplish a correct method of interpretation. Inherent in the mythology of the New Testament is that the cosmos operates according to a dualistic mode, evil must be vanquished by righteousness and darkness eliminated by light. However, Bultmann claims that the task is not necessarily to erase the mythological elements but to produce an existential interpretation of the dualistic mythology of the New Testament.

Bultmann does not believe that the soul is imprisoned by the body as seen in Gnosticism. He discusses the biblical term "flesh" extensively and enumerates the many nuances of this word. The person who lives after the flesh becomes subject to anxiety and the realization that life is ephemeral and fleeting. Man ultimately becomes a slave to that which he hopes to master. In contrast, Bultmann speaks of the authentic life which is based upon intangible realities. This is the life lived in the Spirit or by true faith. It is represented by openness to the future. The true believer is no longer in bondage to the world. The life of faith is not a possession in which the recipient can live a life of ease; there is not only an indicative involved but also the imperative! To be a person of faith is to be between the "already" and the "not yet." There is always an objective to attain. Bultmann cites the fruit of the Spirit in Galatians 5:22, emphasizing that one is meant to live in community, and he can relinquish attempting to cling to possessions.

Bultmann alludes to the fact that some think he is too dependent upon Heidegger, and Bultmann counters this accusation by stating that he believes philosophy and the New Testament are saying identical things about human life. Human nature cannot be known without the help of the New Testament; interestingly, he also includes both Luther and Kierkegaard alongside the New Testament as undergirding modern philosophy. Bultmann has a very high regard for philosophy, and he states that both this discipline and the New Testament together have shown that man has erred. He does, however, say that the New Testament, not philosophy, tells man of his fallen state and that deliverance can only come from God. Without God (Christ) our situation is beyond hope; this is a claim which existentialism does not accept. The New Testament tells people to be holy since they are already so in Christ. Philosophy cannot make this claim. The New Testament makes promises only to believers, to those whose hearts are open to God. The natural man lives a life which in many cases is characterized by despair and hopelessness.

Bultmann mentions the consequences of the Fall, and because of this fact, every thought and act of man without grace springs from impulses of a fallen being. Without Christ one is subject to despair and living in an inauthentic manner. The New Testament portrays man as a rebel, incapable by his own efforts to live an authentic life.

He places a strong emphasis upon the cross and its power to release men from both the guilt and power of sin. The cross is not merely a historical event but is also eschatological, and this event transcends time as the event can be understood as a reality which now can be realized. The cross becomes a reality in the sacraments of baptism and the Lord's Supper. Baptism baptizes one into the death of Christ, whereas with every celebration of the Lord's Supper, His death is proclaimed and realized anew. The cross becomes a *geschichtlich* event. The *historisch* (historic event) is the historical fact of his crucifixion. The cross of history is not as important for us today as it was for the first preachers of the cross. The personal connection for us today cannot be reproduced as it had a unique meaning for those who were acquainted with his historical person.

The resurrection is not a provable event. In fact, Bultmann believes a literal resurrection from the dead is unthinkable. The resurrection is an eschatological event in which Christians participate daily as they live their lives in freedom, hope, and victory. The resurrection is a matter of faith, and Christ meets us in preaching, especially when such a message centers upon the cross and the resurrection of Christ.

Bultmann wrote "The Problem of Hermeneutics" in 1953, and this essay is considered the most thorough statement of his position. One reason for writing this work was because of the criticism he had received for making demythologization a part of his program of existential interpretation in 1941. Bultmann denounces an existential (existentiell) interpretation of exegesis which focuses on the individual interpreter, which is the emphasis in his 1925 essay. Contrary to this method of interpretation, he now emphasizes sixteen years later an existentialist (existential) method. The essay gives a clarification of his early thinking on the topic of demythologization as part of an existentialist interpretation. Here one sees the influence of Heidegger upon Bultmann's method, and in particular, Bultmann attempts to clarify the meaning of faith. "Das Problem der Hermeneutik" was published in *Zeitschrift für Theologie und Kirche* in 1950 and subsequently was included in *Glauben und Verstehen, II* in 1952.

Bultmann commences this essay with citing Wilhelm Dilthey's allusion to "a great historical movement" and the belief that the world is in the midst of such a movement. He states that one major problem is how to achieve the possibility of objectivity in understanding historical phenomena as they are witnesses to human existence; thus, hermeneutics is the science of understanding history, in particular as this history is embedded in literary documents, monuments, and works of art.

Bultmann refers to Aristotle and ancient methods of hermeneutics as still valid—an understanding of structure and style is significant. There should be a relationship between the whole and the parts and vice versa. He refers to the "hermeneutical circle" in which an interpretation moves. There must be an understanding of the grammar of a text, especially if one is interpreting an ancient text; but, even more importantly, one must even go beyond a comprehension of the grammar to understand the author's use of a particular word. By the time of the Enlightenment, the questions grew in sophistication in that one had to comprehend which words were common to particular historical periods.

Schleiermacher earlier emphasized another dimension in interpretation: the psychological. Grammar and stylistic analyses can yield only so much information; thus, there is another significant dimension of interpretation by which one must endeavor to understand the individual's psychological reasons for writing a particular work. Interpretation, then, takes on the form of a re-creation as the interpreter attempts to understand the emotive and psychological expressions of the writer. Dilthey expands on Schleiermacher by stating that the life of the interpreter and of the original writer are intertwined. Interpretation is ultimately a work of art depending upon the gifts of the interpreter.

Bultmann states that a most important aspect of understanding interpretation is the awareness that everyone has presuppositions, and that interpretation is always guided by a pre-understanding of the text. One must have such an understanding in order to ask valid questions, for the questions determine the answers. One must go beyond an understanding of the kind or genre of text and attempt to comprehend the psychical framework of a particular work. Questions grow out of an interest, which is personal to the one asking the questions. But real interpretation does not occur just because the interpreter understands what the original writer was attempting to convey; rather, interpretation happens when both have the same experience of the subject matter. This is the major presupposition of understanding.

Bultmann gives many fine examples of pre-understanding such as interpreting from one language into another and understanding texts of music only if the interpreter has some acquaintance with music. He even states that portions of Doktor Faustus are unintelligible to many readers because of a lack of understanding of basic elements of music! He makes a profound statement claiming that many pieces of literature are essentially not completely understood because of this lack of a life relationship with the written material. It is easier if the questions are determined by what the author wishes to communicate. Genuine interaction with the text is when the reader is gripped by the events and the movement of the story; true participation takes place. If one is interested in the form of a document, the analysis and conclusion will certainly be different than the person who is interested merely in the content.

Bultmann cites J.J. Winckelmann as an innovator in that he emphasizes that it is necessary to attempt to see behind what is objectively said in order to understand the spirit of the piece of art. On the other hand, Dilthey features the fact that we understand ourselves more fully by comprehending history. One must "hear" the questions which are in the work under study, and this should lead to greater possibilities in the questioner's life.

The questioner, even if he has a pre-understanding, must be willing to engage in risk in order to raise his understanding to a higher level. But another step in the process is needed which is allowing oneself to be questioned by the text. Can historical phenomena be interpreted objectively? Bultmann does say that there is a certain ambiguity about history, but if the interpretation is performed in a methodical manner, he claims objectivity can be achieved. The manner of asking questions cannot be termed "subjective" according to Bultmann, especially so if the questions grow out of the history under investigation. The questioner must not read his own conclusions into the text under study, or use the text to confirm what the person already believes. Bultmann states:

> Thus, the demand that the interpreter has to silence his or her subjectivity and quench any individuality in order to achieve objective knowledge could not be more absurd. It makes sense and is justified only insofar as it means that the interpreter must silence his or her personal wishes with respect to the results of interpretation—such as a wish, say, that the text

should confirm a certain (dogmatic) opinion or provide useful guidelines for praxis. Often enough, such wishes have been present in exegesis past and present; and, of course, being without presuppositions with respect to results is as unalterably required in the case of interpretation as in any other scientific research.[37]

He closes the essay with a discussion of what he believes to be Barth's misunderstanding of his position. In defending his own position Bultmann writes: "For such analysis seeks to grasp and understand the actual (historical) existence of human beings, who exist only in a context of life with "others," and thus in encounters. Existentialist analysis endeavors to develop an appropriate conceptuality for just such an understanding."[38] Bultmann appears to be stating that Barth requires of people to engage in a *sacrificium intellectus,* especially pertaining to the physical resurrection of Jesus. To Bultmann, the problem of interpretation is the problem of understanding. In the process of gaining understanding, a testing of one's presuppositions must be performed.

"Jesus Christ and Mythology" represents Bultmann's lectures which were given at several American universities in the fall of 1954. These lectures were revised and became the text for several chapters in *Jesus Christ and Mythology* which was published in 1958. The German translation of this text appeared in 1964. Many believe that these lectures are the most fully developed statements of Bultmann's views on demythologization.

The essence of Jesus' preaching is the subject of the Kingdom of God. About the turn of the twentieth century, the understanding of the Kingdom changed from a spiritual view to an eschatological view, especially that as proposed by Johannes Weiss. Humankind will not bring in the Kingdom; rather, there will be a breaking in of the supernatural activity of God. The emphasis is on transcendence and not immanence. The end of the world will occur suddenly, and then God will bring into existence a new world and all will be blessed. Bultmann believes that an eschatological message is the core of New Testament preaching.

How is one to interpret this Kingdom of God? Bultmann believes:

> For the conception "Kingdom of God" is mythological, as in the conception of the eschatological drama. Just as mythological are the presuppositions of the expectation of the Kingdom of God, namely, the theory that the world, although created by God, is ruled by the devil,

---

[37] Bultmann, "The Problem of Hermeneutics," in *Rudolf Bultmann: Interpreting Faith for the Modern Era,* 152-53.
[38] Ibid., 156.

Satan, and that his army, the demons, is the cause of all evil, sin and disease. The whole conception of the world which is presupposed in the preaching of Jesus as in the New Testament generally is mythological; . . . . In any case, modern science does not believe that the course of nature can be interrupted or, so to speak, perforated, by supernatural powers.[39]

New Testament scholars according to Bultmann are divided concerning the person of Jesus Christ. Did Jesus himself believe that he was the Messiah who would come again and institute righteousness on earth? Bultmann believes that the early Christian community did understand him in a mythological manner. Such views as Jesus born of a virgin and suffering on a cross were widespread in the mythologies of both Jews and Gentiles. One sees a similarity to Gnosticism in the belief that Jesus was preexistent and took on the form of a human being in order to bring about redemption for humans. In this writing, Bultmann wants to know what is the significance of Jesus' preaching and the preaching of the New Testament for the modern person. Bultmann does emphasize that there are many elements in the message of Jesus which would not merit demythologization such as the command to love and to be obedient to God. What should one omit and retain? He suggests a "deeper" meaning which is part of his program of demythologizing the New Testament. He claims that the term "demythologizing" is an unsatisfactory word. Bultmann is adamant in stating that he is not attempting to eliminate the mythological elements but to interpret them, and this method comes under the rubric of hermeneutics. He explains:

> Mythology expresses a certain understanding of human existence. It believes that the world and human life have their ground and their limits in a power which is beyond all that we can calculate or control . . . . It may be said that myths give to the transcendent reality an immanent, this-worldly objectivity. Myths give worldly objectivity to that which is unworldly. (In German one would say, "Der Mythos objektiviert das Jenseitige zum Diesseitigen.")[40]

Bultmann gives an extended discussion of eschatology, which comes from the Greek word *eschaton*, meaning "last" or "end." In theology the word usually refers to the attempt to determine what the future *(Zukunft)* holds for humanity. To Bultmann, eschatological preaching looks at the present in reference to the future. Such preaching reminds men and women

---

[39] Bultmann, "Jesus Christ and Mythology," in *Rudolf Bultmann: Interpreting the Faith for the Modern Era*, 290-91.
[40] Ibid., 293.

that this world is passing and that the eternal is quickly coming. The future will either be a judgment or a blessing to human beings. To Bultmann, demythologizing has its beginning point in the New Testament as seen in the writings of the Apostle Paul but in particular in St. John's writings.

Human beings, according to Bultmann, are in danger of forgetting that love, truth, and obedience to God are more important than their own agendas and also that human life and accomplishments are ephemeral. However, the Word of God can give to humans hope and free them from anxiety (Angst) about their present and future. He makes a profound statement by claiming that only obedience can give a person security.

Bultmann states that the discipline of hermeneutics has been overlooked in German theology since the time of Schleiermacher, though he does acknowledge that Dilthey had revived some interest in the discipline. He reiterates the importance of *Vorverständnis,* and that without such a relationship, it is not possible to understand a text. He asks:

> Now, when we interpret the Bible, what is our interest? Certainly the Bible is an historical document, and we must interpret the Bible by the methods of historical research. We must study the language of the Bible, the historical situation of the biblical authors, etc. But what is our true and real interest? Are we to read the Bible only as an historical document in order to reconstruct an epoch of past history for which the Bible serves as a "source"? Or is it more than a source? I think our interest is really to hear what is the truth about our life and about our soul.[41]

He discusses the argument that man does not have any idea of God until God reveals himself to him. Bultmann, conversely believes that the individual does possess in advance a relationship and understanding of the significance of God. He is careful to add that man does not have a knowledge in advance of the revelation of God in Jesus Christ. However, man is searching for God according to Bultmann; this is true because man is in search of the meaning of his own existence, and to Bultmann the question of God and the question about oneself are identical. He does believe that the Holy Spirit's role is critical, "The personal understanding, in traditional terminology, is imparted by the Holy Spirit, who is not at my disposal."[42] Of course, he strongly emphasizes that we are dependent upon a correct hermeneutical principle which is gained by objective and critical reflection.

He believes that hermeneutics is under the domain of philosophy. But he clearly states that there is no perfect philosophy. There will never be a

---
[41] Ibid., 309.
[42] Ibid., 310.

system which can clear up all the questions and give one complete knowledge. While he appreciates much that is contained within Idealism, which still influenced the theological thinking of his day, he implies that Idealism falls short in understanding what it means to be a person in the crucible of decision making. He believes that an existentialist interpretation is the only school of philosophical thought which directs itself entirely to the human situation. All other worldly beings are only extant *(vorhanden)* says Bultmann; he actually cites Kierkegaard's use of this term. People have a historical existence which determines their present and future. Every "now" is significant to each person. The Bible is concerned with decisions and what it means to be human. Personal existence and choice are each person's responsibility, and he believes that the New Testament contains this mandate. He cites a very clear example of love:

> Existentialist analysis describes particular phenomena of existence, for example, the phenomenon of love. It would be a misunderstanding to think that the existentialist analysis of love can lead me to understand how I must love here and now. The existentialist analysis can do nothing more than make it clear to me that I can understand love only by loving. No analysis can take the place of my duty to understand my love as an encounter in my own personal existence.[43]

Bultmann believes that the miraculous occurs within the world of nature. Miracles are hidden from observation, and are only recognized after the fact, and only the eyes of faith can recognize miracles. He sums up his views on the subject by stating:

> He who thinks that it is possible to speak of miracles as of demonstrable events capable of proof offends against the thought of God as acting in hidden ways. He subjects God's action to the control of objective observation. He delivers up the faith in miracles to the criticism of science and in so doing validates such criticism.[44]

Bultmann believes that God meets us in His Word; the Word allows us to understand the moment, and on this point Bultmann cites Luther. The Word of God is not a statement which is for all time, rather, it must meet one in his concrete, present existence. The Word is eternal, but to Bultmann this means God's presence must be actualized now. The Word acts to cause an encounter; at this point it is the *verbum externum*.

---

[43] Ibid., 312-13.
[44] Ibid., 317.

Bultmann believes that demythologization is similar to Paul and Luther's doctrine of justification by faith alone without the works of the law. As the doctrine of justification, demythologization removes all longing for human security, for Bultmann believes, "There is no difference between security based on good works and security built on objectifying knowledge. The man who desires to believe in God must know that he has nothing at his own disposal on which to build his faith, that he is, so to speak, in a vacuum. He who abandons every form of security shall find the true security."[45]

Bultmann wrote "Is Exegesis without Presuppositions Possible?" in 1955; "Ist voraussetzunglos Exegese möglich?" appeared in *Theologische Zeitschrift, XIII*. Bultmann believes that objectivity is the exegete's aim. He emphasizes that all bring a worldview to the text, and ignoring this fact is not possible; thus, he argues against neutral objectivity. However, he is quick to say that in reality the exegete will approach the text with various questions and a method of going about the task. He explains that the concept without presuppositions means that one is not to speculate what the results will be. It appears that he is arguing that the study must be inductive, or maybe another way of expressing it is that the exegete should not engage in eisegesis.

He rejects allegorical interpretation as a valid method. He does state that personal prejudices must not be accepted, or they will construe the interpretation. All knowledge which is based upon a historical analysis is suspect and is open to subsequent investigation and discussion. One must hear what the text says and not what one desires the text to say.

He speaks about the other sense, or the second sense, of presuppositions and claims that with this understanding there can be no such thing as a presuppositionless exegesis. Especially the historical method of investigating the text cannot be eliminated. This method follows rules of grammar, philology, and style. Every text uses the language of its time and its own particular Sitz im Leben. Bultmann writes:

> This the exegete must know; therefore, he must know the historical conditions of the language of the period out of which the text that he is to interpret has arisen. This means that for an understanding of the language of the New Testament the acute question is, "Where and to what extent is the Greek determined by the Semetic use of language?" Out of this question grows the demand to study apocalypticism, the rabbinic

---

[45] Ibid., 327. Cf. Rene Marle, *Bultmann and Christian Faith* (New York: Newman Press, 1968), 35-43.

literature, and the Qumran texts, as well as the history of Hellenistic religion.[46]

Bultmann believes in causes and effects in history, but he readily says that this does not rule out free decisions of people who determine the course of history. But there is even a cause for a so-called free decision. There is, then, a closedness in history, and Bultmann believes that this fact rules out a breaking in of the supernatural into the natural. Miracles are seen as suspect since such events lie outside of history and are not subject to scientific scrutiny. History can only tell us that there are people who definitely believe in miracles. The world of the Bible must be translated for people today since a very distant world is portrayed. However to translate means that the historian has to make intelligible what he finds, and interpretations by several historians on the same subject matter can have varying results and conclusions. He uses as an example the Reformation stating that it is possible to obtain a one-sided interpretation of the movement by focusing only on economic or political factors. He is arguing for a fully orbed interpretation—this will help to keep the historian from making one-sided and biased questions and conclusions. He succinctly states: "In short, historical understanding presupposes an understanding of the subject matter of history itself and of the men who act in history."[47]

He reiterates that an understanding of the subject matter is presupposed by exegesis. If we come to a problem in history open and alive with questions, then the text will speak to us. It is possible for the past to come to life again in a sense. The knowledge which is gained is such that it can be applied to our lives in the present —it speaks directly to our life situation; indeed, this is an existentiell encounter. When a person is moved by history, then the message can speak to him directly. Historical dates can be fixed, that is, it is possible to cite a specific time and date when a particular event occurred. But the meaning of the event extends into the present and future. He claims: "Hence one must say that a historical event is always first knowable for what it is—precisely as an historical event—in the future. And therefore one can also say that the future of a historical event belongs to that event."[48]

Concerning the issue of a pre-understanding, this does not mean that the questioner must know everything possible about the content of the

---

[46] Bultmann, "Is Exegesis without Presuppositions Possible?" in *Existence and Faith,* 291.
[47] Ibid., 293.
[48] Ibid., 295.

question. For example, concerning the subject of God, the person obviously does not know much about this subject, but his existentiell questioning is sufficient to enable him to move into a deeper understanding. He closes this essay with a significant observation:

> Since the exegete exists historically and must hear the word of Scripture as spoken in his special historical situation, he will always understand the old word anew. Always anew it will tell him who he, man, is and who God is, and he will always have to express this word in a new conceptuality. Thus it is true also of Scripture that it only is what it is with its history and its future.[49]

2. Bultmann's Hermeneutical System

a. Background

In 1948, the collection of essays entitled, *Kerygma und Mythos,* which contains Bultmann's programmatic article, "Neues Testament und Mythologie," was published. This work had the effect of diminishing Barth's theological influence, but also instigated lively debates over the question of the relevance of the message of the kerygma for contemporary humankind. From his teachers, Bultmann learned the historico-critical methodology, and from Barth he learned the primacy of the Word of God. Bultmann's synthesis of these two categories is the immediate history of his existential theology. Henry indicates that it was the consistent extension of existentialism to the dialectical method that enabled Bultmann's ascendancy in Europe.[50] Schubert Ogden concludes that the need for a concise and consistent theological method is an essential presupposition for Bultmann. Ogden states:

> Perhaps more than any other contemporary Protestant theologian, Bultmann has given thorough and extended reflection to the problem of theological method. He has not only done theology, but was unusually self-conscious about what he has done and has tried to work out a mode of procedure—a theological program—that could serve to point directions for the work of an entire generation. In this sense, he is not only the

---

[49] Ibid., 296.
[50] Carl F.H. Henry, *Frontiers in Modern Theology* (Chicago: Moody Press, 1964), 331-332.

contemporary theologian par excellence, but . . . also the contemporary theologian's theologian par excellence.[51]

Bultmann challenged many theologians in particular to consider the multi-dimensional nature of language and thus, its inherent problematic character. Heinrich Ott writes:

> The appearance of dialectical theology signified a theological revolution without parallel. Today, in the continuance of that final revolution, we find ourselves in the midst of a second one signified by the problem of hermeneutics.[52]

Thus, Robinson states the following in the early 1960s: "Germany is just as nearly Bultmannian today as it was Barthian a generation ago," and that his "works and ideas have become Germany's dominant theological export throughout the world."[53]

It can be argued without much opposition that Martin Heidegger (1889-1976) was the person who had the most extensive influence upon Rudolf Bultmann and that this influence revolved around existentialist philosophy. Bultmann even dedicated his *Faith and Understanding, Volume I* to Heidegger. Heidegger's work *Sein und Zeit* appeared in 1927, during the period when he and Bultmann were colleagues at Marburg. Johnson writes:

> While unresolved historical issues from New Testament studies provided the focus for Bultmann's earliest theological development, philosophical concerns soon played an increasing role in his work. The impetus for this new development was the arrival in 1923 at Marburg University of a new

---

[51] Schubert Ogden, "The Significance of Bultmann for Contemporary Theology," *The Theology of Rudolf Bultmann*, ed. Charles W. Kegley (New York: Harper and Row, 1966), 107. Cf. Anthony C. Thiselton, "New Testament Interpretation in Historical Perspective," *Hearing the New Testament*, ed. Joel B. Green (Wm. B. Eerdmans Publishing Co., 1995), 25. Thiselton states: "The basis for Bultmann's distinctive approach to the relation between 'history' and 'faith' arises still more explicitly from a deep suspicion of the 'objective' or 'descriptive' as somehow undermining a genuinely Pauline or Lutheran notion of faith. It risks, that is, transposing faith into observation or reason and turning Jesus and God into mere 'objects' within a Kantian (or more strictly, neo-Kantian) conceptual world of human categories and constructs. The Jesus of historical 'reconstructions' is precisely that: a humanly achieved construct . . . ."
[52] Heinrich Ott, "Theology and Understanding," *Union Seminary Quarterly Review*, (XXI, No. 3 March, 1966), 279.
[53] James M. Robinson, *A Quest of the Historical Jesus* (London: SCM Press, 1963), 11.

professor of philosophy, Martin Heidegger. Heidegger had been working on some theological authors, especially Paul and Luther, and quickly perceived Bultmann's expertise as a valuable resource for his own interests. Bultmann, in turn, discovered in Heidegger a brilliant intellect committed to the development of a fundamental new form of philosophy which could provide an alternative to the several forms of philosophical Idealism long dominant in German thought. Their mutual interests quickly led them into regular discussions with each other, as well as jointly taught seminars. The impact of Heidegger's existentialism began to appear in Bultmann's writings by 1925; two years later, in 1927, Heidegger published Being and Time, one of the most influencial sources of existentialist philosophy in the twentieth century. Heidegger left Marburg in 1928 for Freiburg University, but by that time, Bultmann had already integrated existentialism into his understanding of New Testament eschatology.[54]

b. The Early Heidegger's Influence Upon Bultmann

The existentialist program of Bultmann cannot be understood without some consideration of the genesis of such a program; however, the sources for this program spread widely and penetrated deeply into diverse strata. Certainly, a major influence upon Bultmann's thinking is the philosophy of Martin Heidegger.

While Heidegger taught philosophy at Marburg, from 1923 until 1928, Bultmann saw in his existential analysis a very valuable theological ally. Though Gunkel, Harnack, Jülicher, Weiss, Heitmüller, and Herrmann all impacted the theological development of Bultmann, it was years later as a young professor that another professor at Marburg significantly altered Bultmann's presuppositions and methodology—Martin Heidegger was that colleague. Though Heidegger was five years younger than he, Bultmann realized that existential interpretation was the method for opening up the meaning of Scripture. Smart comments that Barth believes that "Kiekegaard reached Bultmann primarily through Heidegger and with a distinctly Heideggerian cast to his character."[57]

Rene Marle writes:

So Bultmann in no way tries to hide the philosophy which inspires him in his exegetical work and his theological reflection and it is the philosophy of existence ("existentialist philosophy"), especially as M. Heidegger

---

[54] Roger A. Johnson, ed., "Main Themes in Bultmann's Theology," *Rudolf Bultmann: Interpreting Faith for the Modern Era*. (Collins: San Francisco, 1987), 21.

formulated it, which he has adopted. He made his choice neither "arbitrarily" nor because of "personal preference," but because this philosophy belongs to the "historical situation" in which his work develops. A product of our age, it serves the exegete and theologian as well as they can wish. It is not a system that imposes preformed solutions, nor does it require a determined world view. Rather it reminds man that he himself is responsible for the world and for his own existence, and it merely shows him the general conditions under which he can assume this responsibility. Its main point is that man, as a being, realizes himself in action, in "decision," in the act of his existence. This existence is characterized by "historicity" (or temporality), which under- lines the fact that the being of man is identical with "becoming," a "possibility-to-be," and is distinguished in this way from all other beings in nature. It is within this existence, in the context of this "historicity," that all the problems are found and all the encounters occur.[55]

Heidegger's 1927 work, *Sein und Zeit*, had an enormous impact upon the twentieth-century philosophical milieu in Germany. Since this early work had similar themes as those of Sartre, Heidegger has been confused with him; Bultmann, however, does not claim any connection between himself and Sartre.[56]

Heidegger wanted to initiate a new school in philosophy. Though he had been impacted by pre-Socratic philosophers and by Husserl, Kierkegaard, and Nietzsche, Heidegger became a major shaper and prophet for existentialism and phenomenology. These two, Bultmann and Heidegger, focused their attention upon the individual and immediate inner experience of the person.[57] French philosophers were concerned with many of the same themes as was Heidegger. For example, one cannot help but notice the similarity to Heidegger's own work of 1927, *Being and Time,* when one sees the title of Jean-Paul Sartre's classic work, On *Being and Nothingness.* Stumpf claims that Heidegger was heavily impacted by the thought of Husserl.[58] He desires to reexamine metaphysics; he chooses to examine again a preoccupation with human existence. In 1949, he wrote concerning the subject before him:

---

[55] Rene Marle, *Bultmann and Christian Faith*, trans. Theodore DuBois (New York: Newman Press, 1968), 31-32.
[56] James M. Robinson, "The German Discussion," in *The Later Heidegger and Theology*, Vol. I: *New Frontiers in Theology*, James M. Robinson and John B. Cobb, Jr., eds. (New York: Harper & Row, 1962), 2.
[57] Smart, *The Divided Mind of Modern Theology,* 109.
[58] Samuel Enoch Stumpf, *Philosophy, History and Problems* (New York: McGraw-Hill, 1994), 492.

What is to be decided is nothing less than this: can Being itself, out of its own unique truth, bring about its involvement in human nature; or shall metaphysics, which turns its back to its ground, prevent further that the involvement of Being in man may generate a radiance out of the very essence of this involvement—a radiance which might lead man to belong to Being?[59]

Heideggger is concerned with the extrication of Being; he uses a particular word, *Dasein,* translated into English as "Being-there," to convey what it means for a human being's existence. Human beings, unlike animals, are aware of themselves and the decisions which they constantly make. Moreover, human beings understand ultimate issues; the most anxiety producing awareness is that of one's mortality. Heidegger coined some new words, and he helped to remove the mystery from the concept of Being and enabled many to see that this is an issue which concerns every person. He helps to clarify an understanding of our own being. Humans are not like things or objects which have no awareness. They find themselves thrown into the world, and they must choose how to be. To Heidegger a human being is best described not as an object but as a particular mode of being. Heidegger believes that the Greek-derived word *phenonmenon,* translated as "that which reveals itself," enables people to understand the meaning of existence.

John Macquarrie is widely recognized as an interpreter of the relationship between *Sein und Zeit* and Bultmann. Mcquarrie states the following concerning the characteristics of *Existenz*: (1) The person has a relationship to himself; he is not an object or a "thing," but is conscious of his own existence. (2) The person is unlike nature, that is, *Dasein* does not have an essence—his essence is his existence. One has only a history and a future because of the incompleteness of the present and the possibility for decision. (3) Existence cannot be described in a generic manner as each person is unique. Heidegger employs the word *Jemeinigkeit* to convey the idea that existence is always mine. The antithesis of *Existenz* is summarized in the word *Vorhandenheit* which pertains to the world of things. Macquarrie gives further clarification by stating:

> What we have here, then is not an attempt to describe universal properties of *Dasein*—which would be impossible, since *Dasein* is not an object, but

---

[59] Martin Heidegger, "The Way Back into a Ground of Metaphysics," *Existentialism from Dostoevsky to Sartre*, ed. Walter Kaufmann (New York: The World Publishing Company, 1956), 210.

exists—but an attempt to show the horizons of possibility within which the concrete possibilities of every individual *Dasein* must fall.[60]

Dasein, then, is in the world. A person has been thrown into a situation in which he cannot exercise control, and his existence is constantly under threat. Since he is in the world, he is surrounded by the presence of others, and this too causes a dilemma. *Das Man* is the specific word which Heidegger sees as pertaining to the "mere point of intersection of all these prescriptions of the public and external behavior of every day existence. Thus, Everybody and Nobody."[61] Existence becomes depersonalized. Macquarrie writes:

> (1) There is everydayness. . . . It stands for a way of being dominated by unthinking habit, a mechanical following of the ways laid down for us in our established order. . . . (2) Publicity . . . here *Dasein* can forget himself and his responsibility, and so allay his anxiety, by identifying himself with the indeterminate personal multitude. (3) Talking . . . which, instead of disclosing anything as it really is, rather makes it become what the public says it is. . . . (4) scribbling or popular literature. . . . (5) curiosity. . . . the desire to enter into experience without taking the resolve to have them for one's self.[62]

Heidegger describes this condition by the word "fallenness." This word recounts the attempt to escape; thus, there is a loss of the authentic *Dasein* and illusion takes the place of authenticity.

To exist inevitably means that there will be many concerns in this life, but the ultimate anxiety-producing realization is that death is in the future. The meaning of existence in this life is concerned with three temporal movements: past, present and future. Heidegger has a particular view of *Dasein* as an historical being. The past, present and future can be unified. Heidegger makes a distinction between the primary historical and the secondary historical, or man himself who is the subject of history and past artifacts comprise the secondary historical. Artifacts are significant since they signify his being-in-the-world. Man is the subject of history and not nature; therefore, history is to be interpreted existentially. Macquarrie gives insight into this issue by writing the following:

---

[60] John Macquarrie, *An Existentialist Theology* (New York: Harper & Row, 1965), 34. Cf. John Macquarrie, *Principles of Christian Theology* (New York: Charles Scribner's Sons, 1977), 91-95.
[61] William Barrett, *What is Existentialism* (New York: Grove Press, 1964), 56.
[62] Macquarrie, *An Existential Theology,* 91-92.

With this existential understanding of the historical in view, Heidegger contends that the science of history *(Historie)* is concerned with the study of the possible. It is the disclosure of man in his historic possibilities, and the more history understands possibilities, the more penetrating it is. . . . According to Heidegger, it is concerned with man in his authentic possibilities, when he has risen above the level of everyday existence to something great and heroic. And further . . . history is concerned with such authentic possibility as repeatable . . . as possibility for man existing now. The possibility which is studied by history is not taken as a shadowy example, but disclosed as a resolved destiny which can be repeated so that the power of the possible is felt in present existence, that is to say, belongs to its futurity. Though past worlds have lost their significance for our present existence . . . man's authentic possibilities do not perish with his instrumental world, but can be present to us in our world.[63]

Wilhelm Dilthey made a distinction between nature and history; thus, Heidegger also made such a separation. Through the existential method, the essence of man, who is always a subject, can be investigated.

Bultmann also accepts this understanding of history, which is important for understanding his interpretation of the New Testament. Bultmann made a comparable separation between history as objectively verifiable, Historie, and history as existential encounter, or Geschichte; the former refers to linear chronology and the latter to the point-in-time "now" of decision.[64]

Marle gives insight into Bultmann's understanding of history:

> He [Bultmann] feels that we cannot circumscribe the historical nucleus with either precision or certitude. He stresses, especially that for faith and theology it can have only a relative interest anyway. Any project to "objectively" reconstruct the past proceeds from an illusion concerning the very nature of history, because history can never be "considered" objectively, from a distance, in the way that we abstractly consider the phenomena of nature. This is because we ourselves are a part of history, we ourselves are involved in the system of forces that defines its course. We can only regard these forces as solicitations, original invitations addressed to our liberty. It is only in this way that we can begin to speak about the Christian faith and theology.[65]

Bultmann believes that theology always possesses a presupposed framework; thus, it is the task of philosophy to explicate in a scientific

---

[63] Macquarrie, *An Existential Theology*, 162-63.
[64] Robert Funk, *Language, Hermeneutic, and the Word of God* (New York: Harper & Row, 1966), 110.
[65] Marle, *Bultmann and the Christian Faith*, 60.

manner the contents of this underlying conceptual substructure. Historically, there has been a debate concerning the relationship of philosophy and theology. Whereas Tertullian believes that there is no relationship between the two, Augustine believes that theology is sometimes established by philosophy. Hegel believes that in some cases philosophy even supplies content to theology.[66] The compatibility of existentialism with the theological task is based upon Bultmann's belief that the basic religious questions are questions of existence. Since the New Testament is concerned with human existence, questions which relate to existence are put to the text; as a result, the answers are of the same nature. Bultmann is aware that the Bible, even without Heidegger's construct, is to be interpreted existentially. However, for scientific interpretation, the situation is quite different. Bultmann states that it is ". . . a question of relevant interpretation of the inquiry, and that means, at the same time, the relevant interpretation of human existence."[67] [Italics his]. It must lay bare the conceptions in which existence is to be spoken of, which are encompassed in the life relation of the interpreter to the text.[68] Otherwise, theology would simply be a sermon. In Bultmann's method, anthropology and hermeneutics are intimately combined. Since the text requires an existential interpretation, it is thus an anthropological interpretation. Macquarrie writes:

> It is not with any and every philosophy that he is concerned, but with existentialism as that philosophy which offers a conceptual analysis of the structures of human existence. Why should this zone of common interest be of special importance? This depends upon Bultmann's belief that the basic religious questions are questions about our own existence, about which we have to decide . . . . The 'right' philosophy is, quite simply, that kind of philosophical work which endeavors to develop in suitable concepts that understanding of existence which is given with human existence . . . . It does provide the theologian with the conceptual framework which he needs if his work is to have transparency and if it is to be carried out in full awareness of what his questions and answers involve.[69]

---

[66] Millard J. Erickson, *Christian Theology* (Grand Rapids: Baker Book House, 1985), 40-41.
[67] Rudolf Bultmann, *Essays: Philosophical and Theological*, trans. G>G> Smith (New York: The Macmillan Company, 1955), 358.
[68] Ibid.
[69] John Macquarrie, "Philosophy and Theology in Bultmann's Thought," *The Theology of Rudolf Bultmann*, ed. Charles W. Kegley (New York: Harper & Row), 130.

Therefore, the beginning point for understanding the text is the religious question, that is, the understanding of one's own existence. Since understanding is on this level, and not on the level of the biblical thought-world itself, an understanding of what it means to exist is an important theological component. Martin Heidegger furnishes this means of conceptualization.

However, Bultmann does not believe that theology has been relegated to a second-class position in relationship to philosophy. Philosophy enables one to understand what it means to exist before the personal address of the kerygma in the situation of decision. Bultmann writes about the relationship by stating:

> Heidegger's existentialist analysis of being would seem to be no more than a secularized, philosophical version of the New Testament view of human life . . . . Is not this exactly the New Testament understanding of human life? . . . philosophy is saying the same thing as the New Testament and saying it independently.[70]

Bultmann maintains that there is a distinction between ontological and ontic in this relationship.[71] Philosophy attempts an ontological analysis and displays the possibility or non-possibility of such human experiences as love or faith; thus, philosophy analyzes the structures of existence.[72] Philosophy speaks of the "that" of existence, while theology addresses the "how."[73] The theme of philosophy is existentiality, not concrete existence.

Bultmann gives additional insight by stating the following:

> What has been said should have made clear in a provisional way that philosophy and theology have the same object, namely, man, but that they make it their theme in different ways: philosophy by making the being of man its theme, i.e., by inquiring ontologically into the formal structures of human existence; and theology by speaking of the concrete man insofar as he is faithful (or is unfaithful— which is also something positive and not negative), i.e., insofar as his "how" is characterized by the fact that he has been or is to be encountered by a specific proclamation. Thus we can also say that theology as a positive science (in contradistinction to philosophy)

---

[70] Rudolf Bultmann, "New Testament and Mythology," *Kerygma and Myth*, ed. Hans Werner Bartsch, trans. Reginald Fuller (New York: Harper & Row, 1961), 24-25.
[71] Rudolf Bultmann, "The Historicity of Man and Faith," *Existence and Faith,* edited and introduced by Schubert Ogden (New York: The World Publishing Company, 1964), 93.
[72] Ibid., 94.
[73] Ibid.

is in principle a historical science in that it speaks of a specific occurrence in human existence.[74]

Bultmann believes that philosophy can know the nature of authentic existence; therefore, philosophy does not depend upon the New Testament for this insight. What is needed is the knowledge which philosophy discloses of the nature of the true historic existence. Bultmann does maintain that there is a division between philosophy and the New Testament. He states:

> Is this self-confidence of the philosophers justified? Whatever the answer may be, it is at least clear that this is the point where they part company with the New Testament. For the latter affirms the total incapacity of man to release himself from his fallen state. That deliverance can come only by an act of God. The New Testament does not give us a doctrine of "nature," a doctrine of the authentic nature of man; it proclaims the event of redemption which was wrought in Christ.[75]

c. Theologians Who Influenced Bultmann

There were several professors who had a significant impact upon Bultmann, though perhaps none as great as Heidegger. Two professors at Berlin with whom Bultmann studied were Hermann Gunkel and Adolf Harnack. Gunkel used the Religionsgeschichte and Form Criticism methodologies, and it appears that Bultmann was impacted by Gunkel for both Bultmann's *Die Geschichte der synoptischen Traditon* and *Das Urchristentum in Rahmen der antiken Religionen* agree with these procedures.[76] Gunkel also emphasized oral tradition and the meaning of the documents in the life of the people. Bultmann in distinction to Harnack does not wish to eliminate myth, but to interpret it. Harnack, however, did emphasize the necessity to recover the essence of Jesus' religion. One must strip away temporary expressions in order to find that which is of permanent value. In Harnack's book, What is Christianity, he summarizes liberalism. Though Bultmann wrote the introduction to the 1950 edition, he is somewhat critical of Harnack for minimizing the importance of the

---

[74] Ibid.
[75] Rudolf Bultmann, *Kerygma and Myth: A Theological Debate*, ed. Hans Werner Bartsch, Trans. Reginald Fuller (New York: Harper & Row, 1961), 27.
[76] Richard L. Jeske, "Rudolf Bultmann 1884-1976" *Dialog* 17 (Winter 1978):21. Cf. Bruce Corely and Steve Lemke, eds. *Biblical Hermeneutics: A Comprehensive Guide to Interpreting Scripture* (Nashville: Broadman and Holman Publishers, 1996), 22.

History of Religions School and the eschatological theme of the New Testament.[77]

Bultmann's major professors at Marburg were Adolf Jülicher, Johannes Weiss, Wilhelm Heitmüller, and Wilhelm Herrmann. Jülicher and Weiss in particular encouraged Bultmann to study and interpret Jesus' message eschatologically. Jülicher spoke against an allegorical interpretation of the parables. Heitmüller instructed Bultmann to understand New Testament literature by the means of comparing early Christianity with other religious movements of the same period such as Jewish apocalypticism and Hellenistic Gnosticism. Weiss in particular had an impact upon Bultmann's thinking. Perrin writes:

> Weiss was a member of the "history of religions school," a group of scholars who set for themselves the particular task of studying earliest Christianity in its context among the religions of the eastern Mediterranean in the Hellenistic age. Weiss himself was concerned to study the message of Jesus in light of what the key phrase "Kingdom of God" would have meant to Jesus and his hearers, and he revolutionized theological scholarship by demonstrating that the reference would be to God irrupting into history as an overpowering storm to bring to a violent end the world and its history and to create a new and radically different world and history. This was in very sharp contrast to the idea generally held before Weiss that the reference was to a world being gradually transformed by love as men accepted the rule of God in their hearts. In consequence of Weiss' influence, Bultmann consistently speaks of the Reign of God rather than the Kingdom of God so as to stress the fact that the reference is to God and to something that he does, and Bultmann always interprets the message of Jesus as controlled by an imminent expectation of the reign of God.[78]

Wilhelm Herrmann, a professor of systematic theology at Marburg from 1879-1922, also exerted a significant influence upon Bultmann, and Herrmann taught both Barth and Bultmann at Marburg. According to Schmithals, Bultmann acknowledges this legacy and is a more faithful disciple of Herrmann than Barth.[79] Both Karl Barth and Rudolf Bultmann

---

[77] Morris Ashcraft, *Rudolf Bultmann* (Peabody, MA: Hendrickson Publishers, 1991), 19. Cf. James D. Smart, *The Divided Mind of Modern Theology* (Philadelphia: The Westminster Press, 1967), 32-33. Smart believes that Harnack had a considerable influence upon Bultmann.

[78] Norman Perrin, *The Promise of Bultmann* (Philadelphia: J.B. Lippincott Company, 1969), 17.

[79] Walter Schmithals, *An Introduction to the Theology of Rudolf Bultmann* (Minneapolis: Augsburg Publishing House, 1968), 11. Cf. E.L. Miller and Stanley

held Herrmann in high regard. Smart concludes the following about the relationship between Bultmann and Herrmann: "Bultmann, however, shows the influence of Herrmann in his early writings even more plainly than Barth."[80] Hermann emphasized the independence of religion alongside of morality and knowledge, and that faith is essential for daily living.

d. Bultmann's Method

The twentieth-century was marked by technological and scientific advancement as typified by the splitting of the atom and atomic power. In essence, Bultmann asks how can a modern person accept literally what he finds in the Bible. The entire Weltbild in the New Testament is such that a thinking twentieth-century person would have to sacrifice his intellect in order to accept literally what is found there. Bultmann's solution is an existentialist interpretation:

> Our task is to produce an existentialist interpretation of the dualistic mythology of the New Testament along similar lines. When, for instance, we read of daemonic powers ruling the world and holding mankind in bondage, does the understanding of human existence which underlies such language offer a solution to the riddle of human life which will be acceptable even to the non-mythological mind of today? Of course we must not take this to imply that the New Testament presents us with an anthropology like that which modern science can give us. It cannot be proved by logic or demonstrated by an appeal to factual evidence . . . . And this is why we have to discover whether the New Testament offers

---

Grenz, *Introduction to Contempoary Theologies*, (Minneapolis: Fortress Press, 1998), 36. The authors claim that Herrmann impacted Bultmann during his period of study at Marburg. Roger Johnson believes that Bultmann was immersed in the history-of-religions school through the influence of Wilhelm Heitmüller; Johnson, "Introduction: The Formation of Bultmann's Theology" in *Rudolf Bultmann: Interpreting Faith for the Modern Era*, 9.

[80] James D. Smart, *The Divided Mind of Modern Theology* (Philadelphia: The Westminster Press, 1967), 33. Smart believes, "And when we hear Herrmann say, 'God reveals himself to us only in the inner transformation which we experience. . . . The religious man is certain that God has spoken, but what he can say of the event always takes the form of a statement concerning his transformed life. . . since religion is this transformation from what only seems to be life to what is truly life,' we seem to be hearing the voice of Bultmann." Wilhelm Herrmann, *Gesammelte Aufsätze* (Tübingen: J.C.B. Mohr, 1923), 159.

man an understanding of himself which will challenge him to a genuine existential decision.[81]

Bultmann is concerned about communicating the essential message of the New Testament; this is an issue not only for biblical scholars but also for those who gather to hear preaching especially on Sunday mornings. Bultmann attempts to make the message more credible by a method called demythologizing *(Entmythologisierung)*. The goal is to set free the original understanding of existence through expression in a form of conceptuality which is appropriate to it, that is, the existential anthropological categories of Heidegger.[82]

Bultmann acknowledges that what he has attempted is a methodology which has been used before:

> How then is the mythology of the New Testament to be reinterpreted? This task is not the first time that theologians have approached this task. Indeed, all we have said so far might have been said in much the same way thirty or forty years ago, and it is a sign of the bankruptcy of contemporary theology that it has been necessary to go all over the same ground again. The reason for this is not far to seek. The liberal theologians of the last century were working on the wrong lines. They threw away not only the mythology but also the kerygma itself. Were they right? Is that the treatment the New Testament itself required? This is the question we must face today. The last twenty years have witnessed a movement away from criticism and a return to a naïve acceptance of the kerygma. The danger both for theological scholarship and for the Church is that this uncritical resuscitation of the New Testament mythology may make the Gospel message unintelligible to the modern world. We cannot dismiss the critical labors of earlier generations without further ado . . . . Perhaps we may put it schematically like this: whereas the older liberals used criticism to eliminate the mythology of the New Testament, our task to-day is to use criticism to interpret it. Of course it may still be necessary to eliminate mythology here and there. But the criterion adopted must be taken not from modern thought, but from the understanding of human existence, which the New Testament itself enshrines.[83]

Bultmann, then, believes that former attempts at demythologizing were attempted in an inappropriate manner. Earlier critical theology dismissed myth and did not interpret it in a new creative manner.

---

[81] Rudolf Bultmann, "New Testament and Mythology," in *Kerygma and Myth*, 16.
[82] Roger A. Johnson, *The Origins of Demythologization: Philosophy and Historiography in the Theology of Rudolf Bultmann* (Leiden: E.J. Brill, 1974), 2.
[83] Rudolf Bultmann, "New Testament and Mythology," in Kerygma and Myth, 12.

Bultmann mentions some of the earlier methods of interpretation, namely the allegorical, which to Bultmann is to be dismissed because "this method spiritualizes the mythical events so that they become symbols of processes going on in the soul."[84] He also states, "The literal meaning is allowed to stand and is dispensed with only for the individual believer, who can escape into the realm of the soul."[85]

Bultmann is somewhat critical of Adolf von Harnack when he writes: "It will be noticed how Harnack reduces the kerygma to a few basic principles of religion and ethics. Unfortunately this means that the kerygma has ceased to be the kerygma: it is no longer the proclamation of the decisive act of God in Christ."[86]

The history of religions' school commenced a new beginning in interpreting the New Testament. The method used by these representatives demonstrated to what extent the New Testament draws upon various mythologies of religious traditions. The New Testament is viewed as a religious document, arising out of the cultic life of the church and displaying a quality of mystical devotion and "supramundane" religion which was previously unknown in the history of religious development. Myth is seen as secondary to cult. Bultmann states: "The New Testament was thus the abiding source of power which enabled man to realize the true life of religion, and Christ was the eternal symbol for the cultus of the Christian Church."[87] Bultmann believes that this approach helped to correct the subjective idealism of the "older liberalism" and helped to recover the significance of the cultic and religious in early Christianity. However, it avoided the "objectivity" of the mythological; thus, like the liberal approach, this approach does not emphasize the Christ event. Bultmann claims, "So we are still left with the question whether this event and the person of Jesus, both of which are described in the New Testament in mythological terms, are nothing more than mythology."[88] Thus, Bultmann does not agree with these methods to delete myth since by dismissing myth they also exclude the kerygma which occurs through myth. Jesus Christ and the kerygma are described in mythological language and are not easy for the modern person to understand; thus, another approach is needed.

He places hermeneutics within the sphere of historical understanding in general; thus, it appears that historical documents and the New

---

[84] Ibid., 13.
[85] Ibid.
[86] Ibid. (Italics in the original)
[87] Ibid., 14-15.
[88] Ibid., 15.

Testament are approached with a similar methodology.[89] Bultmann, as Heidegger, believes in a person's ". . . radical historicity, in his being delivered over to history."[90] Some would argue that this seems to make the person a pawn in the hand of fate; thus, the conclusion could lead one to nihilism. However, Bultmann has a view of history which places its meaning in the future. The historical understanding of a particular biblical text is constantly open to the future. There is always the possibility of a disclosure of existentiell possibilities; however, Bultmann stresses the individual is responsible for his future. Bornkamm summarizes this perspective as well as explaining Bultmann's hermeneutics:

> History cannot be regarded as an empirical object . . . . There are doubtless facts and events that can be established and chronologically arranged; but history becomes, so to speak, a mass of news items that reveals nothing new . . . . In Bultmann's view the unique meaning of history cannot be understood so long as the historian remains just an observer, for he who endeavors to understand history is himself in the nature of an historical being and can succeed in understanding history as he responds to the challenge of history . . . . the possibilities pertaining to the human understanding of existence become internalized, challenging the interpreter himself to make decisions . . . . In other words, the encounter with history must be in the form of word and response, challenge and decision.[91]

This explanation by Bornkamm leads into the area of the problem of historical understanding.

Bultmann states that literary analysis must continue on the assumption of historical-critical principles which include the following: grammar, words, style, language, and the historical situation.[92] An essential tenet of the historical method is the belief ". . . that history is a unity in the sense of a closed continuum of effects in which individual events are not connected by the succession of cause and effect. . . . All decisions and all deeds have

---

[89] Bultmann, *Essays: Philosophical and Theological*, 234-35.
[90] Heinrich Ott, "Rudolf Bultmann's Philosophy of History," in *The Theology of Rudolf Bultmann*, ed., Charles W. Kegley (New York: Harper & Row, 1966), 42. Cf. Rudolf Bultmann, *History and Eschatology* (New York: Harper & Row, 1962), 11. Bultmann speaks of the person as history and process.
[91] Gunther Bornkamm, "The Theology of Rudolf Bultmann," in *The Theology of Rudolf Bultmann*, ed., Charles W. Kegley, 6.
[92] Bultmann, "Is Exegesis without Presuppositions Possible?" in *Existence and Faith*, 291.

their causes and consequences; and the historical method presupposes . . . to understand the whole historical process as a closed unity."[93]

The understanding of history is related to one's existentiell encounter with it from the vantage point of present existence. It appears, then, that history will always be fluid or possesses an open end. Bultmann gives insight by writing the following:

> . . . historical knowledge is never a closed or definitive knowledge. . . . For if the phenomena of history are not facts that can be neutrally observed, but rather open themselves in their meaning only to one who approaches them alive with questions, then they are always only understandable now in that they actually speak in the present situation. Indeed, the questioning itself grows out of the historical situation, out of the claim of the now, out of the problem that is given in the now . . . . And therefore, one can also say that the future of a historical event belongs to that event.[94]

By this understanding, it appears that history will never be fully realized until its final consummation.

To Bultmann, then, pre-understanding and the asking of questions are vital when attempting to ascertain the meaning of a document. Does not the text of the Bible preclude any pre-understanding since it recounts acts of God? Is not the person ultimately dependent upon God's revelation? Bultmann's answer to this issue is significant:

> Man does have in advance a relation to God which has found its classical expression in the words of Augustine: "Tu nos fecisti ad te, et cor nostrum inquietum est, donec requiescat in te" . . . . Man has a knowledge of God in advance, though not of the revelation of God, that is, of his actions in Christ. He has a relation to God in his search for God, conscious or unconscious. *Man's life is moved by the search for God because it is always moved, consciously or unconsciously, by the question about his own personal existence. The question of God and the question of myself are identical.* [Italics mine.][95]

To be involved in the issues of life such as the questions of choices, salvation, friends, difficulties, happiness, the nature of the world, and one's personal existence is to have an existential awareness of God.[96]

---

[93] Ibid., 291-92.
[94] Bultmann, "Is Exegesis without Presuppositions Possible?" in *Existence and Faith,* 294-95.
[95] Bultmann, "Jesus Christ and Mythology," in *Rudolf Bultmann: Interpreting the Faith for the Modern Era,* 309-10.
[96] Bultmann, *Essays: Philosophical and Theological,* 257.

Thus every man knows what is at issue when we speak of revelation, and yet he does not know it either, because he can only know of it as he knows himself.... Accordingly, therefore, also the answer to the question how revelation is understood in the New Testament cannot be understood as a simple communication, but only as personal address. The question concerning revelation is simultaneously the question concerning man's limitation; and an answer to the question, What is revelation? can only be perceived if the questioner is prepared to let his limitation be disclosed.[97]

When the interpreter addresses the questions of personal existence, one can better understand the intention of the biblical writers. Certainly Bultmann's approach is critical of all attempts to make the ancient worldview of the Bible normative. Bultmann's hermeneutical stance in the final analysis is a result of a spiritual impulse, for Bultmann believes that God is truly present to man in the word which transcends the limitations of history. "Now this means that Jesus Christ confronts men in the kerygma and nowhere else; just as he confronted Paul himself and forced him to the decision."[98]

Historical science reveals nothing of God's redemptive act in Christ. The text continues to offer man a new understanding of himself, and it is not simply a resource for what has occurred in the past; rather, the Bible speaks to one's existence in the present, constantly calling one to decision.

It is not possible to go beyond the kerygma. Bultmann believes that such an attempt is "Jesus Christ according to the flesh." Rather, Jesus' word is a summons to decision, "Nothing that he [Jesus] says is new; but when he speaks, the hour is the decisive hour, the now when the word is spoken, the event of the word.... The word alone, as it supports the hearer in the summons, demands decision."[99]

Bultmann believes that culture is a seductive temptress, and he constantly admonishes to abandon any confidence in self and all attempts to grant fulfillment for the flesh. He is against any attempt to objectify God, or to give permanence to the objects of one's thought; therefore, to Bultmann demythologizing is deobjectifying. Deobjectifying enables one to interpret the biblical speech of God consistently within the limits of existentialist conceptuality with the goal of relinquishing any type of

---

[97] Bultmann, "The Gospel of Revelation in the New Testament," in *Existence and Faith*, 63-64.
[98] Bultmann, "The Significance of the Historical Jesus for the Theology of Paul," in *Faith and Understanding*, ed. Robert W. Funk, trans. Louise Pettibone Smith (New York: Harper and Row, 1966), 241
[99] Bultmann, "The Concept of the Word of God in the New Testament," in *Faith and Understanding*, 291-92.

objectifying thinking about God. Thus, as the kerygma is proclaimed, the hearer is confronted with the demand for a decision in regards to his self-understanding. Authentic existence becomes a possibility as one renounces self-sufficiency and future security. When the kerygma is truly heard and accepted, a person experiences freedom; he is freed from anxiety concerning his past failures and concern for the future.

Bultmann believes that Jesus views man in a crisis before God. The kingdom of God is coming, and with every choice one decides whether he will give to God his whole self. Bultmann believes:

> For the Kingdom of God remains a dark and silent entity, like death, as long as it is not plain that the demand for decision has for man a clear, compre- hensible meaning. Only then is the determination of the present by the future Kingdom not a denial of the present but its fulfillment; only so is the future a controlling factor in the present. Conversely, the will of God, as calling man in the present to decision, is comprehensible only if this will gives man a future. For this decision is no choice between two possibilities which lie equally at man's disposal; it is a true crisis, that is, the Either-Or between two possibilities, in which the "old man" leaves his position of independence and comes under the sovereignty of another. The sovereign in both cases is God, either the angry judging God, or the gracious God. A man becomes through the decision either a sinner or righteous. The real future stands before a man in decision, not the false future over which he already has control, but the future which will give him a character which he does not yet have. This is the meaning of the present instant, that it involves the necessity of decision because it leads into the future.[100]

Bultmann continuously emphasizes the question of the "either-or." He also cites several key biblical passages which emphasize a the need for a definitive decision such as Luke 9:62, Matthew 8:22, and Luke 14:26. Bultmann believes that faith and obedience are combined as one's faith expresses itself in one's daily "walk."[101] The goal of preaching is, ". . . to present the Word in such a way that the possibility of understanding does not appear as a question of theory, of world-view, but becomes an actual possibility which is disclosed by the word and which must be grasped by the will."[102]

---

[100] Bultmann, *Jesus and the Word*, trans. Louise Pettibone Smith and Erminie Huntress Lantero (New York: Charles Scribner's Sons, 1958), 131-32.
[101] Bultmann, *Theology of the New Testament*, Vol. 1 Trans. Kendrick Grobel (New York: Charles Scribner's Sons, 1951), 328.
[102] Bultmann, "The Word of God in the New Testament," in *Faith and Understanding*, 302.

C. Sermonic Exposition

1. Bultmann's Sermons At Marburg

a. Sermons From 1934-1950

Bultmann deems preaching to be highly significant. He states:

> ... it follows that God's Word is a real word spoken to me in human language, whether in the preaching of the Church or in the Bible in the sense that the Bible is not viewed merely as an interesting collection of sources for the history of religion, but that the Bible is transmitted through the Church as addressing us. This living Word of God is not invented by the human spirit and by human sagacity; it rises up in history. Its origin is an historical event, by which the speaking of this word, the preaching, is rendered authoritative and legitimate. This event is Jesus Christ.[103]

Bultmann preached his message, "Der glaube an Gott den Schöpfer" at an academic worship service at Marburg on July 1, 1934, and he drew his message from the biblical text of I Cor. 8:4-6. He begins by addressing the problem of eating meat which had been sacrificed to idols; should a Christian eat that which has been offered to another god (even though a false god)? Some even claimed that though it was offered only to a false god, perhaps this was a demon! The issue is significant

Hitler had been in power since January 30, 1933, and he had already arrested and sent to concentration camps many political opponents. In June 1934, he had conducted a purge and had many of his opponents executed. Bultmann makes some veiled references to the political situation when he expresses that true freedom is an inner attitude, and also the insignificance of anyone who attempts to convince others that he is divine. He makes a veiled reference to the Nazi regime when he states that many are tempted

---

[103] Bultmann, "Jesus Christ and Mythology," in *Rudolf Bultmann: Interpreting Faith for the Modern Era*, 325. Cf. "How Does God Speak to Us through the Bible?" in *Existence and Faith*, 167-68. Bultmann emphasizes the need to hear and make a decision: "Those who are thus ready to hear the word of the Bible will hear it as God's word. Yes *because* they hear it with this readiness, they hear it as God's word. For the call to preparedness is already the call of God through the Bible. The readiness to listen will increase through it; i.e., the word of the Scriptures teaches men to recognize ever more clearly what is "beyond" and the "here." Death and life, flesh and spirit, God and man. ... The church's preaching founded on the Scriptures, passes on the word of the Scriptures. It says: God speaks to you *here*! In his majesty he has chosen *this* place! We cannot question whether this is the right one; we must listen to the call that summons us."

to surrender their freedoms when the promise of dominion over the world is given to them.

Bultmann's objective is to explore the basis for Christian freedom, and that basis or foundation rests upon faith in God as the creator. Bultmann in this sermon is not concerned about only giving a history lesson, but he desires to help people of his day understand the significance of this sermon for their own particular times. He even mentions philosophical Idealism and Positivism as past philosophies which influenced people's thought. He believes that one must be true to himself, and he must freely make authentic decisions pertaining to matters of conscience. He is presenting the word of God in order to help them to be enabled. They are in the world but not of the world.

Bultmann, then, claims that God is above all the powers of history and national life. These temporal powers may lay a certain claim upon us and our lives, but ultimately it is God to whom we give our ultimate allegiance. One cannot serve these temporal powers and also serve the true God! Actually, these powers receive their authority from God and not vice versa. Bultmann gives an extended discussion over the fact that even the person who is considered the greatest and most noble is in fact a creation of God and is nothing in comparison to the ultimate One. Man is in the moment of decision. God demands the whole person, and a divided allegiance is not sufficient.

Karl Barth was the primary individual responsible for the composing of the Barmen Declaration which document was the outcome of the Barmen Synod which met from May 29-31, 1934, in Barmen. This confessional statement declared that there is no revelation of God in German history and politics, and that the true leader is Jesus Christ. After Barmen, the role of the Confessing Church became even more distinguished from the Nazi-controlled German Christian Church; Christians would have a definite standard by which false teachings could be judged.

Bultmann believes that the Christian can participate in civil matters but implies that he should be mindful that God does not want him to become enamored and too "caught up" with such activities and ways of thinking. He quotes Paul's words in 1 Cor. 7:29-31 where the writer speaks about being in the world but living in it in such a manner that one's affections are not controlled by the spirit of the world. He cites one of Paul Gerhardt's hymns encouraging Christians to acknowledge God as the creator. He is encouraging the congregation to realize that though they live responsibly in the world, their ultimate allegiance is to God, and this loyalty expresses itself in decision making which is consistent, authentic, and not alienated from everyday living. An existentialist interpretation does not exclude thinking concerning creation and nature. Nature reminds us of our nothingness. All of creation has its source in God who created ex nihilo. We are in God's hands, but if we forget this fact, our nothingness becomes apparent. One must decide to live a life characterized by faith which will enable one to understand more fully God's love; he will understand God's will for him in the moment.

The Christian is not to seek his ultimate security from that which is temporal or that which does not have eternal significance. A political ideology cannot bring ultimate deliverance, for this is attempting to live according to the flesh. Only by listening to the voice of God in the kerygma and deciding to live a life according to Spirit, is one able to experience true freedom.

The Christian must live as if he has nothing; there is an inner attachment to the things of the world. He is especially open to God's love, and because of this he is able to decide to do the will of God moment by moment. This will lead to authentic decisions. Bultmann suggests that Christians can partake in matters which others might find questionable because behind all of their partaking is their personal faith and relationship with Christ. The Christian should not attempt to cause misunderstandings, however, in the minds of other Christians. If Christians are sincere in their faith and worship, and thus secure in themselves, they can interact freely with the sole ambition of giving honor to God. He is at an either-or situation; either he will trust God completely, respond to his word and live dependently upon him, or live according to the flesh and rely upon something other than God.

On June 7, 1936, Bultmann preached a sermon at Marburg on the biblical text of Acts 17:22-32. He comments on Paul's speech concerning heathendom and states that Paul attacks this mindset because of its vain attempt to appear pious.

By this time, there had been been much talk about the need for Lebensraum—Hitler believed that Germany's borders needed to be expanded. On March 7, 1936, Hitler remilitarized the Rhineland, and he and his generals were in agreement that a war was needed at least by 1940. Göring was given the task of rearmament in April, 1936, and there was the belief that the war would be short—a Blitzkrieg. Just ten days after the preaching of his sermon, Himmler was appointed police chief of the whole of Germany; policing came under the head of the SS. In this sermon, Bultmann urges one to realize that he is not his own master, and ultimately technology cannot save anyone. One must acknowledge his religious awareness; thus leading him to an understanding of the true God. The fact that we are *media in vita in morte sumus* should not cause us ultimate concern because we can trust God realizing our destiny is with him. Only by surrendering ourselves fully to God can we draw near to him.

Bultmann paints a picture of Paul wandering through Athens and seeing the many symbols of the heathen culture, i.e., that the city was full of idolatry. Bultmann suggests that the unregenerate Athenians had a very immature and fallacious concept about the true God and what authentic worship is. He believes that their superstitious concept of religion consists in the desire to engage in polytheism and selfishly attempt to control the divine, which is heinous since this is an attempt to bring the true God down to a human level. Heathen god worship is replete with anxiety and the attempt to overcome anxiety—the more the person attempts to understand divine mystery, the more one realizes the impossibility of such an attempt.

Bultmann is always concerned about applying the message to the life situation in which people currently find themselves; thus, he asks if people attempt to do the same thing today. He believes that many use religion in order to bring a semblance of order into their lives. They have the form of religion but certainly not the substance. Though technology has erased many of the primitive ways in which people understood the cosmos, still by virtue of being human, each one has fears of the unknown and mysterious forces which defy explanation.

Paul reminds them through his words that they are not the masters of their own fate. Centering one's attention on controlling one's environment, others, and even God, leads to a lack of personal peace, which ultimately results in anxiety about one's own existance. He quotes a poem by Nietzsche in which one desires to be his own master. He also refers to the rich man who thought that constructing bigger and better barns and acquiring more material possessions would bring him security, but God's indictment is that he is a fool.

Bultmann stated in 1936 that present-day society is ignoring the discussion of death, living in denial and closed to the future. To Bultmann, this implies that people are ignorant, either consciously or unconsciously, about their relationship with God, who is sovereign both over the living and the dead. Man never escapes the limits of time and space, though he may believe that it is possible because of technology.

God, the ultimate judge, reminds us that depending on technology and not the true God is a means to lose our souls. Modern man does not truly know himself. Bultmann alludes to Ernst Weichert's well known book, *Majorin,* in which book the author portrays contemporary man as not as being terrified at the darkness which lurks in his own heart. He reminds his listeners knowing himself and of some of the atrocities which human beings have inflicted upon one another such as those who were sentenced to camps in Siberia. He then brings the possibility within the reach of all when he challenges them to realize that such inhumane actions lurk within the hearts of all people: "When we have heard of these dark deeds, have we only called God to account, have we not realized that we ourselves were being called to account?"[104]

Man cannot simply live by his unrestrained impulses; rather, he must live in a responsible way and make decisions which are authentic. The voice and judgment of God is terrible, but even more terrible is the means by which persons conceal the presence of God and live out of a *Weltanschauung* which essentially states that God does not exist. One must engage in self-surrender in his relationship with the living God. We see Bultmann's spiritual impulse manifesting itself in a message which encourages his auditors to remember that they live in an either-or situation. The culture is a seductive temptress and promises temporal rewards, but only by listening to God's word and responding, is one able to live authentically.

Bultmann preached a sermon from Matthew 6:25-33 on November 15, 1936, before a congregation in Marburg. The subject matter of the sermon is that one does not need to be anxious. He writes that he chose this particular text because ". . . the times in which we live is full of care and anxiety; but also because this text is difficult to understand."[105] How can one not be concerned about the future? Even when events are going well in one's life, there is still the responsibility to be prepared for the future. Care over our present and future robs one of the joys of the present. In this sermon, Bultmann is reminding especially those whose lives are characterized by a middle-class ethos not to be overly concerned about their economic status. The words of this sermon encourage us to live in such a manner that we transcend the cares of the world, yet we live responsibly.

Many people's lives are characterized by anxiety; however, to live in such a manner is to live according to the flesh. Rather, one must attempt to live a life which has faith as its primary characteristic. Faith will enable a person to live victoriously and without anxiety. Bultmann alludes to Heidegger when he writes, ". . . a philosopher of our day. . . ." Anxiety is the major characteristic of the times, but Jesus encourages one not to be anxious. Anxiety characterizes especially those who attempt to become masters of their own lives. Our main priority must be that we can stand in

---

[104] Rudolf Bultmann, "Acts 17:22-32," in *This World and the Beyond: Marburg Sermons*, Trans. Harold Knight (New York: Charles Scribner's Sons, 1960), 19.
[105] Bultmann, "St. Matthew 6:25-33," in *This World and the Beyond*, 23.

God's presence. This is possible if we seek his kingdom over our own desires. God will give to us "inner freedom and peace."

Bultmann suggests that Jesus is referring to a kind of worry which is destructive; it keeps us from preparing since we become immobilized by such worry. A proper concern encourages us to work and to be prepared, but not to allow anxiety to overcome us or to control us. What we can learn from plants and animals is what they cannot do—provide for themselves and others by their labor. Certainly if plants and animals can live *ohne Angst,* we can as well. Though we do not necessarily see the action of God, since in most cases it is hidden, we can discern the miraculous by faith.

Bultmann is careful to state that we are not sufficient in ourselves; we are not to secure our own future as if we are independent from God and others. He continues to emphasize how ridiculous it is to worry. It makes about as much sense as being concerned about our height; our concern cannot change our physical condition. He believes that the words of Jesus are for two types of people: those who are overly concerned about their existence and the future, as well as those who are overly ambitious. If we cannot change certain physical characteristics, how can we imagine that we can make our future secure? He uses some strong imagery in this sermon by stating that some can lose their very souls by being concerned for material things such as money, food, and clothing. If one is overly concerned about such issues as money, the meeting of physical needs, the future, and death, this is to live according to the flesh and in an inauthentic manner.

He concludes by encouraging us to seek God's kingdom and righteousness. If we will live life as Jesus has suggested, the cares, anxiety, and even catalysts of anxiety will be greatly minimized. We should be ready for self-sacrifice, living simply, and bearing our cross daily. Correct exegesis of this passage is dependent upon an existential encounter with the message. Bultmann closes by stating that the most precious gift God can give is that of inner freedom and peace, and that we must choose to receive them. This choosing means that one surrenders his will and personal ambitions to God and his kingdom. Man is standing in the crisis of decision, and he must decide immediately to choose to do the will of God.

On May 9, 1937, Bultmann preached a sermon from the Old Testament, Genesis 8:22. He begins this message by reflecting that the recent weeks had been especially cold and that it was refreshing to experience the warmth of the spring months. He describes the beauty of nature as blossoms burst forth and the landscape is once again green. He goes beyond a superficial recognition of the changing of the seasons to the fact that all of nature points to God as the creator, and that this recognition must be part of our worldview.

He speaks about a problem in current thinking in that many look to just nature as a type of god and discount the fact of God's revelation in the Bible, and Bultmann reiterates that God has disclosed himself in the Bible. Blood and Soil *(Blut und Boden)* was a philosophical ideology inherent in National Socialism as the connection between Nazism and environmentalism was very strong and pronounced. Bultmann is alluding to his belief that this ecological ideology has supplanted a belief in the God of Christianity.

In 1932 the formation of the German Christians occurred, and the leader was Ludwig Müller. There was, then, a coalition between Nazism and the German Christians as the latter supported Nazi ideology. It was the intention of the German Christians to establish a Reich Church in order that all Protestants in Germany would belong to one large organization. This group was opposed by the Confessing Church, in particular Martin Niemoeller. Bultmann is against the acceptance of pantheism; this view of God he believes can easily lead to the deification of man. This belief also leads to an attempt to objectify God, and of course the attempt to do so is especially repugnant to Bultmann. The action and work of God are mainly hidden, but miracles can be realized by faith. He agrees that God is in nature and nature's marvels are many and wonderful, but nature is not the sphere of God's self-revelation. He is very specific in that he says Christ's presence is in nature, but not his self-disclosure. He cites quotations form both Goethe and Eichendorff which attest to the beauties of this season.

God is not bound to the laws of nature, rather he is above and in control of the natural processes. If we do not acknowledge the God of creation, Bultmann believes that this is a form of idolatry; our admiration of nature must point to the one who is ultimately responsible—God. The tendency for many is to somehow believe that nature is God, and forget the words of Genesis 8:22, which state "While the earth remains . . . . ." The implication is that the earth is temporal and is subject to time; thus, there will eventually come a time when it too will no longer be in existence.

He believes that we must move beyond mere emotionalism as we encounter nature; we must decide to seek God, and if we do not, our piety will soon dissipate. The person who knows God only in nature has a hopeless future. Conversely, the Christian message is one of eternal hope and joy. God will be present for his own not only in nature, but he will be with them when their time on earth is completed. For the Christian, nature is a reminder of a God who is near and who will never leave him. In viewing the temporal, one is reminded constantly of the eternal. Though Bultmann believed that God's presence is only implied in nature, the God of creation whom we know through Jesus Christ is present there. This fact can give to the Christian daily confidence as he lives out the Christian life.

On June 27, 1937, Bultmann preached a sermon on the Pauline text of Philippians 3:7-14. He commences by stating that the end of the term is at hand and that it is a time for looking both backwards and forwards. He raises the question if we are justified in looking back, and then he recounts that Paul too looked back on his life at various occasions. Bultmann initially attempts to answer the question of when we should and should not be concerned about the past. Paul writes about forgetting, but this obviously does not mean that we cannot remember the past. Bultmann believes that the meaning of Paul's passage is we choose what to remember—we are discriminating in what we recollect. If there is something in the past which may cause us to become proud and boast in our own ability, this must be abandoned. However, one episode that Paul will never forget from the past is the event of meeting Christ and the result of possessing a new life. As we encounter the word, we live in expectation and openness to the future. There is an eschatological theme in this sermon as Bultmann reminds his auditors that they are still in the "not yet." The future is ahead of them, and they are not yet what they shall be. They must be decisive in that they must choose not to live in the past, rather, they must claim the future. Every hour is the last hour, and to embrace the future is to decide for authentic living. This theme is very important for the accomplishing of Christian maturity. One is filled with hope concerning the future, and his choices are authentic since they reflect what the person understands to be God's character.

He is aware that there may be some who are feeling discouragement and perhaps believe that the past term has been wasted or that they have not truly been prepared for what the future will bring. If this is the situation, Bultmann suggests that the words of the biblical text are even more appropriate: ". . . Forgetting what lies behind and straining forward. . ." Knowing human nature well, Bultmann says that there may be some who want to hold on to the negative issues in their lives such as anger, disillusionment, and bitterness. Even in this situation Christ is present as he persistently attempts to bring his grace and comfort into the lives of those who believe themselves to be oppressed. When Christ has come upon a person personally, he experiences both empowerment and trials. There will be difficulties for the person who follows Christ after having the Lord's hand laid upon him. Bultmann asks: "Are we ready to receive His grace which liberates us in that it ever anew breaks our lives, shatters over and over again the old man which constantly clings to us? Shatters us with our pride and our indolence, our tense and gnawing self-concern and, on the other hand, our frivolity?"[106] This is a rhetorical question as he does not offer an answer, but the strong implication is that the person is to be ready to abandon all of these immature ways of living and to decide to follow Christ totally. When one makes this decision, he is able to experience life to the fullest extent.

May 15, 1938, Bultmann preached a sermon on a text drawn from John 16:5-15. Only two months before the preaching of this sermon, German troops marched into Austria on March 12, 1938, after Hitler decided on an annexation of Austria. In Vienna he announced the Anschluss, and Austria became a German province.

In this sermon Bultmann's spiritual impulse is evident, for he believes that it is the Spirit which enables one to see that which is truly eternal. God is the ultimate authority, not a political ideology. The Spirit will guide them concerning the truth, but this will require a total dependence upon God. He gives the setting of the biblical text in his introduction. The meal is over, and Jesus will be going to Gethsemane soon. He believes that the text is to prepare the disciples especially for the gift of the Holy Spirit, but the disciples are somewhat disturbed because of the political situation, and Jesus even tells them that he has many things to tell them, but they are not able to accept them. They are filled with anguish because they know that Jesus will not be with them much longer; they have become dependent upon him, and over the short, three years have come to realize that he is no mere mortal man. The coming Holy Spirit will give to them true insight—they will be able to see beyond the mere obvious since Bultmann claims that the Spirit opens one's eyes to the invisible events occurring in the world. Likewise, we too can be enlightened and enabled by the Spirit.

Once again, we see how Bultmann has the ability to translate the historical passage into a meaningful understanding of the present and future for those who are listening. The situation of the disciples is a similar situation in which Christians find themselves today. As the disciples were chosen, so believers today are with Jesus; this means that they can share in the joy of fellowship with him, but it also means that they must suffer as he did. True discipleship means a sharing in the struggle which Jesus faced on earth as the world will mistrust and even hate those who are followers of the Christ. Jesus' message was at odds with the ethos of the world—his message confronts the standards of this world which in many cases is anti

---

[106] Bultmann, "Philippians 3:7-14," in *This World and the Beyond*, 56.

God. Bultmann believes that the term "world" refers to a system which is opposed to God and stands under the domination of the "prince of this world," and when one is dominated by this spirit, his whole life is encumbered and he is subject to the whims of tyranny. It is not only the immoral man but the moral man who must fear that his affections will be caught up by this spirit. People are tempted to believe that somehow what the world has to offer is the ultimate reality, but in the end they discover that it was a mere phantom. However, if anyone decides to set his heart and mind against the world, this person must be very vigilant because the world will attempt to destroy him. Bultmann says that it is the task of the Christian to tell the world that this present age is not the final word and power over men and women. This sermon gives great encouragement to the Christian by reminding him that the world, thus political authorities, has no ultimate claim upon the Christian as he realizes that the Spirit convinces the world of sin, righteousness, and judgment.

In order to be a witness in the world, there does not necessarily need to be preaching since all Christians have a testimony and can share this. The message does not need to even be in words! By virtue of one's existence, he tells the world that there is a God who is the ultimate. What is the world to Bultmann? It is that sphere which is controlled by the "prince of the world." This results in being enslaved to its domination and believing that it is the ultimate reality.

Bultmann believes that some Christians have been duped into somehow believing that the visible is the real; their spiritual eyes have been dimmed by the spirit of the world. He believes:

> Christianity too has often fallen a prey to the temptation to detect its triumphs in the sphere of the visible and to insist on this tangible evidence. Thus people speak of the influence of Christ on the course of world history, of the effects His spirit has had on human manners and morals, of its uplifting and civilizing influence on nations. The world war showed little of all this, and, since it was a war between nominally Christian peoples, many so-called Christians and many pagans became bewildered about Christianity. Rightly so! For we are disastrously wrong when we wish to see the victory and righteousness of Christ manifested in the visible sphere.[107]

Jesus also speaks of judgment because this world does not hold itself accountable to God; that is, it believes it is accountable only to itself. The world will be judged for its rejection of God's claim over all the affairs of the world, or that which many Christians believe to be secular. Finally,

---

[107] Bultmann, "St. John 16:5-15," in *This World and the Beyond*, 68.

there will come a time when the power of the world is broken. But the breaking of the world is not done by the might and power of men, rather, the subduing is because of the proclaiming of the work of Jesus, and those who are weak are able to resist the evil by which they are surrounded.

Bultmann claims that the existence of the church herself is a testimony that the power of the world is not strong enough to dominate and that the church is a symbol of the eternal. This word is not only preaching but also can be works of goodness which Christians perform in order to help others.

Bultmann offered a word of encouragement from Romans 8:18-27 on July 2, 1938. He does acknowledge that this text is one of the most difficult for him in the New Testament, and he says that his goal is to understand its basic thought. This message has an eschatological theme in that the future gives meaning to our present. We are to make authentic decisions in order that we can realize the future God has for us. We must live fully in the present though it is filled with unrest. But as we continue to live in concert with the Spirit, we will experience authenticity.

Ultimately it is God who has a plan and carries this out, fashioning us to be what he desires for us to become. As we wait in the interim, many times our lives are filled with unrest and uncertainty. Bultmann believes that our present existence is provisional, that is, there is a certain tenuousness to our daily lives. Bultmann believes that there is mythical language employed in this passage as Paul alludes to the theme of Adam's fall, which must not be understood literally. The Gospel, according to Bultmann, is that we have been delivered from fallenness, and we can now live authentically in this world. To Bultmann, much of the imagery in this passage is somewhat strange since it speaks of nature "sighing" for redemption. The myth of the fall points to the existential estrangement within human nature.

Bultmann apparently had strong views concerning nature and his fear of her exploitation. He believes in a sense that nature is violated by man and such a violation is seen in the erection of cities and the use of sophisticated technology. The violation of nature reminds us of the fact that our lives are not what they should be. He refers to the desire of many who live in the city to once again decide to retreat to the environs of the pristine beauty and simplicity of nature. He refers to the writings of Adalbert Stifter, whose works were apparently well known, and how the theme of nature is prominent throughout his writings.

Nature reminds us that we are surrounded by evil and that the condition of the world is not as it had been originally intended. He writes, "The survey of the world of nature, disturbed, and defaced by human history, should bring us to consider the drama of human life. Is the life of a man as it should be? Is it not also distorted and corrupted?"[108] He believes that the text is not addressed to people in general but only to those who are waiting for a new world. He believes that all people are in a state of waiting and hoping that the future will bring bright days and a sense of accomplishment.

There is a certain uneasiness when one prepares for the future. After all, it is God's future, and He can determine just what will occur. Some are fearful of the future and their fear keeps them from enjoying the present as a gift of God. Many live in the past, reciting a long litany of either failures or successes which in a profound sense have no relationship to their present lives. He suggests that one should even embrace death and not shrink back in fear!

He closes with the admonition not to live life in one's own strength and with one's personal resources. He preaches encouragingly that it is only the person who makes a decision to love who can be truly free from anxiety concerning the future. There must be a sense of openness to the future. Love shows us not what one is presently, but what he can become. It brings encouragement to us when we are treated in a kind and affirming manner, and our tendency is to believe that this state will continue into the future as well. However, human love is only a reflection of the love of God as seen in the person of Jesus Christ. God's love is a power which indwells us and enables us to meet the future and fulfill our potential. In this sermon, Bultmann emphasizes that God's love ultimately directs us to Jesus Christ.

Bultmann spoke at the end of the term at an evening service on July 27, 1938. He begins this sermon with a quote from J. Chr. Günther which speaks of another day gone and the need to prepare for eternity. In this short homily in preparation for the celebration of the Lord's Supper, he commences by stating that one should be able to look back at his work and see what has been accomplished in the term, and that this shorter period should relate to the entire period of one's life. This reflecting should also enable one to look ahead with anticipation of more accomplishments. The real worth of reflection is attempting to ascertain what has been happening in one's hidden self as he candidly states that one should prepare for death. In this message there is a pronounced eschatological theme. However, he says that it is the now which is significant; now one must decide as this moment is the critical time to hear and obey God. Many live in the past or future, ignoring the importance of the present.

---

[108] Bultmann, "Romans 8:18-27," in *This World and the Beyond*, 75.

He believes that the New Testament does not speak directly to time as we experience it; rather, the New Testament speaks about the subject when the "time was fulfilled," or the "now" when the Word speaks directly to him. He believes, "Hence it would be a mistake to search the Scriptures in the hope of finding a word which is especially appropriate to this evening hour of worship. And we may seek only the word of Scripture, the one word which is the same for all times and which alone makes any time decisive...."[109]

He then tells those who have gathered that he can speak of one word which is significant for the time—peace; he draws this timely word from John 14:27 in which passage Jesus stated, "Peace I leave with you; my peace I give to you. Not as the world gives, give I to you. Let not your hearts be troubled, neither let them be afraid." Here is the promise that though we are subject to time, and the future is unknown, we can still possess God's peace. Bultmann believes that this promise is all encompassing, that is, it is for all. Living by making authentic choices enables one to experience peace.

He concludes by quoting a very short and poignant work by Franz Werfel in which the author acknowledges that his personal nature is not always consistent with righteousness and that he desires to be free from such an existence. But Bultmann encourages those who are gathered not to merely be concerned about themselves and their own seeking after peace. He mentions the millions who are suffering in the Far East and that Christians should be concerned about those who are facing all types of injustice. He also believes that one should not seek the kind of peace which acts as a protection from any kind of evil influence in the world, for this would be a kind of the peace which the world gives. Thus, our faith enables us to live fully in the present, appropriating the grace of God and sharing this love with those who are less fortunate.

He preached on December 11, 1938. Taking his text from Matthew 11:2-6, Bultmann acknowledges the importance of the Advent season.

At the time of this sermon, there was great unrest in Germany, and it seemed as if war was imminent. In September 1938, certain world leaders agreed to the Nazi annexation and military occupation of the Sudentenland. On November 9 and 10, ninety-one German Jews were murdered, most synagogues set on fire, and Jewish property destroyed; this rampage came to be known as *Kristallnacht*, the night of broken glass. Heinrich Müller ordered 20,000 to 30,000 wealthy Jews be arrested and sentenced to concentration camps pending expulsion from Germany. On November 12,

---

[109] Bultmann, "July 27, 1938," in *This World and the Beyond*, 93-94.

80   Chapter One

Hermann Göring decided that 250,000 Jews should pay a fine of 1,000 million marks.

Matthew 11:2-6, the passage Bultmann preached from, refers to John asking if Jesus is the expected Messiah and Jesus' answer which points to all the miracles which he himself is accomplishing; thus, the answer to John the Baptist is that indeed the Messiah is present. Bultmann's message revolves around the issue of the One who is to come and what is implied in that statement. He encourages one to decide for the reign of Christ instead of temporal, material things in order that the person will be able to live authentically before God and others.

Only in recent years, with the advent of science, Bultmann says that the belief in a coming One has been dissipated; he states that this hope has eclipsed a love for and longing of the understanding that a Messiah will come and bring restitution on earth. Bultmann says that it is well if people remind themselves that technology, science, and human ingenuity will never construct that which is eternal—only God has that ability. It appears that Bultmann is reacting against Nazism with this argument. He quotes Isaiah 40:6-8 in which passage the writer speaks about life as passing quickly, but that the word of God will last forever.

He believes that any political system has its shortcomings and that true Christians should not be satisfied with a government which is tyrannical. But Christians know, if they will honestly look into their hearts, that the struggle between good and evil is a perpetual fight as the temptation to engage in impure thoughts seems to be part of the human condition. Each person finds himself in an either-or situation; either he will acknowledge God's lordship in his life or he will allow something else to usurp God's rightful position. True freedom can only be the result of renouncing the evil way and choosing God's way.

In his sermon Bultmann indicated that stories of the miraculous give to us a window into the transcendent. He believes that in many cases miracles are in fact a stumbling, or an offense, to many. He encourages people not to look for proofs of the miraculous: "Where Christ reigns, marvelous things happen; and if we proceed to ask whether this is still the case to-day, we must be careful not to ask for proofs which might relieve us of the burden of decision. There are of course no such proofs."[110] A miracle is in a sense every deed where Christ's mind and the Spirit are prominent and wherever the Gospel is preached and heard. The message is especially pertinent for the poor of this world—to those who have been

---

[110] Bultmann, "St Matthew 11:2-6," in *This World and the Beyond*, 107.

disenfranchised and oppressed by a world which is only impressed with success and material prosperity.

He quotes 2 Cor. 5:17, which is a statement that if anyone is in Christ, he is a new creation. Bultmann believes that this new order is possible for both humanity and the world. The person who truly understands Jesus' coming is not so much concerned with a coming in time as he is aware that his faith sustains him and gives to him victory in the world in which he finds himself. This message encourages one to experience anew eschatological faith and its empowerment for a person's daily walk. Advent reminds one to wait for Jesus, but in waiting one is called to decision. Man stands in history, and an interpretation of history is an interpretation of himself. One's *Weltanschauung* is connected to an understanding of oneself.

An entire year passed until Bultmann preached on December 14, 1939, from John 8:12; 9:39 and 12:35-36. He makes reference to the fact that Germany is at war and that Christmas will be celebrated in the midst of such turmoil. On September 1, 1939, at 5:45 a.m., Hitler issued an order for an attack on Poland which ignited World War II. On September 3, 1939, Great Britain and France declared war on Germany.

He tells them that what they need is true joy, not just something to take their minds off of the difficulties by which they are now surrounded. He preaches:

> No! It must be no ordinary joy, but it must at least be a joy which we would share in common with our fighting men, and which would link us with them. But in any case it cannot be joy of an ordinary kind. For how could any ordinary joy last in face of the distresses of our time? Such joy would be no more than the frivolous pleasures of two or three fleeting days, after which all would seem dark again around us and within us. . . . It would at least have to be a joy which had the power to predominate over anxiety and grief and to become within us a living source of power to transform the darkness around and within into light.[111]

Bultmann in this sermon contrasts the motif of light and darkness. One is able to rise above ambiguous living by choosing the light of life which choice will vanquish the darkness of despair. This choosing of the light over darkness is available to all who decide, and such a choice results in authentic living. He is not certain what the phrase "light of life" ultimately means, but it is understood that this gift is not from this world. A person may have such gifts as nobility of character and beauty, but these can fade, especially in the current state of affairs with the war. Jesus knows that

---

[111] Bultmann, "St. John 8:12; 9:39; 12:35-36," in *This World and the Beyond*, 113.

everyone longs for this ethereal life, even though they cannot exactly explain what it is they desire. He explains that the imagery of light is used since we know how important light is. Light illumines our paths, dispels darkness, and can even bring about a cheery mood. Light represents the vanquishing of our doubts, worries, and anxieties, as well as the torturing mysteries of our lives. It can also represent self-awareness. This does not mean, however, that there will never be doubts and questions in one's life, but it does mean that we are no longer divided within and that problems have lost their sting and control over us—we are able to live above the difficulties and challenges which will always be a part of life. We can freely decide to live in such a manner.

Bultmann issues forth a warning that one should beware of appearance without substance. Perhaps he is thinking of the Latin phrase, *esse quam videri*, as pertaining to this issue. The world has the appearance of genuineness, but on the whole this authenticity is sadly lacking. The Christian is not simply admonished to be a stranger to the world in his attempt to follow Jesus, but he is to live in the fullness of the strength which God promises. He must be willing to admit that he is spiritually blind without the enabling of God; he must pray that God will illumine his thoughts and ways as he attempts to serve him in a world which cares nothing for God's righteous demands.

Bultmann closes by stating that this concept of receiving God's love can be shared with the soldiers who are fighting a war. He calls for a decision and reminds them again that the world is wrapped in darkness, and because of this fact the call to discipleship, or following Jesus, is even more compelling. These words of Jesus are a summons for a decision. The light motif represents self-awareness, walking wisely, and renouncing the way of darkness. This message encourages one to choose to walk in the light which choice leads the person to experience freedom in one's self and in relationships with others. But the person must make this decision now since no one is assured of the future.

Bultmann presented a message from Luke 18:9-14 on August 4, 1940. Two months before this sermon, on June 14, 1940, France fell, and on July 16, 1940, Hitler ordered preparations for an invasion of Britain, code-named "Sea-Lion." On July 19, he made an appeal in a speech in the Reichstag in which he called upon the British government to end hostilities. On August 13, air war over England began but ended by September 16.

Bultmann believes that the story of the Pharisee and the publican is very simple on one level, but he warns against taking this segment of scripture lightly. He believes on the surface there is not too much to explain as it is a parable, and its purpose is to present the contrasts between two people. The parable portrays two classes of people—one who knows himself and is honest before God and others, and one who is self-deceived and living his life in an inauthentic manner. He pointedly asks his auditors which one they resemble. He is pleading that each one choose to live authentically and thereby freely. Bultmann says in this sermon that God is interested in the essential being of a person, not in his outward appearance or his profession.

To the original listener, it was almost maddening for the Pharisee to look inferior to the publican; after all, the latter was despised in Israel during this period. He asks those who are gathered to listen to this scripture to imagine how they would feel if their particular profession was contrasted with another which was generally not respected and yet that person was described as superior to them. Bultmann says that if we too do not feel the emotion and anger, then perhaps we have missed what is being said here. Jesus is very adroit at reminding people that their pride is repulsive to God. The real essence of a man is deeper than his profession, social class or nationality. Bultmann believes that this story shows that the publican knew himself better than the Pharisee knew himself, thus, he possessed better self-knowledge.

If one's life is an attempt to impress others, then his entire life becomes corrupt and meaningless. To attempt to impress people rather than give himself to his work wholeheartedly and for the glory of God will guarantee eventual failure because the quality of his work will become inferior. Bultmann states that the Pharisee's motives were wrong; he was essentially serving self and not God. Bultmann is very good with sermonic application, and he says:

> Let each of us examine himself to see if there is not in him also something of the Pharisaic pattern of life, in some form or other, in some degree or other! Are we truly in our words and deeds filled with the spirit of disinterested honesty and objectivity, of faithful devotion to our work and service? Or are our minds tainted too in some measure with this will to recognition? With the intention of standing forth as distinguished by what we have done? Do we not often eye others with the intention of comparing ourselves with them and fancying ourselves to be better and greater? Or do we eye them sometimes with tenseness and anxiety lest they should get in front of us?[112]

Bultmann says that everyone wants both self-approval and approval by others. To Bultmann, this also means that we are interested in our standing

---

[112] Bultmann, "St Luke 18:9-14," in *This World and the Beyond*, 128.

before God since our search for God is essentially the search for ourselves. God challenges us with the question of whether or not we have lived life as directed by divine principles or in vain. Bultmann says that we all have questions about our ultimate worth, and we live in fear of not measuring up to a given standard. If we do not have the help and encouragement of God, we are to be pitied since all we have is the critique of other humans. But we must have a correct view of God; He is not merely another person that we can attempt to impress. Bultmann says the only answer to this vexing problem is to deny ourselves and place ourselves in the hands of God. Many are fearful to surrender themselves completely to God because it would mean that someone else is master of their lives. They prefer to live inauthentically in self-deception rather than acknowledge that they are nothing without the abiding love and presence of God. This sermon is a strong reminder of the necessity to serve God sincerely and totally.

Bultmann spoke on Revelation 3:14-20 on December 8, 1940. Just weeks before, on November 12, 1940, Molotov traveled to Berlin to present the Soviet Union's war aims. He demanded control of Finland, Romania, Bulgaria, and the Straits of the Bosphorus and Dardanelles; he also suggested that Hungary, Yugoslavia, western Poland, and the entrance to the Baltic should be included later in the Soviet empire. Hitler became convinced because of this meeting that he must conquer Russia.

Bultmann introduces his message with a comment about the significance of the Advent season; he believes that according to ancient Church tradition judgment should be the central theme of the second Sunday in Advent. The text depicts Jesus as standing at the door and knocking; thus, the main idea is that of Jesus summoning individuals to Himself. The Church at Laodicea, according to the text, was neither hot nor cold, and this fact causes God to become angry. In this sermon, Bultmann emphasizes the importance of understanding that our inherent worth is not based upon any external factors. He also admonishes his auditors to renounce this world and seek eternal qualities in order to find their true selves. He encourages Christians to trust God during periods of crises because during such times it is possible to encounter essential being.

Bultmann relates the passage to God summoning not only the world to account but each person. He admonishes the audience at Marburg to realize that this world is not the Christian's true home and that one should be aware that his last day on earth is a future reality. He says that the "I" who is standing at the door is none other than eternity and that the issue at stake is the state of our conditionwhen eternity knocks for us. This person who is described as "neither hot nor cold" is the undecided man, and he believes that this neutral state is actually evil—it would be better for the man to decide against God rather than to take a middle-of-the-road position. This is the person who in his choice not to make a decision actually does decide. In his attempt at neutrality, he chooses not to be a person of faith and obedience. This person does not fully desire God and his reign; he has an opportunity to gain a new understanding of Him, but he relinquishes this invitation. Bultmann believes that the one who struggles with God implies a measure of connection with God, and he cites Friedrich Nietzsche as an example. That God should find an enemy is not as bad than if he should find nothing or no one there! This is another way of stating that He may find the person who has lost his soul through the cares of the world and is living as if God does not exist. Some people can lose their souls through the various distractions by which all are surrounded. Rather than emphasize a final judgment, Bultmann emphasizes a present judgment as man attempts to justify himself before God.

He asks a rhetorical question whether or not this summoning of us is fantasy and has nothing to do with the issues of the moment. After all, people have daily responsibilities, and many would say that such a question about eternity is impractical and frivolous. But he believes that such thinking is humanity's problem—living for the moment and not for eternity. The summons can clear a person's mind and remind him that in eternity there are much larger questions over which one must be concerned. He says:

> How often are we involved in the blindness of pride! Eternity knocks at our door, yet we do not hear it because we suppose that we have subsumed eternity in our life in this world and that it lies at our disposition—whether it be that we talk of eternal values which lend the radiance of eternity to our lives, whether it be that like the builders of the tower of Babel we wish to erect a tower reaching to heaven, that we dream of creating works of abiding value. For us men eternity is not a possession but a bar of judgment; it spells the end of our planning, organizing and creating. Do our works give eternal meaning to our life? . . . Though the monuments we erect were to last to the remotest conceivable times and not rather fall long before into ruins? Is then eternity endlessly protracted time? In any case such an eternity would not be ours, for we are not endless.[113]

What we call "normal" is only the superficial Bultmann preaches. We love to have our days go as planned, and somehow we think that this routine will go on ad infinitum, but of course, this is not the situation.

---

[113] Bultmann, "Revelation 3:14-20," in *This World and the Beyond*, 139.

He makes a profound observation in that it is not only the threat of judgment which reminds us of eternity, but also the pleasures and joys which we experience as well. A look of love, the beauties of nature, and friendship remind us of the eternal. But if we refuse to accept these or intentionally overlook them, then we are left empty and we lose the blessing. He says that the realizing of love is more important than the accomplishments and deeds which a person achieves.

The word of the Bible is never outmoded, but is always relevant in our daily lives. When we hear the tolling of the church bells, it should be a reminder that the Word of God is to be preached, and we will hear from God if we choose to do our part.

June 22, 1941, found Bultmann declaring a message from the Gospel of Luke 14:16-24. Germany's attack on the Soviet Union, Operation Barbarossa, began on June 22, 1941. He states that all are shaken by the news of the invasion of Russia. He says that if he had known this before beginning to prepare his sermon, he may have chosen a different text from the Bible. He admonishes those who are present to attempt to reflect on the message in calmness of heart.

He gives the cultural background of the text stating that it was a common custom for a wealthy person to invite many to a banquet. However, in this parable there are many who do not take the invitation seriously—they are caught up in matters of everyday living which are not as important in the long run as is the invitation to the banquet of this powerful person. Angry, the host opens the invitation to anyone who will come, even beggars and those who are not esteemed in society are given a special invitation.

Bultmann believes that the meaning of the parable is that the call from God is extended in order to invite people to come into his kingdom. Again the spiritual impulse of Bultmann is seen as he speaks to the issue of the "decisive now." We must be inwardly detached from all worldly possessions and passions. It is a solemn tone as those who were originally invited are not extended another invitation; each in a sense is viewed as a persona non grata. Bultmann explains that the people who were initially invited in this parable are representative of the religious members of the various divisions of Judaism, such as the Pharisees, who at times acted as if they were with Jesus, but then turned in defiance and even hatred against him. They choose, but they make the wrong decision since they choose the temporal over the eternal. These people were in the presence of the kingdom. It was the decisive moment of confrontation, yet they chose not to follow; thus, they were unwise. They will not experience freedom but bondage or enslavement to the flesh and anxiety concerning the future. They are snared by the concerns and pleasures of the world.

Relating this passage to those who are gathered to hear him, Bultmann says it may speak to some who are present:

> But if Jesus is speaking to us to-day through this parable, then He is summoning us also to consider whether we do not belong to the category of the original guests, who have long accepted God's call and God's invitation but who, when the matter becomes serious, calling for decision in the present moment, prefer to be absorbed in private affairs and to despise God's summons.[114]

He alludes to the fact the Germany heard the summons a long time ago by means of the preaching of Martin Luther in the sixteenth century, and he also refers to the fact that not too many years previously the country was dominated by the Church. He suggests that many of the churches are now only monuments to a time when Christ was preached and people took seriously their personal faith. In fact he says, "We all know that Germany is no longer a Christian country; that church life is now a surviving remnant and that many desire and hope that even this remnant will shortly disappear."[115] Why is this the situation? Because, he states, many are concerned with making money, gaining power, and enjoying the pleasures of the world over seeking to serve God. Bultmann is preaching in order to help us make a decision for eternal values and not merely the temporal.

This is a message given to individuals, for it is the individual who has not heeded the call. This passage can also pertain to those who have rejected to help their brothers and sisters who are in need. He says that if the Church had been doing what it should have concerning the crisis in housing and other social problems, then the number of people who are angry with the Church would be greatly minimized. This is true not only of the physical needs of citizens in the country but also of their spiritual needs. This sermon admonishes Christians, whom have heard and responded to the call to enter the kingdom, to continue to listen and decide for the kingdom and eternal matters rather than for the mere temporal.

But one should also be vigilant that worldly success does not quench the presence of God. He quotes Agnes Günther who writes that sometimes through darkness God calls men to himself. We must remember how uncertain are our good fortunes. It is not enough simply to consent to various doctrines and beliefs; we must live out our faith and grow stronger

---

[114] Bultmann, "St. Luke 14:16-24," in *This World and the Beyond*, 145.
[115] Ibid., 146.

each day. We do not fully understand matters which are transcendent. What we do understand is our present life and twhat we think, say, and do will determine our and future. Our worldview influences our daily decisions, which in turn affects our future. One must be aware that there could be a false call which is not God at all but fate which desires to bring the person to nothingness. The definitive question each should ask is whether he is ready. He closes with an indirect comment about the war and the need for inner detachment from all that the world promises, Detachment enables us to recognize daily the need to be prepared for eternity.

On July 13, 1941, Bultmann's message was drawn from Luke 5:1-10, and in this sermon he delves into the meaning of the miraculous. Is it part of the Christian faith to believe in miracles? He reminds the congregation that they live in a period of time when perhaps most people do not believe in the miraculous. There is the law of cause and effect in the world, and people could not function if they did not pay attention to this basic law. There are unknown forces at work in the world that cannot be quantified or understood, and perhaps these can be called miracles, Bultmann suggests. The miraculous, as an action of God, remains hidden and is only seen by faith.

This sermon encourages us that the miraculous can occur in our lives, but we must be willing to relinquish any desire for control. We must be aware that we are not masters of the world. Such a view will enable us to grasp a new understanding of the miraculous. Bultmann is emphasizing the need to abnegate the old life which is sinful and manifests itself in self-centered living. Bultmann says that a literal interpretation of the New Testament miracles is not a precondition for true Christian faith. He references Luther's belief that the essence of faith is belief in Christ as the one who brought victory over law and death. He summarizes his view of the account in Luke 5 about Peter's large catch of fish:

> Yet having made it plain that Christian faith does not consist in accepting as true the miracle stories of the New Testament, we must make it equally plain that Christian faith implies faith in miracles, faith in the miraculous action of God, and the readiness to experience God's miracles in our lives. And our story is meant to enable us to understand what this means. . . . Hence we are not discussing whether this story represents the account of a true happening or whether it is merely legendary, a pious fiction. In order that no one may misunderstand me I will say that I myself consider it to be a pious fiction.[116]

---

[116] Bultmann, "St. Luke 5:1-10," in *This World and the Beyond*, 158.

The catch of fish is not the real miracle, but it does point to something even more miraculous—God will use mere human beings to proclaim his word! We see the de-objectifying emphasis here substituted with a spiritual accentuation. It is a person's life which is dramatically changed as he decides to respond to God's grace.

The story of Peter's catch of many fish is a reminder to follow and depend upon God. The story also teaches that in the moment of our despair, Jesus comes to give to us advice and consolation. If we wish to become new creatures in Christ, we must put away our old habits and ways in which we typically handle issues of a given day. To the one who acknowledges the power of Jesus, as did Peter when he bowed before Jesus, the miracle is made known. In Peter's case, he became a fisher of men! His life had been changed, and he was never the same again. Certainly Peter was not perfect; he even denied his Lord later. The one who has seen the miraculous will be beset at times by temptations of the flesh and desires to give up on the faith, and at such a time one must again surrender his will to God. Deeds for others and for self are viewed in a different manner, for they are no longer performed for recognition and self-ambition, but rather for the glory of God. He is not anxious about results since he commits these into the hand of God. A person whose life is characterized by joy, love, and peace, Bultmann says, is really a miracle to others since the natural person does not have the capacity to exude such qualities.

Bultmann closes by stating that this is the last academic service of the term and that while they have been pursuing their studies, many of their loved ones have been on the battle fields and are living in great stress and danger. He suggests that it is a miracle that they too have been able to carry on their responsibilities as students.

In the midst of the war years, May 10, 1942, Bultmann extended a message drawn from Luke 17:7-10. The Nazi doctrine of racial purity had been finalized less than four months previously at the Wannsee Conference; the Final Solution was now a reality in Germany.

He commences the message with a quote from Matthias Claudius who believed that these words of Christ are like an eternal fountain. This message is a reminder to Christians that though life may be difficult at times, and it is tempting to question the goodness of God, we can truly be filled with hope and joy because of the grace of God. Bultmann says that those who actually heard these words of Jesus knew what it meant to be a slave during that period of time and that he was not making any kind of judgment about slavery. What was new for those who heard Jesus was that he was likening this master and slave arrangement to the relationship of the Christian to God—indeed, this was strange especially to people of Jesus' time as they regarded man as God's servant, not His slave, and that they would be rewarded because of their labor and faithfulness. To them, this message was most offensive!

The facet of God which is described here seems to take away the aura of his compassion and gentleness, and for some this is an offense. The reasoning is that surely God would give a person some authority in saying how his own life should be governed. Bultmann says that he believes we are to complete this parable; that is, we must compare it to the other parables and not simply see this one in isolation from the others. We must interpret this passage with others in order to obtain a clear and concise conclusion on the issue. This parable is not speaking about God as the judge, nor is it stating a fact about a servant who has done a half-hearted or poor task. Bultmann believes that the phrase "unworthy servant" means essentially the person is "wretched." He quotes one of Luther's hymns concerning the pardon of sin. Bultmann claims that this passage is actually a word of grace in that ". . . . it teaches us that we wretched human beings cannot live otherwise than by the inspiration of God's grace."[117] There is no partiality with God. After we have seen our true standing before God, we become more aware of his love and grace. The person who admits his true position before God gains a new understanding of himself. Our entire worldview needs to be adjusted. We should be grateful to God for life itself, and not believe that everything revolves around us. He says that he is aware that there are some people who because of certain limitations and conditions find it almost impossible to praise God, but Bultmann offers a solution to such a person—he must give up the notion that he has a right to life since life itself is a gift bestowed and not earned. This will enable the person to transcend the world, but yet live responsibly daily.

Any human society can only be as sound as its members, and the citizens should realize that they have obligations and responsibilities, but he suggests that a higher motivation is love and trust rather than mere duty. Genuine character shows forth the love of God and does not make a pretense of hardness and strength. This parable is a word of grace and true strength. He refers to the soldiers in the present battle and the fact that those who are involved in studies at Marburg are in relative ease and do not have to worry about direct conflict in war. But he does say that what they will need nevertheless is resolve. He uses the Latin imperative, *Rogate,* pray for yourselves and others. He then closes this first academic service of the term with a prayer petitioning for peace and purity of heart.

---

[117] Bultmann, "St. Luke 17:7-10," in *This World and the Beyond,* 171.

Perhaps the main theme of the prayer is to take the path of self-surrender to God, which will result in relinquishing selfishness and grasping after that which is temporal. The decision to relinquish self-will and anxiety about the present and future results in confidence, joy and peace. This is a revolutionary shift in self-perception, but it is the only means to ultimately experience the grace of God.

On May 30, 1943, Bultmann presented his message from John 16:22-33. In February 1943, German troops surrendered at Stalingrad; on February 18, 1943, Goebbels made a speech for total war.

In this sermon, Bultmann preaches that it is possible to possess true freedom though one may be living in very oppressive circumstances. This freedom means even freedom from ourselves since at times may our desires and choices are not conducive to God's will for our lives. Jesus' promise of "that day" can become for us a present reality.

Bultmann begins by stating that the text has been assigned according to the lectionary and that the subject is prayer. Once again he uses the Latin imperative *Rogate,* which signifies a command to pray. In this passage, he focuses on the phrase "that day" and attempts to explain its significance. He says that this word was apparently well known by the early community and that it ultimately refers to the day of his return, or the day when the world will come to an end. Another phrase for this is "the day of the Lord."

According to Bultmann, the first thing which the text explains is that a true Christian looks forward to the end of this age. The believer is already spiritually removed from the world, and he chooses to live a life characterized by joy. He refers to the difficulties of the present days, and that Christians of his day understood well what the difficulties were for the early Christians. He cites Luther, Kierkegaard, Hölderlin and C.F. Meyer consecutively as he explains the importance of joy. But what is this joy? Obviously, it is not earthly joy, rather, it is the anticipation of an eternity with God in whose presence there is joy forever. The present joy is somewhat of a foretaste of that eternal heavenly joy. Rejoicing is an individual experience since there is no formula for one to follow in order to experience this emotion; there is no particular object of earthly joy because that would mean being dependent on temporal things.

Bultmann says that perhaps the closest earthly experience to the heavenly is that of freedom, specifically freedom from the bondage to the world and what it has to offer. It is also freedom from self. We no longer have burdens which drag on our spirit and cause us to feel depleted of emotion and spiritual energy. The promise is for those who find themselves in the midst of struggles and difficulties. He quotes John 17:15

where Jesus said that he would pray for his own to be kept from the evil one.

To experience this joy, we must feel comfortable in being alone with God. He says: "We must be ready to enter into a solitariness in which the world fades away, in which all relationships, even the most binding and the dearest, are loosed and where we stand confronted by God alone . . . . and the God who meets us in such loneliness may wear to us the appearance of the annihilating power of death."[118] One must decide now in the present for this joy.

We must be willing to suffer with Christ; he actually died on the cross, and only those who will follow him are qualified to share in the joy. But we must live in this world, and it is necessary to relate to others in a distinct manner. Always our lives will be marked with an awareness of "that day." One must live his life with the awareness that the kingdom of God is coming. Man continues to find himself in an either-or situation.

He concludes with asking what is the right method of prayer. To pray in the name of Jesus means always being aware of the cross and the ultimate victory over the world and anything which is anti-God. Also, if we pray in his name, we will be free from bondage to ourselves.

The text for Bultmann's December 12, 1943, message came from Matthew 5:3-10. He believes the main theme of the beatitudes is that of the promise of deliverance for those who feel oppressed for whatever reason. Speaking to the contemporary situation in Germany, he says that many can relate especially to the promise of "blessed are those who mourn, for they shall be comforted." On the other hand, he states that the beatitudes all belong together, and it is not necessary to isolate them. This message displays Bultmann's spiritual impulse with its emphasis upon seeking God's kingdom over that which is material. The kingdom of God is man's ultimate deliverance, but it confronts him as an either-or situation. Bultmann accentuates that one must decide to live with an inner detachment to that which is material because our possessions can divert us from that which is eternal and of ultimate importance. A person may not literally leave his home and family, but he has decided that his affections will not be dominated by earthly and temporal responsibilities.

Speaking about the first beatitude, Bultmann says to be poor in spirit means to admit that we are to be aware of our poverty in comparison to God. This fact must be known not only cognitively, but it must be a part of our entire being. Many try to hide this poverty and amass great sums of wealth, but it could be that these people are especially in spiritual poverty.

---

[118] Bultmann, "St. John 16:22-33," in *This World and the Beyond*, 194-95.

He cites Luther who said that to be poor in spirit is when a wealthy man acts as if his possessions are nothing. He refers to the war and that many are now ready if God should take what they have acquired. Those who are poor in spirit do not have spiritual pride.

He believes that the beatitude, *blessed are the meek for they shall inherit the kingdom,* doesn't resemble the other seven beatitudes and that textual criticism reveals it may have been added later into the text.Those who search for righteousness will be filled. Bultmann gives an extended discussion of what it means theologically to be righteous. There is a blessing for those who realize their own shortcomings and who do not try to hide these especially before God. The beatitude is for those who wait for God's approval.

The first four beatitudes speak about waiting upon God and being blessed for waiting while the latter four emphasize how waiting bears fruit in a person's life. The last four remind us to be free from the present and to understand that the future is in God's hands; thus, we are released to be what God would have us to become.

The merciful, or those who are actively bringing God's grace into others' lives, will themselves be recipients of God's mercy. He suggests that such a person can bear sorrow with a certain ease.

The pure in heart, he believes, are those who live life without pretense, and these people have no ulterior motives. They have a certain inner truthfulness about them—they are trustworthy.

The peacemakers are those who desire to be harbingers of peace no matter what the situation. They are able to bring people together in order to promote the possibility of peace. Finally, there is a promise for those who are experiencing persecution: they will be involved in that which is eternal and has ultimate significance. Their lives will be free from anxiety even though their current, outward situation is not easy.

He likens the Christian to a pilgrim who is somewhat homesick and is on the route to home. He has turned his back on the world, and he is stepping into the future which God has created for him. We see an eschatological emphasis in that he believes, "To be a Christian means to be one who waits for God's future. Hence for the Christian perhaps all seasons are essentially an Advent season. For Advent is characterized above all by this note of expectation."[119] Openness to the future is life lived in the Spirit. Man is related to God in his search for God. As one responds to the message of the kerygma, he gains self-understanding as he lives in his own concrete situation. This message is of great

---

[119] Bultmann, "St Matthew 5:3-10," in *This World and the Beyond*, 210.

encouragement in that it reassures us that waiting characterizes the life of the one who follows Christ, but we can have joy now and embrace the future with confidence and great expectation. Our entire existence is to be characterized by the spirit of Advent which is primarily that of promise. Though the ultimate fulfillment is yet to come, we are now able to celebrate life now in light of what is to come.

Germany surrendered on May 7, 1945, and on June 5, the Allies formally took control of Germany. The war was over in Germany, but that there is much work to be done is a theme which is found in Bultmann's June 17, 1945, message on the biblical text of 2 Corinthians 4:6-11. He emphasizes that victory over the difficulties is not always outward but is inward. Yes, the country should be concerned about rebuilding and making a better life for the next generation, but one's heart should also be guarded and strengthened. Again, we see the emphasis upon maintaining an attitude of inner detachment. It will never be possible to remove all trials, but it is possible to respond to them in manner which brings glory to God. Bultmann believes that whoever can take these words of Paul to heart and truly live them out will be the most effective in building for the future. Bultmann preaches that it is possible to experience victory in the present as one encounters external distress.

He believes that Paul's spiritual strength came from the fact that he lived in two worlds, the one which is decaying and the one which is eternal and bright. The various trials and difficulties of his present situation made him all the more certain of the glorious future—he had tenacity and was filled with great hope; thus, we can choose to live in such a manner. At times, however, one is tempted to give up living in two worlds, and it is possible to feel almost schizophrenic because of living in the present world and looking ultimately to eternal matters. This too is an either-or situation. He writes:

> His empirical ego is in fact the battle-ground of the struggle between the powers of the spirit and the lower impulses. His ego is rent in twain; it lacks unity and purity. It needs cleansing, purification from the stains of the old man, emancipation from its disharmonies, regeneration; in a word, it needs divine grace.[120]

The person who lives in light of eternity is willing to renounce the material and is capable of making authentic decisions. Bultmann believes that the people of his time have forgotten the importance of obedience to the faith in such a world. He refers to false doctrines which have taken the

---

[120] Bultmann, "2 Corinthians 4:6-11," in This World and the Beyond, 215.

place of previous doctrines which once were influential in the country. The concept of power has been accepted over the view of what is right; love for blood and soil, a not-too-subtle reference to Nazi ideology, is viewed as more significant than the world of the spirit. A belief in absolutes has been abandoned, and the concept of the will to power is seen as prominent. He speaks strongly against National Socialism. He comments on how religion and matters of faith have been ignored for a long time, and in his opinion people are reaping the consequences of such beliefs and actions. This is an admonition for us today to ascertain that our worldview is not based upon that which will crumble.

He encourages especially Christians to continue to realize their dual citizenship; they are citizens on earth, but they ultimately belong to the sphere of grace. "If we live in the pain and distress of these days without that inner treasure which the eternal world . . . of grace bestows, then we are lost and must despair. But if we realize that our highest and truest life consists in this inner treasure of spiritual life, then in all our darkness we have a light, in all the agony of our time we have a solid ground of hope."[121] He believes that living in two worlds is not a curse, but is a wonderful measure of grace as it reminds us to depend upon God for all things. The beginning point of a relationship with God is an understanding of one's own existence. In the midst of darkness, if we choose, we can have the spiritual treasure of inner light. But we must make a conscious decision for a spiritual life which is characterized by grace.

On June 23, 1946, Bultmann brought a message from Lamentations 3:22-41. During this period, relations between the democratic government of West Germany and the communist government of East Germany began to deteriorate, thus, paving the way for the Cold War.

This sermon highlights the importance of waiting for God's ultimate deliverance. In our waiting it is possible to develop the quality of patience; This characteristic means that one has decided to place his ultimate confidence in the Lord. Bultmann reminds the congregants to rejoice every morning for the new day and to constantly thank God for his many mercies in their lives. He says that they may be surrounded by suffering, but that there is always something for which they can be grateful. Bultmann says that the writer of Lamentations is neither deceived nor neurotic; rather, he sees the trouble in light of hope, "The Lord is my portion." He speaks about the fact that God's work is many times hidden from us, preventing us from seeing the results of our hard labor for

---

[121] Ibid., 218-19.

righteousness. Bultmann believes that though miracles are not able to be scientifically observed and explained, God is still present.

He again alludes to the fact that they are surrounded by destruction and that what is necessary at this point is great patience and perseverance. Impatience is actually harmful according to Bultmann. "Impatience only makes things worse and leads you to embittered and foolish thoughts. Impatience is harmful too for the community. How much anger and abuse of others arise from our impatience!"[122] Impatience is an expression of living after the flesh, and may be the reason for heaping verbal and physical abuse upon others. Patience is a choice, and by such a decision one can gain inner freedom.

He believes that they must be patient with the foreign troops who are now occupying their land. Patience will help the rebuilding process and will enable good will between those now who are occupying their land and those whose land it is. He believes that all share in guilt, though certainly not in the same measure. Bitterness and arguing must be abandoned in order that reason and true patience can prevail.

He gives an extensive quote from Eichendorff which speaks to the prospect of happier times, but the poem also reminds one of the difficulties of life as well. He believes that his message to the professors and students at this time is essentially one of God's grace, for life's difficulties produce qualities as described in Romans 5:3-5.

Certainly the issue of the transitory nature of life was foremost in the thoughts of those living in Germany during this period. This is a very helpful message as we are reminded that the present as well as the past has meaning. Humans have a tendency not to live fully in the present by either dwelling on the past or merely anticipating the future. Though our last hour is hidden from us, *ultima latet,* we can still live confidently with the expectation of a meaningful future. However, we are to live fully in the present moment, making responsible and authentic decisions, free from self-preoccupation, opening our eyes to the eternal and living in fulfilling relationships.Mark 13:31-33 was the biblical text on which Bultmann preached on the date of July 25, 1950, and in this text Jesus informs his disciples of his impending death. On the final service of the term, Bultmann tells the students at Marburg that it is difficult to part from one another. He admits that the Bible does not say a great deal about transitional times in our lives such as events in families, seasonal changes, and even the end of a particular term. He says that in reality our entire life

---

[122] Bultmann, "Lamentations 3:22-41," in *This World and the Beyond,* 229.

is a continuous process of saying goodbye to one another, yet another reminder that we are in time and learning about eternity itself.

In fact, he says that one's entire life is transitory in nature. The heathen as well as Christians have written about this fact over the centuries. He quotes Tibullus and Hoffmannsthal as well as Pascal. He asks what is it that really controls the quality of our present moments. "All this which gives content and substance to our life, passes away. And does not the curse of transience render it all vain and meaningless? Is life an exciting drama but a drama which dies away to nothingness? Or has it all an eternal import, or can it have such?"[123]

Again, we see Bultmann's emphasis upon an eschatological interpretation. One is to be vigilant concerning the future as he finds himself in an either-or situation. One must truly hear the kerygma as the word of God; such hearing will enable one to make authentic decisions. He believes that the passage from which he is preaching is a call for us to surrender that which is fleeting and unimportant in our lives and to embrace that which has eternal significance. The future toward which we are headed is in essence God's future, and it is from this perspective that life has meaning. We stand in history and an interpretation of history is an interpretation of ourselves.

b. Summary

Bultmann's messages abound with themes of grace and divine love. He believes that true freedom is an inner quality. One is always at the moment of decision; he finds himself in the crucible of the either-or situation. To Bultmann, one must live in the now, deciding for the kingdom and not temporal matters. One must live with an inner detachment in regard to the world. His sermons appeal to the admonition that one must not seek his ultimate security from the temporal, for to do so is to "live according to the flesh." Rather, the person must live with an inner detachment from the world. One is to renounce the claims of the world upon him, and he is to be vigilant that he does not lose his soul to the cares of the world. Paramount for him is to encourage others to seek authentic decisions which are a result of attempting to determine God's will. As the individual views creation and nature, he is reminded of his nothingness and that ultimately he is in God's hands. We are not our own masters—ultimately technology cannot save us. Though death awaits in

---

[123] Bultmann, "St. Mark 13:31-33," in This World and the Beyond, 242.

the future, this fact should not cause one to be distressed because his future is in God's hands.

Were it not for God's grace, every human being is capable of committing atrocities. One must engage in a constant surrender to God. The culture is like a seductive temptress and promises great rewards, but only by listening to God's word and responding in a practical manner, can one live authentically.To be a person who life is characterized by anxiety is to live according to the flesh. The goal is to have a life which is characterized by faith, which quality allows one to live life victoriously, making it possible to discern the miraculous in one's life. The person must surrender his will and choose God's will, and he will experience true freedom.

Bultmann preaches against any concept of pantheism, which belief can result in man's deification. Any idea of objectifying God is also offensive to Bultmann. God's work in most cases is hidden, but miracles can be realized by faith. Christ's presence is in nature but not his self-disclosure. The awareness of God's presence can give to the individual confidence which is needed for daily living. As the word speaks to us, we are filled with expectation and openness to the future. No one knows his last hour, however, to embrace the future rather than to shrink from it, is to make a choice for authentic living. Difficulties and trials always will be a part of living, and many times one brings upon himself trials by his pride and self-obsession. But receiving God's grace can bring liberation. Those who choose God's way are enabled to see beyond the exterior, for God's Spirit brings to light that which is eternal and has ultimate significance. One should live his life in expectation as life lived in the Spirit is openness to the future. A true disciple of Christ will experience hatred from those who reject him. The Christian is not to retreat, but he must announce to the world that there is a higher authority. There will come a time when the world's power is broken, but in the interim, a Christian does not need to search for evidence of God's power in the natural realm.

The promise of the Gospel is that one's fallenness does not need to dominate him; rather, the person can live authentically in the present. A human being does experience existential estrangement, but this separation from God, others, and himself can be overcome. True freedom is an inner awareness that one's meaning in life is not dependent upon exterior circumstances. The person who chooses to allow love to become a dominant characteristic of his life is able to minimize anxiety. God's love enables him to meet the future confidently. As one reflects on the past, he should be able to understand more fully the course of his life. What is important is to determine what has been occurring in one's innermost being. But the past or the future is not as important as the present, which our faith allows us to fully actualize. Living in the present and making authentic decisions allows one to possess peace. Choosing God's way results in joy.

Deciding for the reign of Christ is more important than having a desire for the temporal. He speaks against National Socialism. Though the Christian lives in two worlds, he can realize the spiritual treasure of the inner light if he chooses to do so. While he waits for the eternal, it is possible to develop the quality of patience. Science and technology will never be able to replace the eternal. Either one will acknowledge God's sovereignty or he will attempt to find something else to steal his affections away from God. A person does not need to search for miracles since he experiences the miraculous whenever the Gospel is preached.

He is against making the ancient view of the Bible normative. He preached some messages from the Old Testament but primarily from the New Testament, especially the gospels. He uses logical and exegetical skills and displays a great deal of knowledge concerning textual matters. Always his messages speak to the needs of people who are present to hear him preach; thus, his ability in application of the message is timely and helpful. He especially emphasizes the either-or situation in which one finds himself, and the necessity of making an authentic decision now. Bultmann advocates that the Christian must have an attitude of inner detachment from the world, and that one should live with the sole ambition of knowing God. Jesus' word is a summons to decision.

As the word is preached, the eschatological "now" occurs as the cross and resurrection become realized. The incarnation, Easter faith, Pentecost and the Second Coming all converge in a singular Augenblick. As one responds, the transition from inauthentic to authentic existence occurs. One abandons all securities and chooses the eternal over the temporal. Man receives the forgiveness of sins by faith; thus, he is delivered from himself and is capable of an authentic existence. No longer does one live "in the flesh."

2. "Gospel" in Bultmann's Sermon

a. Background

Bultmann is ultimately concerned about communicating in such a manner that the person listening to what he is stating will determine that the subject matter is believable and helpful in his life, enabling the person to make authentic decisions. Bultmann certainly does acknowledge that he himself faces a dilemma. He knows that he cannot preach the message as if his audience were a first century person, though it is certainly helpful to know the cultural setting and the *Sitz im Leben* of a particular biblical passage. However, Bultmann also knows that it is not intellectually honest to require a person of his generation to believe and accept all the miracles of the Bible since this is not essentially part of the gospel. Ευαγγελιον is the New Testament Greek word for "Gospel," and essentially the word means "good news." The following is helpful concerning this word:

> Most of the NT references to euangelion are in Paul. His use of to euangelion shows that the concept is now a fixed one both for himself and his readers. As one may see from 2 Cor. 8:18; Phil. 4:3, 15, it refers to the act of proclamation, but 1 Cor. 9:14 shows that it may also refer to the content. This twofold sense is especially plain in Rom. 1:1: "set apart for the gospel of God," for while Paul is set apart to preach the gospel, the clause that follows (vv 2-3) describes its content. . . . The gospel records a historical event, but this event transcends ordinary history. Similarly, it consists of narratives and teachings, but it also relates to human reality and shows itself to be a living power. The "for our sins" of I Cor. 15:3 makes it a message of judgment and joy. The "resurrection from the dead" of Romans 1:4 shows it to be the initiation of the general resurrection. If the gospel is witness to salvation history, it is itself salvation history, for it comes into human lives, refashions them, and constitutes the communities. It cannot be grasped in the ordinary way (2 Cor. 4:3); divine revelation takes place in it. Through the gospel God calls us to salvation through the preacher (2 Th. 2:14), summons us to decision, and claims our obedience (Rom. 10:16; 2 Cor. 9:13). We shall be judged by our attitude toward it (2 Th. 1:8). The gospel is no empty word; it effects what it says, since God is its author (Rom. 1:1 etc.).[124]

In order to appeal to the modern person, then, Bultmann asserts that demythologization of the gospel must occur. It is not sufficient to preach a history lesson of the culture of the first century. Likewise, it is not intellectually honest to expect the twentieth-century person to ignore logic, the scientific method, and what many would say—common sense. Bultmann strongly believes that it is dishonest to require anyone to commit a *sacrificium intellectus*. Thus, Bultmann suggests that one must find a third means, a method which goes beyond liberalism and orthodoxy; this is the method of demythologization. With this method, Bultmann claims that the kerygma is still intact, the essentials of the gospel are still present, but it removes many of the blatant stumbling blocks for a thinking

---

[124] *Theological Dictionary of the New Testament*, eds. Gerhad Kittel and Gerhard Friedrich, Trans. Geoffrey W. Bromiley (Grand Rapids: William B. Eerdmans Publishing Co., 1992), 270-71.

person in order that such an individual can honestly and authentically accept the gospel. Prenter gives clarification concerning the process of obtaining an understanding of the gospel:

> To demythologize the gospel means to replace the clothing of mythological images in which the gospel is presented in the New Testament with an existentialist interpretation of the mythology. This program was intended to satisfy the whole present problem, for on the one hand existentialist philosophy is the form of self-understanding peculiar to our time, and on the other hand the true intention of the gospel itself, in Bultmann's opinion, is to give us an understanding of existence and not a mythology.[125]

Bultmann believes that the historical Jesus is not concrete and is enshrouded in myth and legend. It is not possible to locate the historical Jesus because of the mythological element. Much of what is contained in the gospels is but an invention of the Hellenistic Church. Bultmann is not like theologians who predated him in that Bultmann acknowledges Jesus as the decisive figure in salvation. However, the basic doctrines which fundamentalists in particular interpret in a literalistic manner have no meaning for Bultmann. The belief in the pre-existence of Jesus and a virgin birth, one ". . . can dispense with the objective form in which they are cast."[126] This is a simplistic manner for a modern day person to view what the gospels are telling us about Jesus. The belief in a literal resurrection is not necessary since this is not a fact of history which can be objectively established. We must employ existentialist language in order to engage in truly theological dialogue about God and salvation. All theological statements have reference to the situation of the person himself; thus, every statement about God is one about us as well.

Some have questioned why Bultmann would desire to retain Jesus Christ as the focal point of the Christian faith. Should not the person of Christ be demythologized too? Bultmann gives insight into this issue by writing:

> The distinctive idea in the New Testament, in contrast to the Old, is . . . to be described as this: that the relationship of men to God is tied to the person of Jesus. Is this idea mythology? Certainly, expressions of the sonship of God in the metaphysical sense and the return on the clouds of heaven at the Last Trump might be mythology. But should the idea that

---

[125] Regin Prenter, "Myth and Gospel," in *Kerygma and History: A Symposium of Rudolf Bultmann*, eds. Carl E. Braaten and Roy A. Harrisville (New York: Abingdon Press, 1962), 121.

[126] Bultmann, "New Testament and Mythology," in *Kerygma and Myth*, 35.

God has achieved the world's forgiveness through the cross of Christ also be eliminated as mythology? Or does the Christian faith stand and fall with that belief? Moreover, in making this assertion, the New Testament asserts also that the new age has broken in with Jesus Christ, that is, the New Testament divides the whole of history into two halves of a basically different kind: prophecy and fulfillment. How far is the mythology to be eliminated? How far is it essential for the Christian faith?[127]

Scholars have gone their separate ways on this issue. John Macquarrie is critical of Buri and Jaspers for understanding Bultmann's thought in an extreme manner, and thus promoting a blending of theology with a philosophy of existence.[128] While Macquarrie has some disagreement with Bultmann in how far to carry the program of demythologization, Schubert Ogden, conversely, believes that Macquarrie is somewhat confused concerning the topic, and he supports Buri and Jaspers. Ogden attempts to explain what some see as Bultmann's inconsistent attempt to demythologize the New Testament's miracles, Virgin Birth, angels and Second Coming with Bultmann's insistence on the necessity of Jesus Christ. Ogden claims that Bultmann believes that Jesus Christ is only one of numerous possible historical solutions for coming to a non-mythological understanding of God.[129] Carl Braaten believes that Ogden is the one who is confused, and states, "A more complete misunderstanding of Bultmann could not be imagined."[130]

Bultmann seems to part with Heidegger and secular existentialism which insists that the person can experience self-actualization by willing to do so. Bultmann, however, insists on the Christ event primarily because he believes the New Testament witnesses to such an event. He states:

> But the New Testament speaks of an event through which God has wrought man's redemption. For it, Jesus is not primarily the teacher, who certainly had extremely important things to say and will always be honored for saying them, but whose person in the last analysis is immaterial for those who have assimilated his teaching. On the contrary,

---

[127] Rudolf Bultmann, "The Significance of the Old Testament for the Christian Faith," in *The Old Testament and the Christian Faith: Essays by Rudolf Bultmann and Others*, ed. and Trans. B.W. Anderson (New York: Harper and Row, 1963), 11.
[128] John Macquarrie, *The Scope of Demythologization* (New York: Harper & Row, 1960), 130-85.
[129] Schubert Ogden, *Christ without Myth* (New York: Harper & Row, 1961), 156.
[130] Carl Braaten, "A Critical Introduction," in *Kerygma and History*, eds. And trans. C.E. Braaten and R.A. Harrisville (New York: Abingdon Press, 1962), 13, n. 2.

his person is just what the New Testament proclaims as the decisive event of redemption. It speaks of this person in mythological terms, but does this mean that we can reject the kerygma altogether on the ground that it is nothing more than mythology? That is the question.[131]

Bultmann answers in the negative to this particular question and attests to the Christ event and the kerygma, which is announced in the New Testament. He states:

> If we ask for plain convincing reasons why God speaks actually here, in the Bible, then we have not understood what God's sovereignty means. For it is due to his sovereign will, that he has spoken and speaks here. The Bible does not approach us at all like other books . . . . It claims from the outset to be God's word. We did not come across the Bible in the course of our cultural studies, as we came across, for example, Plato or the Bhagavad-Gita. We came to know it through the Christian church, which put it before us with its authoritative claim. The church's preaching, founded on the Scriptures, passes on the word of the Scriptures. It says: God speaks to you here! In his majesty he has chosen this place! We cannot question whether this place is the right one; we must listen to the call that summons us.[132]

Bultmann believes that God addresses the person through the preaching of the Christ event. To Bultmann, the Christ event ". . . . must denote an act in a real, objective sense, and not just a symbolized or pictorial expression."[133] He also believes that the Christ event is unique as a saving event. 1 John 4:10 states: "Herein is love, not that we loved God, but that he loved us, and sent his Son to be the propitiation for our sins" (cf. 1 John 4:19, John 3:16). Since the Christ event is a saving event, it ". . . . is therefore the revelation of the love of God."[134] Galatians 2:20 speaks of God's saving action in terms of faith: "I have been crucified with Christ; yet I live; and yet no longer I, but Christ liveth in me: and the life which I live in the flesh I live in faith, the faith which is in the Son of God, who loved me and gave himself up for me" (cf. Rom. 8:22, Gal. 1:4). The Christ event is the essential corollary and ground of faith. Bultmann states: "Here then is the crucial distinction between the New Testament and existentialism, between the Christian faith and the natural understanding

---

[131] Bultmann, *New Testament and Mythology*," in *Kerygma and Myth*, 14.
[132] Bultmann, "How Does God Speak through the Bible?" in *Existence and Faith*, 168.
[133] Bultmann, "Bultmann Replies to His Critics," in *Kerygma and Myth*, 196.
[134] Bultmann, "New Testament and Mythology," in New Testament and Mythology," in *Kerygma and Myth*, 32.

of Being. The New Testament speaks and faith knows of an act of God through which man becomes capable of self-commitment, capable of faith and love, of his authentic life."[135]

To Bultmann, faith must have an object or a corollary. He believes in the non-demythologization of God's saving event in a tangible, historical person since faith cannot operate independently from revelation and faith is intimately associated with *Geschichtlichkeit*. There are, then, at least two reasons for Bultmann's retaining Jesus of Nazareth at the center of the Christ event, and they are as follows: 1. God addresses humankind in the preaching of the church, and it is necessary for there to be a synthesis between the historical *(Historie)* and the historic *(Geschichte)* in order that Christianity will not be merely an Existenzphilosophie; and 2. The Christ event in the person of Jesus is a primary revelation of God's love.

For Bultmann the critical issue is not ". . . whether that particular event in which the New Testament sees the act of God and the revelation of his love—that is, the event of Jesus Christ—is essentially a mythical event,"[136] but rather to what extent is Jesus of Nazareth in the saving act of God and what is to be the scope of the demythologization of the Christ event? Bultmann states: "Now it is beyond question that the New Testament presents the event of Jesus Christ in mythical terms. The problem is whether that is the only possible presentation. Or does the New Testament itself demand a restatement of the event of Jesus Christ in non-mythological terms?"[137] He is not arguing that God's saving event in Jesus Christ is mythical, but as it is depicted in the New Testament, its Weltanschauung, is mythological.

According to Bultmann, many beliefs, which are held by conservative scholars, concerning Jesus are not significant to the Christian faith. The pre-existence of Christ, his Virgin Birth, deity, miracles and the empty tomb are all mythical in Bultmann's understanding. One cannot know the facts of the historical Jesus since historical-critical research has displayed that such an attempt is invalid. Bultmann states:

> As a result of this investigation it appears that the outline of the life of Jesus, as it is given by Mark and taken over by Matthew and Luke, is an editorial creation, and that as a consequence our actual knowledge of the

---

[135] Ibid., 34.
[136] Bultmann, "New Testament and Mythology," in *Kerygma and Myth*, 32.
[137] Ibid.

course of Jesus' life is restricted to what little can be discovered by individual scenes constituting the older tradition.[138]

Remarking on his thoughts about historical skepticism, Bultmann comments:

> I have never yet felt uncomfortable with my critical radicalism; on the contrary, I have been entirely comfortable. But I often have the impression that my conservative New Testament colleagues feel very uncomfortable, for I see them perpetually engaged in salvage operations. I calmly let the fire burn, for I see that what is consumed is only the fanciful portraits of Life-of-Jesus theology, and that means nothing other than 'Christ after the flesh'.[139]

Bultmann does acknowledge that there is a measure of historical *(historisch)* significance concerning the person of Jesus Christ, and this is the fact "that he proclaimed." Bultmann terms this historical fact the "dass" of Jesus; that is, Jesus was a historical figure whose eschatological message birthed the initial decision of authenticity on the part of his disciples. Bultmann states: "The great enigma of New Testament theology, how the proclaimer became the proclaimed, why the community proclaimed not only the content of his preaching, but also and primarily Christ himself . . . that enigma is solved by the realization that it is the fact, 'that he proclaimed', which is decisive."[140] Bultmann believes that Jesus' message is condensed to a neutral "that," and that the essential substance of what Jesus preached is very similar to what the ancient Jewish prophets preached.[141] To Bultmann, it really does not matter if Jesus was aware that he was the Messiah or not. What is significant is that God "sent" his Son into the world "in the fullness of time" to live among humans in order that they might live authentically. The "that" (dass) is translated on the existence domain into the here, initiating and sustaining a recurring present dynamic of *Geschichtlichkeit*. Bultmann states:

> The proclaimer must become the proclaimed, because it is the fact that he proclaimed which is decisive. The decisive thing is his person (not his personality), here and now, the event, the commission, the summons. When the primitive community called him Messiah they were confessing

---

[138] Bultmann, "The New Approach to the Synoptic Problem," in *Existence and Faith*, 34.
[139] Bultmann, "On the Question of Christology," in *Faith and Understanding*, 132.
[140] Bultmann, "The Christology of the New Testament," in *Faith and Understanding*, 283.
[141] Ibid.

that he was the decisive event, the act of God, the inaugurator of the new world.[142]

The four-letter word dass, "that he proclaimed," then, is very significant as this word helps to form a link between the historical *(Historie)* and the historic *(Geschichte)*, or between what is objective and what is existential. This is important in order that there will not be a complete merger into an *Existenzphilosophie*. The dass transcends time and brings the *Vergangenheit* and the *Gegenwart* together; it is the primary means of authentic living. Bultmann believes that it is not necessary to attempt to go beyond the dass since such an inquiring is an attempt to ascertain "Christ after the flesh," and there is no need to be curious about such. He writes: "But the 'Christ after the flesh' is no concern of ours. How things looked in the heart of Jesus I do not know. . . ."[143]

It is not necessary to construe a biography of Jesus since the crux of the issue *(crux interpretum)* is intimately connected with the cross and the resurrection. These two issues Bultmann discusses in his article on "New Testament and Mythology."[144] The redemptive works of Christ are demythologized; the Christ event is objective, but it is not considered objectivizing. The cross and the resurrection must be interpreted existentially in terms of *Daseinsanalyse*. Bultmann claims:

> To speak of the act of God means to speak at the same time of my existence. Since human life is lived out in time and space, man's encounter with God can only be a specific event here and now. This event, our being addressed by God here and now, our being questioned, judged and blessed by him, is what we mean when we speak of an act of God.[145]

Thus, the belief in the pre-existence of Christ, the God-man who takes on the sins of the world and makes a payment for sin on the cross is shrouded in a mythological portrayal of the Jesus of Nazareth. Bultmann believes, "This mythological interpretation is a mixture of sacrificial and juridical analogies, which have ceased to be tenable for us today."[146] Bultmann gives an extended discussion of these analogies, and he states that their genesis is from expiatory sacrificial language of Judaism and the

---

[142] Bultmann, "The Christology of the New Testament," in *Faith and Understanding*, 284.
[143] Bultmann, "On the Question of Christology," in *Faith and Understanding*, 132.
[144] Bultmann, "New Testament and Mythology," in *Kerygma and Myth*, 22-44.
[145] Bultmann, "Bultmann Replies to His Critics," in *Kerygma and Myth*, 196-97.
[146] Bultmann, "New Testament and Mythology," in *Kerygma and Myth*, 35.

redeemer myths of Gnosticism.[147] The resurrection is not believed to be an objective event of the past since the idea of ". . . a resurrection from the dead is utterly inconceivable."[148]

The cross becomes a reality in the present, existentially, when the believer realizes his co-crucifixion in Christ. We see here an emphasis upon sanctification themes in Bultmann's thought. In the sacrament of the Lord's Supper, he believes that individuals are baptized into the death of Christ; believers partake of his body which was crucified and of his blood, which was spilled. The believer acquires two results by taking possession of the cross by faith. First, he is freed from the tyrannical powers of this world. Second, he is able to overcome human passions and lust.

The historic event of the cross acquires cosmic dimensions. And by speaking of the cross as a cosmic happening, its significance as an historical happening is made clear in accordance with the remarkable way of thinking in which historical events and connections are presented in cosmic term. For we see in the cross the judgment of the world and the defeat of the rulersof this world (I Cor. 2:6ff.). The cross becomes the judgment of ourselves as fallen creatures enslaved to the powers of the world.[149]

Now one is free from the enslavement of the world. Secondly, the cross empowers the believer to have mastery over human passions and lusts; he quotes Gal. 5:24, which states: "They that are of Christ Jesus have crucified the flesh with the passions and the lusts thereof." Bultmann believes that "the crucifying of the affections and lusts includes the overcoming of our natural dread of suffering and the perfection of our detachment form the world."[150] We see in the statement the existential theme of becoming, as the believer embraces the future making authentic decisions. The lure of the world will entrap one and keep that person from becoming a self-actualizing person.

Concerning the resurrection, this event is inextricably connected with the cross. Bultmann believes, "Cross and resurrection form a single, indivisible cosmic event which brings judgment to the world and opens up for men the possibility of authentic life."[151] Both the cross and the resurrection are accepted by faith, and Bultmann believes that, ". . . the resurrection cannot be a miraculous proof capable of demonstration and

---

[147] Bultmann, *Theology of the New Testament*, Vols. 1, 2, 1:166, 174-76; 2:6, 12-32, 66-69.
[148] Bultmann, "New Testament and Mythology," in *Kerygma and Myth*, 39.
[149] Ibid., 36.
[150] Bultmann, "New Testament and Mythology," in *Kerygma and Myth*, 37.
[151] Ibid., 39.

sufficient to convince the skeptic that the cross really has the cosmic and eschatological significance ascribed to it. . . . The resurrection of Jesus cannot be a miraculous proof by which the sceptic might be compelled to believe in Christ."[152]

Bultmann agrees with Karl Barth at least on one issue—I Cor. 15:3-8 does not prove the *historisch* fact of the resurrection. The eye witnesses merely guarantee Paul's preaching concerning the risen Christ is existentially the same as the preaching of the first apostles and not the historical veracity of the resurrection of Jesus of Nazareth.[153] Bultmann states: "The eyewitnesses therefore guarantee Paul's preaching, not the fact of the resurrection."[154] His conclusion is as follows:

> The real Easter faith is faith in the word of preaching which brings illumination. If the event of Easter Day is in any sense an historical event additional to the event of the cross, it is nothing else than the rise of faith in the risen Lord, since it was this faith which led to the apostolic preaching. The resurrection itself is not an event of past history. All that historical criticism can establish is the fact that the first disciples came to believe in the resurrection. The historian can perhaps to some extent account for that faith from the personal intimacy which the disciples enjoyed with Jesus during his earthly life, and so reduce the resurrection appearances to a series of subjective visions. But the historical problem is not of interest to Christian belief in the resurrection. For the historical event of the rise of the Easter faith means for us what it meant for the first disciples—namely, the self-attestation of the risen Lord, the act of God in which the redemptive event of the cross is completed.[155]

The resurrection is an existential faith issue of God's saving climax in the cross, and this event is inseparable from the New Testament kerygma. The Christ event is ". . . the eschatological event par excellence."[156] He believes:

> How do we come to believe in the saving efficacy of the cross? There is only one answer. This is the way in which the cross is proclaimed. It is always proclaimed together with the resurrection. Christ meets us in the preaching as one crucified and risen. He meets us in the word of preaching

---

[152] Ibid.
[153] Ibid.
[154] Bultmann, "New Testament and Mythology," in *Kerygma and Myth*, 39.
[155] Ibid., 42.
[156] Ibid., 41

and nowhere else. The faith of Easter is just this—faith in the word of preaching.[157]

The foundation of faith, then, is the Christ event proclaimed by the community of Christians. As one makes a decision of obedience in true faith, he renounces the claims of the world; the various entanglements no longer control an individual who has made such a decision. When this experience is appropriated and actualized in a person, that individual experiences the resurrection-Easter faith which Paul and the early Christians knew.

b. Select Themes Pertaining to the "Gospel"

For Bultmann, the significant issue is to re-experience the gospel and to express that experience in terminology and a mind set which is understandable for his day. Bultmann believes that the true message of the gospel is the kerygma and the call to renounce all worldly securities and live in radical faith and commitment to the unseen God. His sermons encourage us to make decisions which are consistent, authentic, and practical, enabling the Christian to live out the Christian faith in such a manner that one is not alienated from everyday life. One must be able to live by means of a worldview which allows him to transcend the cares of the world, but still live responsibly. A person's worldview can retain the miraculous, but one should not look for an obvious manifestation of miracles; they are real but hidden, and miracles are realized by faith. Bultmann always preaches with a goal in mind—to enable one to make authentic decisions. We are in history; therefore, an interpretation of history is an interpretation of ourselves. Our search for God is essentially a search for ourselves.

One major theme found in Bultmann's preaching is that the human being is subject to Angst; this anxiety is caused among other things by an acute awareness of his finitude and the fact that ultimately the individual is not in control of his destiny. There are unforeseen difficulties and snares which can cause problems and even destruction in one's life. Bultmann's solution is not to pretend that the fear is not there, but to face such a fear and to determine to live authentically. He suggests that one must give up the constant attempt of controlling his environment and situation in life. Bultmann states: "Man will never be free from anxiety by seeking to illuminate the world, by seeking to control and organize it in his own interests, but only by facing the question which his anxiety suggests, by

---

[157] Ibid.

giving due recognition to his religious awareness, so that it may ultimately lead him to the knowledge of the one God who is Lord of heaven and earth."[158]

But it is primarily the subject of physical death which is a cause of such anxiety for most people. The fact that we are finite, not in control of our daily lives, but subject to mortality, this fact can evoke a certain sense of dread in our experience of life. Bultmann states that even though the belief in a final judgment by an austere God is not believed by the majority today, still there is a dread which can overwhelm a person. However, there is an element of God's judgment which is pertinent today, and that is all of us are ultimately responsible to live in an honest manner and not to allow worldly temptations to entice and jeopardize our relationship with others and God.

Bultmann does sound a clear warning in that he states the temptation is to attempt to overcome finitude with technology, and in his opinion this only leads to the illusion that one is secure and not finite. He preaches the need to trust and to self-surrender: "And on what basis shall we dare to penetrate the darkness of this self-surrender? With what justification shall we allow ourselves to sink deep into this darkness trusting that God's hand will enfold and keep us with gracious strength? . . . but really for this reason, namely, that the unknown God has made Himself known to us in His word."[159]

The theme of human anxiety is also the subject of his November 15, 1936, message in which he spoke on the familiar Mattthew 6:25-33 passage. In this particular message, he discusses the fact the humans are subject to time, and time is something over which ultimately we have little or even no control. Of course, the primary concern in this passage is that of daily sustenance. Will we have enough food, proper clothing and shelter now and into the future? Bultmann emphasizes the promise that God makes for his own. That is, they are infinitely more valuable than the birds and the lilies, and they will be cared for by a loving God.

Intermingled in this particular sermon is another major Bultmannian theme: the kingdom of God. Our ultimate concern should not be for the material. God honors his word, and he will care for those who place him first on their list of priorities. Bultmann states:

> But we can win the strength to bear the burden of these mysteries, if we do not allow ourselves to be mastered by tormenting fears about the material side of life, but rather seek with all our hearts and minds the kingdom of

---

[158] Bultmann, "Acts 17:22-32," in *This World and the Beyond*, 13.
[159] Ibid., 22.

God and His righteousness. In that case we shall not only gather the strength to bear the burden of the mystery but more and more shall we come to realize what gift God wishes to bestow on us through the burden of the mystery: inner freedom and peace. And we shall become ever more aware what gift He has bestowed on us in Jesus Christ, who in His word calls us to this freedom of the spirit.[160]

Bultmann apparently had a great capacity for appreciating the aesthetic. His message on Genesis 8:22 is filled with references to the glories of nature, and that essentially nature mirrors a magnificent God. He apparently believes that we cannot find God in a salvific manner in nature, though nature can give us an awareness of divinity. He preaches: "Whoever sees God in nature only is acquainted with a type of piety which is episodic merely."[161] But such an experience can awaken us to the reality of the eternal and to the forgiveness which is promised in Jesus Christ. This message ". . . declares that God forgives and has forgiven the fundamental sin of our whole existence, the one essential sin which is that we have separated ourselves from God. . . . When we have this faith, then God is present for us not only in nature but in the world and life as a whole . . . in the humdrum world of every day as well as in the relaxation of festival days.[162]

In a message Bultmann preached on the text of Philippians 3: 7-14, he speaks of striving to successfully finish various responsibilities, not only the various academic responsibilities but also the multitude of others. He speaks of resurrection power: ". . . may the gift of the term to us be that we who are weak are learning to let His grace make us strong, that we are coming to know the power of His resurrection and the fellowship of His sufferings, that we are pressing on . . . ."[163]

Bultmann speaks about the world as being a place which is not home for the Christian. We must continue to perform our responsibilities in the world, but our ultimate allegiance is to God. In John 16, he understands the concept of the world here is not that of nature, but as a domain which is under the influence of the "prince of this world." This world can actually become a god, and we must pay attention to our lives in order that worship of this false god will not occur. He speaks of the enabling of the Holy Spirit in the life of the Christian. This is more of a theme related to the issue of sanctification, but the gospel message is one that also gives

---

[160] Bultmann, "Matthew 6:25-33," in This World and the Beyond, 35.
[161] Bultmann, "Genesis 8:22," in *This World and the Beyond*, 48.
[162] Bultmann, Ibid., 48-49.
[163] Bultmann, "Philippians 3:7-14," in *This World and the Beyond*, 56.

freedom from encumbrances to sin. He states: "The very existence of the Christian Church, with its proclamation of the gospel of Christ in the world, proves that the power of the world is broken. The Church is a symbol of eternity in the midst of the self-sufficient world. The word of the gospel resounds in the world and does not allow it to rest in its illusions."[164]

Bultmann preaches constantly about the fact that the gospel offers hope for the present and the future. This is clearly seen in his July 2, 1938, message on Romans 8:18-27. He believes that ultimate hope is not for the unbeliever but only for the believer. Intertwined with hope is what Bultmann refers to as "inner freedom." This is the opposite of the person who does not embrace the promise of the future; this person is characterized by concern and even anxiety. On the other hand, a person characterized by inner freedom is able to live expectantly and confidently welcomes the future. He says, "The faith of the Christian is that the future will bring him his true self, which he can never capture by his own self-appointed courses. In other words, readiness for my fate, for that which God designs to do with me."[165] He states that it is only the power of love as expressed in Christ which can take away the power of fear in a person's life.

In his July 24, 1939, message on Matthew 11: 28-30, Bultmann speaks about Sunday not only as a day of rest but as a reminder of our reconciliation to Christ. He says, "We must remember that the Lord's Day is the Day of the resurrection of Christ; the day on which the new world of life in the spirit victoriously broke in upon the old world of sin and death, and so initiated a new beginning for all who honor the Risen Lord as their Saviour and Master."[166] Sunday is a sign of assurance and forgiveness.

The hope of the Gospel is repeatedly mentioned in his message on Matthew 11: 2-6. He speaks about the message of the Gospel being offered to the poor of the world, or those who are afflicted and are waiting for freedom from the present difficulties of living. He quotes 2 Cor. 5:17 and takes seriously the promise that all are a new creation in Christ. Bultmann apparently enjoyed preaching sermons during the season of Advent; his messages are aglow with themes of hope, faith and joy.

Bultmann's message on Luke 18:9-4 is a most memorable one in that he addresses the issue of intent of the heart. Why serve God, and if one's motives are not pure, how can one overcome the tendency to be more concerned about the favor of man over God? He suggests that by "fleeing

---

[164] Bultmann, "St. John 16:5-15," in *This World and the Beyond*, 69.
[165] Bultmann, "Romans 8:18-27," in *This World and the Beyond*, 78.
[166] Bultmann, "St. Matthew 11:28-30," in *This World and the Beyond*, 90.

from themselves and seeking refuge in God" they can find ultimate security and an awareness of the fathomless love of God for them. He believes, "If our parable persuades anyone to adopt this new way of life, on such a one Jesus has exercised His liberating power."[167]

Bultmann believes Rev. 3:14-20 teaches that it is better to be against God than to be neutral concerning him since if one is against God at least that person acknowledges him. In this sermon we find the emphasis upon the importance of decision. Even the ringing of the church bells is a reminder that we are to make a conscious decision for authentic living. He speaks of the Holy Scriptures summoning us also to the moment of decision.[168] He admonishes, "For here God speaks to us through His word, in which He has fully disclosed His being to us, and through His Son whom he has sent into the world that in Him we may apprehend the full manifestation of divine love."[169]

The gospel invitation is particularly striking in his message preached June 22, 1941, from Luke 14:16-24. He believes that the call of the rich man inviting guests to the banquet symbolizes God's call for people to come into his kingdom. Bultmann has the ability to draw his listeners into the narrative of the parable, and he even suggests that Jesus is speaking to those who are gathered to hear this message. He believes that the gospel summons can come at times when we least expect such a call. He admonishes, "Hence I can give only a general warning that each of us should be prepared and vigilant and alert both to hear the summons and to obey it."[170]

Bultmann does not claim it is necessary to believe that many of the miracles as recounted in the New Testament literally occurred. To him it is not necessary for us to accept this account in order to be a Christian. He believes:

> In the first place, that belief in the miracle stories of the New Testament is not in fact the essence of the Christian faith. Christian faith means rather faith in the grace of God which has been manifested in Christ. As Luther has already said, the real work of Christ consists in His victory over the law and death. And to believe in Christ means to believe in Him as the One who frees us from the tyranny of the law and from the reign of death;

---

[167] Bultmann, "St. Luke 18:9-14," in *This World and the Beyond*, 133.
[168] Bultmann, "Revelation 3:14-20," in *This World and the Beyond*, 141.
[169] Ibid., 142
[170] Bultmann, "Luke 14:16-24," in *This World and the Beyond*, 149.

but it does not mean considering the miracle stories of the New Testament to be true.[171]

To believe in miracles means to be open to the miraculous in our lives and to believe that such episodes can convey to us something of the very presence of God. Bultmann states that the creative myths convey the miraculous. He quotes Luther several times especially in regard to God as the Creator. Bultmann believes that the account of creation contains the essence of the Christian faith. Speaking of God as Creator, Bultmann says:

> The man who is able to confess this is also able to realize what a gift God has given to the world in Jesus Christ. Such a one encounters Jesus as the manifestation of the redeeming grace of God in the world, and the word which promises this grace to the sinner finds its way into our heart. All this is made vividly clear to us in our story. When Peter in obedience to the command of Jesus has let down his net and made the wonderful catch of fish, he falls to his knees before Jesus and says: "Depart from me, for I am a sinful man, O Lord." Jesus, however, does not reject his adoration but promises: "Do not be afraid; henceforth you will be catching men." Thus to the prostrate sinner the miracle is made known, and the real miracle is just this—that Jesus calls to His service sinful man, and that He transforms the being of sinful man making him a new and pure creation.[172]

Bultmann believes that whoever with a willing heart hears the message of God's grace is freed from the hold of bondage to sin and self.

In his message from Luke 17:7-10, Bultmann acknowledges that we Christians are not only unworthy servants but actually wretched ones. The message of this parable is that, "It is a liberating and saving word because it frees us from the illusion that we might, because of what we are and achieve, lay claim to some justification in the sight of God. Only he who surrenders all presumption to right and claim before God, only he can live by God's grace."[173] The theme of surrendering oneself to God's call in the gospel is an incessant theme with Bultmann.

Upon reading Bultmann's sermons, one is struck with the fact that joy in relationship to the Gospel is a constant theme. One even finds this theme in his sermons which were preached during the period of World War II. In his message on John 16: 22-33, he states: "What then is the joy which no man can take from us? It is no joy connected with anything which this world and life within it can bestow, even the most precious and highest things of the world. It is a joy imparted by what lies beyond this

---

[171] Bultmann, "Luke 5:1-10," in *This World and the Beyond*, 157.
[172] Ibid., 164.
[173] Bultmann, "St. Luke 17:7-10," in *This World and the Beyond*, 171.

world; and we experience it only when we stand beyond this world . . . ."[174] He speaks of the Resurrection as canceling out the grief of the cross.

> He gives the example of Paul who experienced God's grace. And it is just this which has become luminous for Paul in the face of Jesus Christ: the grace of God which has made a new creature. "For it is the God who said, 'Let light shine out of darkness', who has shone in our hearts to give the light of knowledge of the glory of God in the face of Christ." As the new man in Christ, Paul of course remains involved in the two worlds as long as he leads his life on earth. But this life has acquired for him a new rich meaning: life in the spirit is also life in the grace of God, and so in a new sense too he has become victorious over life in the visible world.[175]

He speaks of the fact that the gospel signifies two worlds, and that the Christian must be aware of living his life in reference to the eternal and not the temporal.

Bultmann preaches constantly about the significance of the cross. Rather than center on this as an historical event, he compares the Christian's life to that of bearing one's cross. He believes that the person who faces life's difficulties and lives honestly is honoring God. He says: "I do not know whether any one to-day is thinking on these lines, to-day when all of us are involved in suffering and deprivation, and when even those who are better off than most have to bear their cross."[176] We must look to the hope of the invisible world especially during times of trials. Bultmann's sermons resound with the Gospel. Intertwined are many themes such as love, faith, hope, perseverance, decision, authenticity, and eschatology.

D. Hermeneutics and Preaching: Conclusion

1. Hermeneutics

Bultmann believes that only an existential hermeneutic will both yield a sound understanding of a given text and the awareness to apply the new insights in one's life. One cannot study a particular text in a manner which is unconnected to his being; rather, the interpreter recognizes the life-changing import of the passage under consideration. A detached, unrelated-to-life, strictly exegetical method is completely inadequate for Bultman. The interpretation arises out of the personal experience of the

---

[174] Bultmann, "St. John 16:22-33," in *This World and the Beyond*, 191-92.
[175] Bultmann, "2 Corinthians 4:6-11," in *This World and the Beyond*, 215-16.
[176] Bultmann, "Lamentations 3:22-41," in *This World and the Beyond*, 234-35.

interpreter; thus, there is a sense in which Scripture does not speak definitively on a particular topic.

As the exegete interprets the New Testament, he is aware that there is much material therein which must be demythologized through the process of *Entmythologisierung* since the writers themselves were heavily influenced by especially Jewish Apocalypticism and Gnosticism. Bultmann believes that the contemporary person, who has been heavily influenced by contemporary science and technology, cannot be expected to accept literally the mythological elements. However, scripture does give to one further insight concerning the transcendent. Though Bultmann holds philosophy in high esteem, he believes that only the New Testament has the ultimate answer for deliverance—Christ.

One always approaches the text with a particular pre-understanding, and the interpretation is guided by this pre-understanding. If the writer and the interpreter have the same experience of the subject matter, there is a much greater probability of a precise interpretation of the text under consideration. Methodical interpretation of the biblical text, guided by a pre-understanding that is ideally shared by both author and interpretor, enables the interpretor to attain an authentic conclusions. Bultmann believes that a human being has an existential knowledge of God; therefore, it is justifiable to believe that one possesses a pre-understanding of God.

Bultmann asserts that the primary theme of Jesus' teaching is that of the kingdom of God. Eschatological preaching obviously emphasizes the future, but this particular type of preaching also encourages the person to live fully in the present, the now. He must be involved in making authentic choices; fully engaged in his faith, he is able to renounce the temporal and live for the eternal. One must not allow that which is material to hold him in bondage.

Scriptural interpretation should not produce a definitive conclusion. Conversely, interpretation of the text is ongoing, arising out of the personal experience of the interpreter. Human experience is seen as more credible than emphasizing the invasion of the supernatural or the miraculous. The interpreter is in a relationship with the text as he is with an existing person. The basic religious questions are inquiries concerning one's own existence about which the person is constantly in a process of decision.

The subject of hermeneutics was a life-long concern for Bultmann, for he realizes that the presuppositions and methodology behind interpretation will determine one's conclusions. In particular, Bultmann realizes the significance of both *Vorverständnis* and an openness to the meaning of man. He does not believe that either the allegorical method of interpretation or the orthodox exegetical method, namely the historical-grammatical method, is sufficient to enable one to come to valid conclusions. He believes that the essential meaning of any particular piece of literature is what it has to say about the individual in his existential context. Bultmann's hermeneutical position is the result of a spiritual impulse since he believes that God is present to man in the preaching of the Word. The text continues to offer man a new understanding of himself as he is constantly called to decision.

The primary reason for emphasizing the mythological *Weltanschauung* is because the modern person is so indebted to the scientific method and means of interpreting phenomena; thus, it is not possible to simply restate in a literalistic manner what one finds in the New Testament, especially the many accounts of the miraculous. The cosmology of the New Testament must be reinterpreted in a mythological manner since to continue to preach and teach these literalistic beliefs is one major reason for the skandalon of the Gospel. Mythology according to Bultmann is the human attempt to explain the other world in terms of what we understand in our present experience. The *existentielle* situation connects the question of God and the question of one's personal existence. To Bultmann, the universe is self-contained; hence, divine incursions of the miraculous cannot be documented. We should not be concerned about the historicity of Jesus as much as Jesus who is preached in the kerygma. We can only know the Christ who is preached. When the Word is preached, the cross and resurrection become present for us.

He does not believe that demythologization is a method which is forced upon the New Testament; rather, this method is found in the New Testament itself. He is concerned with the issue of what the text is saying to one at a particular moment, and in tandem with this issue is the necessity for the person to respond to this knowledge. Bultmann is critical of Naturalism which has a tendency to view the person as subject to the forces of history so that both history and human beings are causally determined. He is also critical of the History of Religions School with its tendency to obscure doctrines. He believes that it is possible to interpret only in accordance with one's own personal position and situation in life. Historical and psychological exegesis merely convey what has been thought at a particular period, but they do not reflect on the meaning of what has been said. We must confront history in order that we may experience its claims upon us.

Bultmann has a high regard for philosophy, and his indebtedness to especially Heidegger is seen in his thinking. He does state that the New

Testament and not philosophy tells the person of his fallen state and that deliverance can only come from God. The person must be delivered from especially himself, and this is where the Christ can bring deliverance.

He believes that everyone has presuppositions and that the interpretation of a text is always guided by a pre-understanding of the text. However, we must go deeper than just understanding a particular genre of a text; rather, we must attempt to understand the psychical framework of a given work. He suggests that the interpreter engage in a measure of risk in order to raise his understanding to a higher level. The past can come alive again, and the knowledge which is gained can be applied to his present situation. This is the existentiell encounter.

He believes that demythologization is similar to Paul's and Luther's doctrine of justification by faith alone. As justification by faith removes any possibility of pretense for self-sufficiency, so demythologization removes security which is built upon objectifying knowledge.

2. Preaching

While Bultmann in his sermons gives the historical and cultural settings, and it is obvious that he is very knowledgeable concerning the exegetical issues of a given biblical passage, his primary concern is how a person is to understand the text in the moment and the application of this understanding in his life. The historical context from which he preaches is translated into the now of decision. Bultmann believes that the word of God understood, accepted and applied to everyday living will enable one to live authentically; his decisions will be based upon the eternal and not the temporal. Many of his sermons have an eschatological emphasis in that they encourage the person to live fully in the present while being ever mindful that the future is coming. His sermons place a demand upon the person for a decision pertaining to his self-understanding. He challenges his auditors to abandon human security and to realize that ultimate security is only in God. But the questions posited by the preacher concerning God are questions which relate to the person himself. Christ confronts the person in the kerygma.

He preached many of his sermons to a community of colleagues and students at Marburg. These sermons are practical, rigorous, joyful and encouraging. Most of them were preached in the years leading up to and during World War II. Bultmann is concerned about the application of the sermon to the person's situation in life. One theme which he openly discusses is that of mortality, but even with this topic he skillfully imparts hope and expectancy pertaining to the future. His messages enable one to have a new understanding and awareness of God; thus, one has a deeper understanding of himself. For Bultmann, preaching is the result of sound exegetical studies as he attempts to determine how the message can be presented to enable the individual to live authentically. Ultimately, the person himself is responsible for his actions. Though one is thrown into the world, and this can be the cause of great anxiety, and the decadence of a world of enticement and decadedence of the flesh, every person has the capability to appropriate his freedom. Such freedom means that the person is free from his past and the remembrance of inauthentic decisions; he is also free from the dread of the future which is unknown to him, though he knows that the specter of death is a future occurrence. However, it is possible for the dread of death to no longer control his thinking, and he becomes free to extend genuine love in his relationships with others.

He rarely preached from the Old Testament, but preferred either the Gospels or Pauline epistles. Sometimes he would discuss issues which are controversial for the Christian such as the subject of Christian liberty. He preaches in such a manner to enable his auditors to understand their personal existence. Bultmann's preaching enables one to understand his own humanity.

He is concerned about applying the message to the life situation in which people find themselves; he points them to Christ. He is aware that he is preaching to people who are very aware of their own mortality; after all, many of the sermons were presented during the war years. He openly discusses death since he believes that not to do so displays one is fearful of the subject. Constantly he admonishes the congregants not to be anxious.

He reminds those who are gathered throughout the many years he preached in Marburg to listen to God. He says that this is more important than in previous times when people had less leisure time. Technology has given to human beings many advantages. However, in the security of technology, the temptation is to forget God, and such a forgetting of God is a means of losing one's soul. He believes that people of his day are tempted to rely too heavily upon mass media, ideologies, technology and reason at the expense of losing their essential being and authentic living.

Bultmann even preaches concerning ecology. He displays his appreciation for the beauty of nature; though to Bultmann, nature is not a means of revelation. Nature can serve as a reminder to us that there is something much stronger than we are.

He tells the congregants that if they follow Christ there will be trials and challenges in this life. They should be sensitive to life's pressures; the difficulties will enable them to grow stronger in their faith. He warns against human pride and declares that difficulties in a person's life have a way of humbling him.

Repeatedly, Bultmann encourages his listeners not to be duped regarding what is truly authentic. They should be aware of looking only at the appearance and, thus, perhaps missing the essentials. He also admonishes them to strive for authenticity in regards to themselves and others.

He is very gifted in his ability to give the cultural setting of the passage under consideration. Such an explanation helps those who are hearing the message understand more fully the passage's original intent, but he then skillfully relates the message to the setting of his current times. He even gives illustrations from sermons which his father preached many years previously!

His sermons cause his listeners to search their own souls in order to determine if the message has revealed something which has been overlooked in their lives. People are encouraged by the messages because they know that they are forgiven and loved. His messages enable one to have a new understanding and awareness of God; thus, one has a deeper understanding of himself. The person now lives in a state of openness with God who continues to be present with him in his contemporary situation. Though he has been thrown into the world, and his existence is threatened, he is able to live fully in the present while aware that the future is coming. He realizes that he is responsible for his own existence and his future. Bultmann preaches in such a manner to enable his auditors to understand their personal existence.

Chapter Two

Dietrich Bonhoeffer's Practical Exegesis and His Hermeneutics

A. Introduction

Bonhoeffer did not have the opportunity to engage in research in the same manner as did Bultmann. He finished his academic work when he was only twenty-four years of age, and for the next fifteen years, he would be involved in teaching, pastoring, organizing an underground seminary, traveling, writing, and resisting what he believed to be the personification of evil—National Socialism. One always has the impression that Bonhoeffer was perpetually involved in people's lives as a teacher, pastor, mentor or friend, and in his thirty-nine years he was able to extract meaning from each moment as few people who live twice his years have the capacity to do who. His life was extremely compact and full. Though he was born into the high middle class, his persona is reflected in the lives and hearts of people from all walks of life. Perhaps he fairly easily could have obtained a professorship and contributed to the study of theology and its practice in a strictly academic setting, but it appears that from early on he had determined to be involved in ministry outside of academia.

Bonhoeffer is somewhat enigmatic and contradictory. A large and powerful man, he impressed people with his gentle mannerisms; a churchman, yet, at least early in his calling, he did not attend church regularly; reared in a family which did not take the Church too seriously, the subject of the Church became paramount with him; warm and friendly, he could also be distant and competitive; emotionally secure, he could also express self-doubt; and he was a pacifist, but was also involved in a plot to kill Hitler.

His close friend and biographer, Eberhard Bethge says the following insightful words about him:

> In conversation, he was an attentive listener, asking questions in a manner that gave his partner confidence and led him to say more than he thought he could. Bonhoeffer was incapable of treating anyone in a cursory fashion. He preferred small gatherings to large parties because he devoted

himself entirely to the person he was with. He kept a certain distance from others out of respect for their privacy, and he saw to it that he was treated likewise. . . . When he was angry, his voice grew softer, not louder. The Bonhoeffer family considers anger indolent, not impertinent. They had a strong sense of what was proper; they also had the quality, often ascribed to the British, of treating the daily routines of life very seriously; whereas the really disturbing matters, where all was at stake, were treated as if they were quite ordinary. The stronger the emotions, the more necessary it was to dress them in insignificant words and gestures. Dietrich Bonhoeffer was able to work with total concentration. He did whatever work had to be done without hesitation. Yet this ability was accompanied by a willingness to be interrupted, and even a craving for company when playing music. . . . He liked children and took them seriously. . . . It was said that Bonhoeffer was a particularly intense child. He remained intense in the way he set about everything: reading, writing, making decisions and giving the reasons for them, helping people or warning them. In short: throughout his brief life, he dealt with whatever happened and was demanded of him.[1]

One wonders if he had lived longer, would he have written a concise systematic theology? Or would he have continued the themes in *Sanctorum Communio* and *Akt und Sein?* It is interesting that "in the index to *Act and Being* Heidegger took second place only to Luther—even before Barth; Husserl, Scheler, Griesbach and Tillich were also discussed."[2] One cannot help but wonder at this heavy allusion to Heidegger since he was somewhat critical of Bultmann's dependence on him.

Bonhoeffer seems to transcend theological categorizations; that is, he is accepted by orthodox and non-orthodox theologians alike. Although John A. T. Robinson refers to him as the first neo-liberal,[3] many others emphasize that Bonhoeffer defies any kind of theological classification. William Hamilton says the following of Bonhoeffer, "He disturbs liberal and neo-orthodox, pious and worldly alike."[4] Marle suggests that there is a certain ambiguity about Bonhoeffer. He writes:

---

[1] Eberhard Bethge, *Dietrich Bonhoeffer: A Biography* (Minneapolis: Fortress Press, 2000), xvii-xviii.
[2] Ibid., 133.
[3] John A. T. Robinson, *The New Reformation?* (Philadelphia: Westminster Press, 1965(, 23.
[4] William Hamilton, "Bonhoeffer: Christology and Ethic United," *Christianity and Crisis* (October 10, 1964), 195-96. Cf. Martin E. Martin, "Problems and Possibilities in Bonhoeffer's Thought," in *The Place of Bonhoeffer* (New York: Association Press, 1964), 14-15.

The name of Bonhoeffer is now among those often referred to in religious discussions. There are many people almost everywhere ready to make him into a latter day prophet. Yet their basis for doing so is often slight enough . . . . Even those who have actually read some of Bonhoeffer's writings, especially *Letters and Papers from Prison,* in general still have only a somewhat fragmentary knowledge of the man and his work. It is all too likely, then, that the true significance and scope of the bold themes in his last reflexions from prison—which have with good reason awoken so many echoes in recent years—will be only imperfectly grasped.[5]

Wind also suggests something contradictory about Bonhoeffer when she states,

The question of Dietrich Bonhoeffer's own identity often comes up in his *Letters and Papers from Prison.* In the summer of 1944, he wrote a poem "Who am I?" In it we find the portrait of someone made up of contradictions, who emerges from his cell "calmly, cheerfully, firmly, like a squire from his country house," and who at the same time, like his fellow prisoners, gets "stir-crazy," and has to fight against anxiety and depression. Under the pressure of the interrogation prison, which goes on for months, urgently waiting for the overthrow of Hitler which he has had a share in preparing—and which will then go wrong, only a few days later—Dietrich develops as a theme the way in which he is torn in two directions, between self-confidence and doubt in himself. This contradiction dogged him all his life, and it was never just a problem for him as an individual. The reason why Dietrich felt this problem so strongly was that during the course of his life traditional values were both put in question and put to the test.[6]

One has the impression that his most stable years were up to about 1930, the year in which he completed *Akt und Sein,* thus, qualifying him to be a university lecturer. However, Wind suggests that there was an underlying conflict in the home in some measure because of the aloofness of Dietrich's father who was both sensitive and detached.[7] From 1930 until April 9, 1945, Bonhoeffer's life was divided between teaching, writing, and traveling to such places as Spain, England, Sweden, and the United

---

[5] Rene Marle, *Bonhoeffer: The Man and his Work,* trans. Rosemary Sheed (New York: Newman Press, 1967), 9. Cf Dietrich Bonhoeffer, *Reflections on the Bible,* ed. Manfred Weber, trrans. M. Eugene Boring (Peabody, MA: Hendrickson Publishers, 2004), 4. Weber alludes to Bonhoeffer's comment that the Bible ignites doubt and not faith.
[6] Renate Wind, *Dietrich Bonhoeffer: A Spoke in the Wheel,* Trans. John Bowden (Grand Rapids, MI: William B. Eerdmans Poublishing Company, 1995), X.
[7] Ibid., 5.

States. He was a leader in various ecumenical councils and conferences, and he certainly was one of the most influential leaders in the Confessing Church. But it seems that he was a marked man after his February 1933 address in which he stated that the *Führer* could become a *Verführer*; thus, the next five years would find Bonhoeffer in a number of activities—from helping to plot the downfall of Hitler to involvement in a multitude of facets within ministry. One is amazed that he was able to write so many works while engaged in a variety of other activities.

Bonhoeffer became known to British and American theologians during the decade of the 1960's, and his writings found a ready welcome by especially John A.T. Robinson, Paul van Buren, Harvey Cox, William Hamilton and Thomas J.J. Altizer. These individuals took Bonhoeffer's thought into another direction beyond neo-orthodoxy into a movement which spawned various theologies. One wonders what Bonhoeffer would have written had he lived for another three or four decades. Would he have again emphasized ecclesiology as he did in his early twenties, or would he have continued with themes of discipleship? Bethge states:

> Dietrich Bonhoeffer had no opportunity to mature and perfect his life-work and it is a laborious task to reconstruct his ideas, after the event, from his books and collections of many of his essays, letters and notes. Some of these make light and stimulating reading, others are almost incomprehensible except to the specialist.[8]

The difficulty of reading Bonhoeffer has tended to keep many completely away except perhaps to find pithy quotes or phrases to help support various theological views. Concerning his habilitation thesis, one reviewer remarked: "Reading it is an act of self-discipline if not of penance."[9]

Not only is his style at times somewhat cumbersome, but also there is a reactive nature to his writings, a tendency to base his beliefs around his environment and current events in his life. His writings, then, reflect three particular periods of his life which are as follows: the university period, 1927-1933; the Confessing Church period, 1933-1940; and the period of political activity, imprisonment and martyrdom, 1940-1945. Bonhoeffer has a desire to place theological thought in what he termed "concreteness;" he wants to apply theology to the present, the "now," and to "this world."

---

[8] Eberhard Bethge, *Costly Grace*, trans. Rosaleen Ockenden San Francisco: Harper and Row Publishers, 1979), 141.

[9] Dwight P. Adler, "Bonhoeffer: What Was He All About?" *Eternity* 21 (February 1970): 48.

Contemporary events must be given significance in Bonhoeffer's thought.[10]

There are some who argue that the only reason Bonhoeffer has been elevated to such a standing is because of his martyrdom at a young age. Still others claim that he died for a political cause and not a religious one; therefore, he should not be held in such high esteem among theologians. While there may be some validity to these statements, the fact is he was a theologian and pastor who in a limited amount of time lived out his faith effectively and courageously.

Bonhoeffer is close theologically to Barth. Dr. G. K. A. Bell, Bishop of Chichester wrote a recommendation for Bonhoeffer on November 16, 1933, in which he states concerning Bonhoeffer:

> ... I should however like to suggest a man who would do the article with great ability and first-hand knowledge. He is Dr. Dietrich Bonhoeffer. ...
> He spent a year in U.S.A. for theological purposes. He knows the personnel of the German church at Berlin extremely well and is a follower of Karl Barth.[11]

Nearly all students of Bonhoeffer agree that Barth is the most significant theological influence on Bonhoeffer, and he always speaks very highly of him. In a letter to Erwin Sutz, dated July 24, 1931, he states concerning Barth: "For he is really all there. I have never seen anything like it before and wouldn't have believed it possible. . . . There's really someone that one can get things out of! And to think that I'm sitting in poor old Berlin and moping because there's no one to learn theology from. . . ."[12]

Bonhoeffer also admires Reinhold Niebuhr, though not to the extent that he does Barth. He sees Niebuhr as the right balance between neo-orthodoxy and true liberalism; however, he is somewhat critical of Niebuhr in that Bonhoeffer believes he lacks a strong christological emphasis. He writes: "He [Niebuhr] sees the right way between neo-orthodoxy, for which Jesus Christ becomes the ground for human despair, and a true liberalism, for which Christ is the Lord, the norm, the ideal and the revelation of our essential being."[13] Though he thinks highly of

---

[10] P.H. Ballard, "Bonhoeffer on Providence in History." *Scottish Journal of Theology* 27 (August 1974): 268

[11] Dietrich Bonhoeffer, *No Rusty Swords*, ed. Edwin H. Robertson, trans. John Bowden (William Collins Sons & Co., 1977), 253.

[12] Ibid., 116.

[13] Ibid., 112.

Niebuhr, he would conclude that, "God has granted American Christianity no Reformation," and he would eagerly return to Germany.

Bonhoeffer's life experiences force him to search the Old and New Testaments in order to find a source to give to him guidance. Unlike Bultmann who for many decades had a stable academic position, Bonhoeffer's life is characterized by tentativeness and transience. Whereas for Bultmann exegesis leads to preaching, this seems to be reversed in Bonhoeffer; that is, his preaching leads him to exegetical studies. This can be seen more specifically in his *Cost of Discipleship*.

B. Bonhoeffer's Method

1. Old Testament

a. Introduction

Bonhoeffer had already studied Hebrew before he was a student at Tübingen for one year beginning in 1923. The year of study at Tübingen widened his awareness of theological studies, but he did not display interest in any particular field of study. However, Bethge believes that his year there was characterized ". . . by a persistent exploration of the epistemological field."[14] He attended a class which was taught by Volz, who lectured on the Psalms, and he also showed an interest in Old Testament theology which course was taught by Bultmann. He especially enjoyed the "passion of the prophets."[15]

Almost a decade later, Bonhoeffer lectured on the first three chapters of Genesis in which he discussed the issue of conscience and orders of creation. He referred to the creation story as a "legend." His two-hour lecture was divided between discussing recent theology and the topic "Creation and Sin: A Theological Interpretation of Genesis 1-3."[16] Bonhoeffer's major field was systematic theology, and it seems that he was aware that he must not "invade" the field of the professional Old Testament scholars; nevertheless, he apparently believed that he was competent to involve himself in a scholarly manner in Old Testament studies. *Creation and Fall* would become his first minor literary success, and he received an excellent review in the *Kreuzzeitung*.[17]

---

[14] Bethge, *Dietrich Bonhoeffer: A Biography*, 56.
[15] Ibid., 54.
[16] Ibid., 215.
[17] Bethge, *Dietrich Bonhoeffer: A Biography*, 216.

His 1936 study on Ezra and Nehemiah, however, did not enhance his reputation as an Old Testament scholar. Bethge claims:

> His exegesis on The Reconstruction of Jerusalem according to Ezra and Nehemiah was affected by the fact that his professional status as an Old Testament scholar, of course, was weaker. Both the essay and the exegesis, however, sprang from the same impulses; both sought to clarify and strengthen the minds of those who had become confused. This makes them absorbing reading, even if the principles of exegetical scholarship applied by Bonhoeffer are not entirely defensible.[18]

Bethge defends Bonhoeffer by stating that, "His Bible study was more of a sermon than a critical examination of the text."[19]

Bonhoeffer makes no distinction between the Old Testament and the New Testament as containing the Word of God. One is impressed of the high regard which he expressed concerning the entire Bible. Bethge refers to a statement made to a student, Herr Kanitz, in 1932 near Alexanderplatz in Berlin in which Bonhoeffer stated that every word of the Holy Scripture was like a personal love letter from God to human beings.[20] One may find it remarkable that Bonhoeffer, who had been trained in systematic theology, devoted so much of his study and writing to both the Old and New Testaments. His works can be divided among the following: (1) exegetical studies; (2) sermons; and (3) essays, letters, and papers concerning themes and/or texts from the Bible. One of his best-known, if not the most well-known, is his *Nachfolge* (*The Cost of Discipleship*) which is essentially christologically centered.

Interestingly, it is not only the New Testament in which Bonhoeffer finds christological themes, but according to Harrelson,

> In Bonhoeffer's other writings it is made clear that the entire Bible is to be interpreted in relation to Jesus Christ. The Old Testament is no less the Bible of the Church than is the New Testament. Traditional ways of relating Old and New Testaments are not satisfactory to Bonhoeffer (Law and Gospel, Promise and Fulfillment, Old Testament messianic references and the like). He insists that Christ is found in the Old Testament as well as in the New Testament, and not alone in those passages which herald the coming of the Messiah.[21]

---

[18] Ibid., 526.
[19] Ibid., 527.
[20] Ibid., 204
[21] Walter Harrelson, "Bonhoeffer and the Bible," in *The Place of Bonhoeffer*, ed., Martin E. Marty (New York: Association Press, 1964), 117. Cf., Dietrich

Bonhoeffer's earliest exegetical work, *Creation and Fall* (1933) contains a christological interpretation. However, themes pertaining to Christology are seen in his Bible study entitled "König David," as well as in his study of Psalms. At this point Harrelson is somewhat critical of Bonhoeffer when he writes:

> Here we need only say that Bonhoeffer's christological interpretation seems to us to be unnecessary. Would it not have been more consistent for Bonhoeffer to have argued that the Bible *may or may not* bear witness to Christ? Why should he not have summoned us to do our exegesis with *no* key at all, not even the christological key to the Bible's meaning? Is Bonhoeffer not violating his own warning that we bring nothing to the Bible save our own readiness to hear God address us? Is he not insisting upon a dogmatic presupposition that *only* in Jesus Christ may man know God? Is such a presupposition defensible?[22]

In Bonhoeffer's prison letters, one sees his preoccupation with the Old Testament, and according to Woelfel, the Old Testament dominated his theological thinking during his years of imprisonment and that his reflections on the Old Testament during this period constitute a central element in his "religionless" interpretation of Christianity.[23] Bethge records the prison letters he received from Bonhoeffer from April 14, 1943, to January 17, 1945. The following Old Testament books are cited by Bonhoeffer in his prison correspondence: Genesis, Leviticus, Numbers, Job, Psalms, Proverbs, Ecclesiastes, Song of Songs, Isaiah, Jeremiah and Lamentations.

His first reference to the Old Testament is contained within his May 15, 1943 letter in which he quotes Jeremiah 17:9 regarding the human heart as wicked and deceitful. However, in this same letter he also refers to Psalm 2, 13, 31, 47 and 70. It is in this letter that Bonhoeffer states he is reading the Bible in its entirety, and in particular that he reads from the Psalms daily.

Bonhoeffer, *Reflections on the Bible*, ed. Manfred Weber, trans. M. Eugene Boring (Peabody, MA: Hendrickson Publishers, 2004), 93-99.
[22] Ibid., 119. Cf. James W. Woelfel, *Bonhoeffer's Theology* (New York: Abingdon Press, 1970), 223-236. The author claims that the Old Testament dominated Bonhoeffer's thinking during his years of imprisonment, and that he had a concern for the penultimate. He especially favored the books of Ecclesiastes, Proverbs, Job, Song of Songs, and to some extent Isaiah and Jeremiah.
[23] James W. Woelfel, *Bonhoeffer's Theology* (New York: Abindon Press, 1970), 223.

In a letter simply dated May, 1943, he cites Genesis 2:18, but he also quotes four verses from Proverbs. Many today might say that Bonhoeffer's views of marriage and the family are somewhat antiquated; nevertheless, his high view of the family is very obvious, and he supports this perspective by numerous Old Testament quotes.

It is interesting to note that Bonhoeffer's references to the Old Testament gradually increase—the longer he is imprisoned, the more he makes use of the Old Testament. Many times these references refer to encouragement not to worry but to trust in God. He has an especially poignant interpretation of Ecclesiastes 3 when he writes:

> These last words probably mean that nothing that is past is lost, that God gathers up again with us our past, which belongs to us. So when we are seized by our past—and this may happen when we least expect it—we may be sure that is only one of the many 'hours' that God is always holding ready for us. So we ought not to seek the past again by our own efforts, but only with God.[24]

His first letter of the New Year on January 23, 1944, Bonhoeffer quotes for the first time from the book of Job; in fact, there are two references. Though the letter is filled with concern about the war and even the "Jewish problem," the general tenor of the letter is optimistic.

There is a shift in his April 30, 1944 letter which contains references to the essence of Christianity. He writes:

> You would be surprised, and perhaps even worried, by my theological thoughts and the conclusions they lead to. . . . What is bothering me incessantly is the question what Christianity really is, or indeed who Christ really is, for us today. The time when people could be told everything by means of words, whether theological or pious, is over, and so is the time of inwardness and conscience—and that means the time of religion in general. We are moving toward a completely religionless time; people as they are now simply cannot be religious anymore. . . . and if therefore man becomes radically religionless—and I think that that is already more or less the case (else how is it, for example, that this war, in contrast to all previous ones, is not calling forth any 'religious' reaction?)—what does that mean for 'Christianity'?[25]

---

[24] Dietrich Bonhoeffer, *Letters and Papers from Prison,* (New York: The Macmillan Company, 1978), 169.
[25] Ibid., 279-80.

He asks in the same letter such questions as, "How can Christ become the lord of the religionless as well?"[26] In this letter he claims that the New Testament is seldom read and understood in light of the Old Testament, and it is in this context which he uses the term "religionless Christianity."

In both his May 9 and May 16, 1944 letters, Bonhoeffer is concerned about locating an appropriate biblical passage for the sacrament of baptism, and he suggests only one New Testament passage, but three from the Old Testament. One would initially believe that Bonhoeffer would prefer a New Testament passage. This preponderance of emphasis on the Old Testament certainly displays at this point in his life that he is very involved with the Old Testament, and that he views both Testaments as essential. He writes, "I'm still writing something for the baptism. What would you think of Ps. 90:14 as a text?"[27]

He writes an interesting letter on May 20, 1944, in which he extols human romantic love and cites Song of Songs 7:6. He believes that the love of God should be primary, and this love is a *cantus firmus*. He believes the following:

> Even in the Bible we have the Song of Songs; and really one can imagine no more ardent, passionate, sensual love that is portrayed there (see 7.6). It is a good thing that the book is in the Bible, in face of all those who believe that the restraint of passion is Christian (where is there such restraint in the Old Testament?).[28]

On the baptism of Dietrich Wilhelm Rüdiger Bethge, Bonhoeffer writes a lengthy letter in May, 1944. In this particular letter, he uses passages from the Old Testament extensively. This letter has scripture from the following Old Testament books: Ecclesiastes, Proverbs, Jeremiah, Lamentations, Job, Psalms and Isaiah; there are sixteen Old Testament references, but only four New Testament! Again, one is amazed at his involvement with the Old Testament as opposed to the New Testament especially when the subject of the letter is baptism. One readily obtains the impression that Bonhoeffer gained hope and consolation during this period of his life by immersing himself in the Old Testament. It is also somewhat surprising that he applies these scriptures directly to his situation. This is perhaps the most poignant of Bohoeffer's letters as he anticipates that the baby who has been baptized will perhaps one day read this letter and its encouraging words of how to live a life which is pleasing

---

[26] Ibid., 280.
[27] Bonhoeffer, *Letters and Papers from Prison*, 292.
[28] Ibid., 303.

to God. Throughout the letter, Bonhoeffer cites various Old Testament passages which speak of courage, trust, hope, friendship and deliverance.

Bonhoeffer encourages Bethge on July 16, 1944, to preach in the future from the following Old Testament passages: Psalm 62:1, 119: 94a, Jeremiah 31:3, and Isaiah 41:10. The only suggested New Testament passage is Matthew 28:20b. In his letter dated July 18, 1944, Bonhoeffer believes that Jesus fulfilled Isaiah 53.[29] Bonhoeffer preached from Isaiah 53:5 on April 5, 1945, emphasizing the clause, "and with his stripes we are healed."[30]

Bonhoeffer loved the Old Testament. He knew Hebrew and was able to perform exacting exegesis on the text, but one readily obtains the impression that he was content to read the Old Testament in German and make direct application to his life situation as the text spoke to him. His December 5, 1943 letter states that his thoughts and feelings are similar to those contained in the Old Testament, and it is in this testament that Bonhoeffer especially believes that the concept of *Diesseitkeit* or "this worldliness" is found. Perhaps his best skills were in the areas of systematic theology and New Testament, but it is as if he could not confine himself only to these disciplines. To Bonhoeffer, God speaks in both the Old and New Testaments, and to exclude one is to lose a genuine message from God. His method of interpretation is such that the message of the Old Testament makes application to the life situation in which he finds himself, especially the last two years of his life in prison. Bonhoeffer is not a literalist, and he believes that much of the Old Testament is not *Historie*.

b. *Schöpfung Und Fall*

Bonhoeffer lectured on the topic of "Creation and Fall: Theological Exegesis of Genesis 1-3" during the winter term of 1932-1933. Bethge explains:

> The lectures made such an impression that Bonhoeffer's students persuaded him to have them published. He had given little thought to making it a proper book, as is shown by the fact that he did not take the trouble to verify the biblical and literary references with footnotes, as he had done in his previous books as a matter of course. Only the title was changed, to

---

[29] Bonhoeffer, *Letters and Papers from prison*, 361-62.
[30] Bonhoeffer, *Letters and Papers from Prison* (New York: The Macmillan Co., 1967), 232. The earlier edition includes a section, "The Last Days," which is not included in the newer (1978) edition.

avoid confusion with Emanuel Hirsch's *Creation and Sin*, published in 1931,though the remainder of Hirsch's title, ". . . in the natural reality of the human individual," was very different. Thus Bonhoeffer's work was published as *Creation and Fall*.[31]

Bonhoeffer attempts a theological interpretation of Genesis 1-3, not an exegetical analysis of the text. It would have been interesting to see how he would have interpreted some of the more controversial issues of these first chapters, but an exacting exegesis is not his purpose. *Creation and Fall* was the first book which Bonhoeffer wrote that Barth read, and though he was somewhat critical of the work, Barth stated that *Creation and Fall* at times ". . . showed greater fidelity to the biblical text than the parallel passages in Wilhelm Vischer's book."[32] However, according to Bethge "the exegetes regarded the work as systematics, and the systematicians viewed it as exegesis. One group was indignant and the other took no notice."[33] In fact, the November 1934 *Kirchliche Anzeiger für Würrtemberg* stated that Bonhoeffer's method could be described as *credo quia absurdum*! There were many who apparently believed that Bonhoeffer should leave Old Testament studies to those who were considered the authorities in this particular field of studies.

In *Creation and Fall,* Bonhoeffer's indebtedness to existentialism is seen. He writes of living in relation to the center of existence, and this is portrayed by the tree of life in the Garden of Eden. Man lives in freedom before the event of experiencing sin and separation from God. He lives in freedom before, God, others and even to himself. But the consequences of the Fall bring estrangement and even a certain knowledge of death. For Bonhoeffer, death in this context means that life is no longer a gift but a commandment. Harrelson gives insight into Bonhoeffer's existentialist thinking at this point:

> These traces of the author's existentialist thought are pointed out only to indicate that Bonhoeffer—departing from his own method—*has* brought something to the text other than Jesus Christ. The existentialist philosophical theology, which Bonhoeffer later abandoned, is a powerful exegetical instrument in his hands. What he has to say about Genesis 1-3 is highly illuminating and often quite original. It is a good thing for his exegesis, in fact, that he comes to the text with this particular interpretive

---

[31] Bethge, *Dietrich Bonhoeffer: A Biography,* 216.
[32] Ibid., 217. Cf. 527.
[33] Ibid.

key. And quite apart from this existentialism he has cast light upon the familiar text at many points.[34]

However, Harrelson is critical of Bonhoeffer's exegesis in that he believes there is no warrant to conclude that the references to Christ are appropriate. He writes: "If we are to go beyond the meaning of the text for Israel, should we not distinguish this Christian import of the text from its meaning for the community in which the text first took shape?"[35]

Creation and Fall is concerned with a christological interpretation of creation. Reist gives insight by stating the following about the work: "The treatment of Genesis 1-3 has to do with the understanding of creation.... He is attempting a *theological* interpretation of these chapters. His broad point is a striking one: There is only one link between God and the world, and that is Christ's freedom. *This* freedom is known in Christ."[36] Bonhoeffer's program is concerned with a concept of *analogia relationis*, or with the issue of analogy. Some theologians believe that this is the greatest theological problem—how does one speak of the relationship of divinity to humanity? Is human language sufficient since the issue of God's transcendence is ever before us? The Hebrew word for "God" in Genesis 1:1 is *Elohim,* and this word points to God as the ultimate high one. Man is mortal and finite; thus, the problem seems to be unsolvable.

Genesis 1:27 reads, "So God created man in his own image, in the image of God he created him; male and female he created them."[37] There continues to be lively debates concerning the Hebrew words for "image" and "likeness" with the majority of theologians claiming that the two words are very close to each other in meaning, and that this image is not material but incorporeal. Bonhoeffer is arguing not for an *analogia entis* (analogy of being), but an *analogia relationis* (analogy of relationship). Reist believes concerning this issue in *Creation and Fall:*

> With Christology as the clue to the doctrine of creation, the focus is on Freedom. One could put it this way, then: In creation minus man God could behold his work but not a reflection of himself. "Only in something that is itself free can the One who is free, the Creator, see himself" (CF 36). If this freedom is a reflection of the Creator's freedom, then the freedoms must correspond. If Christ is the clue to the nature of God's

---

[34] Walter Harrelson, "Bonhoeffer and the Bible," in *The Place of Bonhoeffer,* 120.
[35] Ibid., 121.
[36] Benjamin Reist, *The Promise of Bonhoeffer* (Philadelphia: J. B. Lippincott Company, 1969), 49.
[37] *New International Version* (Grand Rapids, MI: Zondervan Bible Publishers, 1985)

freedom, he is also the clue to the nature of man's freedom. And this is of immense import. For God in Christ is understandable only in his relationship to man. So man in Christ is also understandable only in relationship to God.[38]

Reist continues:

As the relational character of man's creaturehood is the free gift of the God who in freedom creates, so is the analogy of relationship. It derives from and is dependent upon God's act. In the light of the knowledge of this act, however—in the light, that is, of God as he is known in Christ—it can be said that man in his freedom for the other is man in the image of God.[39]

Bonhoeffer works through the first three chapters of Genesis. One perhaps wishes that he had cited the actual verses, but it is possible if one has the biblical text to determine upon which particular passages he is commenting. Bonhoeffer's high regard for scripture is evident as he introduces this work:

The Bible is nothing but the book upon which the Church stands. This is its essential nature, or it is nothing. Therefore the Scriptures need to be read and proclaimed wholly from the viewpoint of the end. Thus the creation story should be read in church in the first place only from Christ, and not until then as leading to Christ. We can read towards Christ only if we know that Christ is the beginning, the new and the end of our world. Theological interpretation accepts the Bible as the book of the Church and interprets it as such. Its method is this assumption; it continually refers back to the text (which has to be ascertained with all the methods of philological and historical research) to this supposition.[40]

As previously stated, many would find his Old Testament scholarship somewhat lacking, but his intention is to interpret this section of the Old Testament in a theological manner.

As one reads through this work, the initial impression may be that Bonhoeffer should have dealt more with the Hebrew grammar. The meaning of specific words and their nuances could have provided a deeper meaning of the text. The various tenses of the Hebrew verbs could help one to understand the original intent of the writer. But this is not Bonhoeffer's purpose.

---

[38] Benjamin Reist, *The Place of Bonhoeffer,* 51.
[39] Ibid., 52.
[40] Dietrich Bonhoeffer, *Creation and Fall* (New York: Macmillan Publishing Co., 1978), 12.

Bonhoeffer believes that humans inherently think about the beginning: "The Bible begins in a place where our thinking is at its most passionate. Like huge breakers it surges up, is thrown back upon itself and spends its strength."[41] He believes that it is somewhat irritating to speak of the beginning since we were not there; nevertheless, it is a question which is inherent to the human condition, though humans can only conceive of the beginning as something which is temporal, and to Bonhoeffer truly understanding the beginning is not possible. Bonhoeffer refers to Hegel, but he denies that Hegelian thought is helpful with the question of beginnings since Reason would take the place of God.

Humanity finds itself in the middle, not at the beginning nor at the end. Bonhoeffer is concerned with eschatology, though he does not offer any specific answer or solution to how and when the end will occur. It is impossible for the person to fully comprehend both the beginning and the end, he knows only that his life is controlled by both. Bonhoeffer contrasts humans with the animal kingdom:

> The animals do not know about the beginning and the end; therefore they know no hatred and no pride. Man, aware of being totally deprived of his self-determination—because he comes from the beginning and is moving toward the end without knowing what this means—hates the beginning and rises up against it in pride.[42]

No one can understand the concept of the beginning. Perhaps the evil one himself will attempt to convince man of the possibility of possessing such knowledge, but it is one great lie. Only the One who is in the beginning, i.e. God, can understand what such a state is.

Bonhoeffer believes that God bears witness of himself in the Old Testament. God is both transcendent and imminent—He makes himself known to human beings through scripture. But we can only hear the beginning in the middle—that is, in our present situation. "There is no possible question which could go back beyond this 'middle' to the beginning, to God as Creator. Thus it is impossible to ask why the world was created, about God's plan or about the necessity of creation."[43] There is no particular date for the creation, and there is "nothing" between the Creator and that which is created; thus, there is no law of cause and effect, but only freedom, and this freedom occurs through the void. In other

---

[41] Ibid., 13.
[42] Ibid., 14-15.
[43] Ibid., 17.

words, God is compelled to create. Bonhoeffer is clear; this nothing is nothing—the void is not a substance out of which God can create.

One perhaps wishes that at this point, Bonhoeffer would have looked at the various possibilities of the Hebrew word, *bara*. Does this word point to *creatio ex nihilo* or not? Did God create out of a preexisting substance or not? Though Bonhoeffer does not discuss the word, he clearly holds to the belief that there was no preexisting material out of which God fashioned the world. To Bonhoeffer, even the void itself is obedient to the will and action of God; the void has no power on its own.

Bonhoeffer writes concerning the resurrection of Christ from the dead, and he compares this to creation:

> The fact that Christ was dead did not mean the possibility of the resurrection, but its impossibility; it was the void itself, it was the *nihil negativum*. There is absolutely no transition or continuity between the dead and the resurrected Christ except for the freedom of God which, in the beginning, created his work out of nothing.[44]

The Bible addresses humanity which is in the middle, and this gives hope that despair will not triumph. The tendency is to experience anxiety, but the Gospel, even Christ will be with us as we move toward the end. Bonhoeffer uses words such as "mercy," "grace," and "forgiveness" in the context of God's presence with his people.

The earth in its formlessness waits for the work of God to bring order out of the chaos. Bonhoeffer seems to personify the word, describing it as slumbering and resting. Bonhoeffer does use the Hebrew word, *tehom*, to help give a better understanding of this formlessness and darkness. His christological interpretation is evident as he states: "The dark deep. That is the first sound of the power of darkness, of the Passion of Jesus Christ."[45] He continues to emphasize God's transcendence as he is over the creation and not one with it. The purpose of creation is to bring glory to the creator. God gives great power to creation, and this expresses itself in form. Bonhoeffer is aware of mythologies, but Bonhoeffer is careful to bring out the distinctive nature of the creation story as contained in the book of Genesis. There is no hint of pantheism in Bonhoeffer's view of cosmology, and in this context, Bonhoeffer alludes to God's sovereignty. The only relationship of God to his work is that of command.

At this point, it seems that Bonhoeffer sounds somewhat like Barth with his strong emphasis upon the Word. He writes: "He is in the world as

---

[44] Ibid., 19.
[45] Ibid., 21.

Word, because he is the really transcendent, and he is the really transcendent because he is in the world in the *Word.* Only in the Word of creation do we know the Creator, in the Word in the middle do we have the beginning."[46]

He has an interesting discussion of what "God speaks" means. To Bonhoeffer "Word" is not a symbol or an idea, but refers to God's work itself—imperative and indicative are combined. However, his Word does not act as the imperative since it is issued out of total freedom and authority. We cannot speak of cause and effect in regard to the creation since it was done in complete freedom in the Word. The Word has inherent power to create and to dissolve chaos. Bonhoeffer's christological interpretation leads him to identify the light as that of Christ. "If that word from the darkness upon the deep was the first reference to the Passion of Jesus Christ, so now the freeing of the submissive, formless deep for its own being by means of the light is the reference to the light that shines in the darkness."[47]

Bonhoeffer believes that preservation of the work is connected to creation, but to him, this is one *Augenblick,* as there is no thought of sequence here. He believes that the meaning of God seeing his work as good is that He sees even the fallen world as good, and because of this perception on His part, the world will not be destroyed is critical of Kant as the latter had a somewhat negative view of the world and the work of God. Bonhoeffer believes that it is this world in which the kingdom of God will eventually come to fruition, and because of this, God's preservation continues. He argues against a *creatio continua,* and believes there is a vast difference between this belief and preservation. He does believe that there is a distinction of preservation in regards to the original creation and the fallen one.

One would have liked to see an exegetical discussion concerning the Hebrew word for "day," *yom,* however, Bonhoeffer omits this. Instead Bonhoeffer discusses "day" in a very philosophical manner depicting day as rhythm and power, and not a certain period of time which can be measured. He refers to some of the descriptions as "scientific *naivete,*" and remarks that the early writer lacked scientific awareness. It is in this context that Bonhoeffer remarks, "The idea of verbal inspiration will not do."[48] His exegetical and hermeneutical methodology at this point in his career was indebted to existentialism. On the other hand, one senses at times an almost pietistic emphasis in the writings of Bonhoeffer.

---

[46] Bonhoeffer, *Creation and Fall,* 23.
[47] Ibid., 24.
[48] Bonhoeffer, *Creation and Fall,* 29.

He writes of the stars and the fact that they do not take part in the everyday life of the person, and in this sphere number rules. But the world of number can actually be constricting for man. "It is peculiar to man to know that the higher he can rise in the world of number the more rarefied the air is around him; it becomes more restricted, and thinner, so that he cannot live in this world."[49] Man instinctively wants to seek comfort in the world of the tangible, but this world too is ultimately dependent upon God and his protective care. Number is also a creation of God and is seen as subservient to him. The light of creation is from God: "The light *per se* of the creation, the light which lay formless over the formless darkness, is bound to form, to law, to the fixed, to number; but it remains in God, it remains God's creation, and never itself becomes calculable number."[50] Bonhoeffer does not accept any concept of deism with its belief that God wound up the universe, allowing it to continue by the laws which are inherent within it—God is far removed from his work according to deism. Instead, Bonhoeffer states that God is intimately concerned and involved with his work, i.e., the world. In fact, he states that if God would withdraw himself, the world would vanish into nothingness. The goodness of the work is because it is from the hand of the Creator and gives glory and honor to him.

He has an interesting discussion of Genesis 1:26, in which he states that God does not see Himself in His work. This work comes out of his freedom, but it is strange to him. Bonhoeffer does explain that the Hebrew plural is used in this context, "Let us make man in our image. . . ." To Bonhoeffer, this has nothing to do with Darwinism; rather, this event is truly unique. We cannot know the condition of the first person; only as we stand in the middle, in Christ, can we comprehend our true nature. He states freedom is found only in relationship: "In truth freedom is a relationship between two persons. Being free means "being free for the other," because the other has bound me to him. Only in relationship with the other am I free."[51] He ties this freedom to the message of the Gospel. God views himself in man in that man is in God's image. At this point Bonhoeffer mentions the reality of pneumatology, that is, the Holy Spirit is involved in the life of man. The fact of *analogia relationis* ". . . means that even the relation between man and God is not a part of man; it is not a capacity, a possibility, or a structure of his being but a given, set relationship; *justitia passiva.*"[52]

---

[49] Ibid., 30.
[50] Ibid., 32
[51] Ibid., 37.
[52] Bonhoeffer, *Creation and Fall*, 39.

The person receives his authority to rule from God; he is free *from* the world but free *for* others. Humans were created to rule the world, but the converse has taken place. Man is held by technology. "We do not rule because we do not know the world as God's creation, and because we do not receive our dominion as God-given but grasp it for ourselves."[53]

Bonhoeffer commences Genesis 2 with a discussion about the significance of rest, stating that the idea of rest is completion, peace and perfection. The day of rest is as essential for us today as it was for Adam. In the New Testament this day of rest is the day of victory—Jesus' conquering of death and resurrection from the dead.

Bonhoeffer believes that the two creation accounts picture the same event, but they are expressed from differing vantage points. The first account is from God's perspective while the account in Genesis 2 is from the human viewpoint. The first depicts God as Lord; thus, his transcendence is portrayed. The second shows him as near, and his immanence is obvious as he is seen as a fatherly God.

In the context of Genesis 2:7, Bonhoeffer discusses the distinctions between Yahweh and Elohim, believing that the former is God's real name while the latter is but a generic name. He discusses the use of anthropomorphisms on the part of humans in attempting to describe who this God is. In fact, Bonhoeffer states that the anthropomorphisms become intolerable, especially when one reads of the descriptions of how God fashioned man. But though the language seems unsophisticated, Bonhoeffer is convinced that this is *the* story of creation, and it displays God's wonderful sovereignty and craftsmanship in making the human being. He believes that man is body and soul, and he uses the term "spirit" as well in referring to the incorporeal aspect of the person. He believes that

> . . . God enters into the body again where the original in its created being has been destroyed. He enters it in Jesus Christ. He enters into it where it is broken, in the form of the sacrament of the body and of the blood. The body and blood of the Lord's Supper are the new realities of creation of the promise for the fallen Adam. Adam is created as body, and therefore he is also redeemed as body, in Jesus Christ and in the Sacrament.[54]

Concerning the primal earth, Bonhoeffer has some difficulties with a literalistic understanding of the events described. "How should we speak of the young earth except in the language of fairy tales?"[55] He does not suggest that this primal place could have been literally between the Tigris

---

[53] Ibid., 40.
[54] Bonhoeffer, *Creation and Fall,* 48.
[55] Ibid., 49.

and Euphrates River, though he does say, "Who can speak of these things except in pictures? Pictures are not lies: they denote things, they let the things that are meant shine through. . . . They are true to the extent that God remains in them."[56] The "magic garden" experience does not last and humanity becomes too familiar with sin. The Fall is an event which is beyond history. (Bonhoeffer has a tendency to use *Historie* and *Geschichte* interchangeably). He writes: "It is the beginning, destiny, guilt and end of every one of us: thus speaks the Church of Christ."[57]

He is not certain of the sources of the story of the two trees in the garden; the story may come from a variety of sources. As Bonhoeffer describes the events leading up to the taking of the forbidden fruit and the consequences, he describes the episode as if it is rooted in history. He has an extended discussion of the words "good" and "evil," or the Hebrew *tob* and *ra*. He quotes Hans Schmidt who believes that these words though opposites are inseparably linked with one another.[58] Bonhoeffer believes that this story describes the situation of humanity today. The death spoken of in this passage is to live life by commandment and not by grace—life is no longer a gift. Such a person must live life in his own strength, and life becomes a drudgery and one is alone. Bonhoeffer claims that this story reminds all who are fettered by contradiction and living in a torn world to realize that our history is with Christ and not as Adam's history was with the serpent. We can know about the new life, ". . . from the new middle, from Christ, as those who are freed in faith from the knowledge of good and evil and from death, and who can make Adam's picture their own only in faith."[59]

His existentialist interpretation draws on the theme of solitariness—as Christ is alone, so is Adam, and also in a sense every person knows the experience of being alone, and he uses some strong language to describe this aloneness. Bonhoeffer emphasizes the kinship that humans have with the animal kingdom, and he states that no other religion emphasizes this as much as found in Genesis 2. He is still alone even though the animals have been created. Adam's helper is created from his own rib, and Eve and Adam are one, but yet two.

> It is best to describe this unity by saying that now he belongs to her because she belongs to him. They are no longer without one another; they are one and yet two. The fact of two becoming one is itself the mystery

---

[56] Ibid.
[57] Ibid., 50.
[58] Bonhoeffer, *Creation and Fall*, 57.
[59] Ibid., 57.

which God has established by his action upon the sleeping Adam. They were one from their origin and only when they become one do they return to their origin. This becoming one is never the fusion of the two, the abolition of their creatureliness as individuals. It is the utmost possible realization of their belonging to one another, which is based directly upon the fact that they are different from one another.[60]

Bonhoeffer has a lengthy discussion of how Adam and Eve complete each another, and the importance of love in the relationship. Each knows that the other is a gift from God. He states that we are the Adam—this is a story about our situation. The ultimate expression of belonging to one another is seen in sexuality which points to one being both an individual but also belonging to the other person. He describes this relationship by writing: "Here the community of man and woman is the community derived from God, the community of love glorifying and worshipping him as the Creator. It is therefore the Church in its original form."[61] Bonhoeffer seems to be equating community with church at this point.

Bonhoeffer is careful to say that Genesis 3:1-3 cannot be interpreted in a simplistic manner; that is, it was neither the devil who caused the problem of the Fall, nor man's freedom for either good or evil. He writes against any *diaboli ex machina.* He is not certain about the passage, especially that pertaining to the serpent. Bonhoeffer believes:

> It is not the purpose of the Bible to give information about the origin of evil but to witness to its character as guilt and as the infinite burden of man. To ask about the origin of evil independently of this is far from the mind of the biblical writer, and for this very reason the answer cannot be unequivocal and direct. It will always contain two aspects that as a creature of God I have committed a completely anti-godly and evil act, and that for that very reason I am guilty—and moreover inexcusably guilty. It will never be possible simply to blame the devil who has led us astray. . . . The guilt rests upon me alone, I have committed evil in the midst of the primaeval state of creation.[62]

In his belief concerning theodicy, Bonhoeffer places the sole responsibility upon the person. He refers to Luther and Catholic dogmatics with its emphasis upon Adam as the first victim of Lucifer, but Bonhoeffer holds that Adam's actions are inexcusable.

The rhetorical question "Did God say," is for Bonhoeffer the godless question, but it is also more enticing since it comes from a religious

---

[60] Bonhoeffer, *Creation and Fall,* 60.
[61] Ibid., 62.
[62] Bonhoeffer, *Creation and Fall,* 65.

vantage point; this question is clothed in righteouness, but it is actually the antithesis. Bonhoeffer warns that one should be on guard against such a question, for it comes in many forms and has the power to destroy: "Let us be on our guard against such cunning exaggerations of God's command. The evil one is certainly in them. The serpent's question immediately proved to be *the* satanic question *par excellence,* the question that robs God of his honour and aims to divert man from the Word of God."[63] In this discussion, Bonhoeffer's respect for God's Word is apparent.

Bonhoeffer refers to Eve's conversation with the serpent, ". . . the first religious, theological conversation," and that it is merely speaking about God and not calling upon him in prayer. The promise that "You shall not die" soon becomes the pronouncement that "You will die," thus, begins the conflict between God and humanity who is in the *imago dei.* The person, according to Bonhoeffer, now stands in the middle which means he is now left to his own resources and strength—the oneness of fellowship with God is no longer his experience. Bonhoeffer states that the temptation for man is to be *sicut deus*, but God wishes to address him in his creatureliness:

> He can address man in his never-abolished creatureliness, and he does this in Jesus Christ, in the Cross and in the Church. He speaks of the creatureliness of man only as the truth which is spoken by God and which, because of God, we believe in spite of all our knowledge of reality.[64]

Bonhoeffer speaks about such a person going beyond the Word of God and attempting his own means of knowledge of God. Bonhoeffer seems almost to be ridiculing theological theories of sin when he states: "No theory of *posse peccare* or of *non posse peccare* can apprehend the fact that the deed was actually done. Every attempt to make it understandable is merely the accusation which the creature hurls against the creator."[65] However, Bonhoeffer believes fully that the Fall impacted humanity and the world in a disastrous manner: "The Fall affects the whole of the created world which is henceforth plundered of its creatureliness as it crashes blindly into infinite space, like a meteor which has torn away from its nucleus."[66]

The Fall results in division—in the person, in nature, between Adam and Eve, and assuredly between them and God. "Passion and hate, *tob* and

---

[63] Ibid., 68.
[64] Bonhoeffer, *Creation and Fall,* 73.
[65] Ibid., 75-76.
[66] Ibid., 76.

ra—these are the fruit of the tree of knowledge."[67] He now has conscience and somehow believes that it is possible to hide from God, but he is his own worst enemy. Bonhoeffer says this experience is also the plight of human beings: "We have all had the dream that we desire to flee from something horrible and cannot. This is the ever-recurring knowledge in our subconscious of this true situation of fallen man."[68] However, as Adam and Eve would not take responsibility for their actions, so is the condition spiritually of many today. The ramifications of the Fall continue to escalate.

Quoting Faust, Bonhoeffer says the biblical text is stating just the opposite of rebuilding the fallen world; Genesis speaks of irreparable damage, and one is condemned to live between curse and promise—he is subject to a life of *tob* and *ra*. However, there is always the promise of Christ, who can enable one to overcome this divided life. Again we see that Bonhoeffer is very comfortable with speaking of Christ's personal promise to Adam and his descendents: "The tree of life, the Cross of Christ, the middle of the fallen and preserved world of God, for us that is the end of the story of paradise."[69]

2. New Testament

a. Introduction

Bonhoeffer's best-known book perhaps is *Nachfolge* (*The Cost of Discipleship*), which work he published in 1937; however, the work has its roots in several years previous to this date. It seems that Bonhoeffer is on firmer ground when he writes on New Testament themes rather than Old Testament topics. Bonhoeffer as early as 1932 began outlining his thoughts concerning the future work, *The Cost of Discipleship,* and the book reached its completed form in 1936.[70]

Bonhoeffer studied New Testament with Adolph Schlatter in Tübingen during the summer term of 1923, and he took copious notes on the Gospel of John. Bethge states:

> Theologically, Bonhoeffer and Schlatter shared the desire to accept the concrete world as fully as possible; Bonhoeffer was also drawn to Schlatter's distinction allowing for the good in the New Testament and for

---

[67] Ibid., 78.
[68] Bonhoeffer, *Creation and Fall,* 81.
[69] Ibid., 94.
[70] Bethge, *Dietrich Bonhoeffer, 862-63.*

responsibility toward the natural, and not merely equating the latter with the night of sin of the Reformation. Bonhoeffer may have forgotten this distinction at times, but even during the *Discipleship* (originally published in English as *The Cost of Discipleship*) period he never failed to draw his students' attention to Schlatter's assessment of the good and the just in the New Testament: that goodness and justice would not be transformed into wickedness and deception.[71]

Bonhoeffer also attended Adolph Deissman's seminar for two semesters on the New Testament in Berlin. But it is not clear how much of an influence Bonhoeffer received from these two professors, especially regarding his work *Nachfolge*. Bethge claims: "Discipleship emerged from Bonhoeffer's own path, which he had pursued long before the political upheaval of that year [1933]. He had already expressed these things to his students. . . ."[72] He gave two series of lectures at Finkenwalde on the subject of discipleship: "Thus Bonhoeffer did not appear at the preachers' seminary with a manuscript ready for publication; but entire sections of his lectures went straight into the book. He continued to make alterations and deletions and to insert whole new chapters until the last page of the manuscript was delivered."[73] *The Cost of Discipleship* contains the quintessential thought of Bonhoeffer; many of his previous works were theoretical and contained the concepts of other theologians, but this work portrays the essence of his beliefs concerning what it means to be a disciple of Jesus Christ.

Bonhoeffer speaks later in life in a very positive manner about the Old Testament, and he even made some unusual comments about the New Testament. In his December 5, 1943 letter from Tegel prison he writes: "My thoughts and feelings seem to be more and more like those of the Old Testament, and in recent months I have been reading the Old Testament much more than the New. . . . In my opinion it is not Christian to want to take our thoughts and feelings too quickly and too directly from the New Testament."[74] However, in his March 9, 1944 letter he writes that he believes, "We so like to stress spiritual suffering; and yet that is just what Christ is supposed to have taken from us, and I can find nothing about it in the New Testament . . . ."[75] It appears that he is claiming that the New

---

[71] Bethge, *Dietrich Bonhoeffer*, 53-54.
[72] Ibid., 210.
[73] Ibid, 451.
[74] Dietrich Bonhoeffer, *Letters and Papers from Prison*, 156-57.
[75] Ibid., 232. In his March 24, 1944 letter, Bonhoeffer appeals to the New Testament claiming that it has no particular law about infant baptism. Cf., Woelfel, *Bonhoeffer's Theology*, 238.

Testament is authoritative over the Old Testament, though this is an argument from silence since he never explicitly states that in this letter.

Bonhoeffer believed that it is necessary for the Christian to study both the Old and the New Testaments. He writes in his April 30, 1944 letter, ". . . . we still read the New Testament far too little in the light of the Old."[76] Was Bonhoeffer speaking about himself when he wrote "we?" Or is this simply a rhetorical question? It appears that he wants to retain the authority of both testaments. He makes some interesting comments in his June 8, 1944 letter to Eberhard Bethge: "My view is that the full content, including the 'mythological' concepts, must be kept—the New Testament is not a mythological clothing of a universal truth; this mythology (resurrection, etc.) is the thing itself—but the concepts must be interpreted in such a way as not to make religion a precondition of faith (cf. Paul and circumcision)."[77] He seems to equate the two Testaments when he writes in his July 28, 1944 letter concerning the subject of blessing, "Indeed the only difference between the Old and New Testaments in this respect is that in the Old the blessing includes the cross, and in the New the cross includes the blessing."[78] It would have been fascinating to read more concerning this subject, but he immediately goes into another issue.

Marle claims the following about Bonhoeffer's premise concerning reading and understanding the Bible: "Bonhoeffer even goes so far as to give practical details on how best to read the Bible intelligibly without imposing one's own subjective personality on it. . . ."[79] Marle believed that for Bonhoeffer, "It [the Bible] must be read from beginning to end in a Christological perspective. . . . the light of Revelation, fully accomplished in Jesus Christ, is the only thing that can show us the whole meaning of Scripture, just as it is the only thing that can explain the meaning of the mystery of the Church and of our own lives."[80] More insight into Bonhoeffer's view of scripture is revealed by his following words:

> Holy Scripture is more than a watchword. It is more than "light for today." It is God's revealed word for all men, for all times. Holy Scripture does

---

[76] Bonhoeffer, *Letters and Papers from Prison*, 282.
[77] Bonhoeffer, *Letters and Papers from Prison*, 329. Cf., Bonhoeffer wrote on June 27, 1944, that "This world must not be prematurely written off; in this the Old and New Testaments are at one." He writes in this same letter that he must substantiate his recent thoughts in detail from the New Testament. He did not mention the Old. (He also states in his outline for a book, that he would like to look at the subject of example and its place in the New Testament), 383.
[78] Ibid., 374.
[79] Rene Marle, *Bonhoeffer: The Man and His Work*, 87.
[80] Ibid., 71-72

not consist of individual passages; it is a unit and is intended to be used as such. As a whole the Scriptures are God's revealing Word. Only in the infiniteness of its inner relationships, in the connection of Old and New Testaments, of promise and fulfillment, sacrifice and law, law and gospel, cross and resurrection, faith and obedience, having and hoping, will the full witness to Jesus Christ the Lord be perceived.[81]

Bonhoeffer speaks of the New Testament as the completion of the Old, and always his interpretation is christological. He believes:

The New Testament is the testimony to the fulfillment of the Old Testament promise in Christ. It is not a book of eternal truths, doctrines, norms, or myths but is a single united witness to the incarnation of God in the man Jesus Christ. It is as a whole and in all its parts nothing else than this witness to Christ—his life, death, and resurrection. This Christ is witnessed to not as the Eternal in the temporal, as Meaning in the accidental course of things, as the Essence of the transient! Rather Christ is testified to as the simply unique human being in whom God has become human, the one who died and was raised from the dead, and this unique, once-for-all character of the Christ event fills the whole New Testament. Here there is no distinction between *didactic* texts (in the epistles or sayings of Jesus) and the *narrative* texts. . . . In the miracle story just as in the parable or a command in the Sermon on the Mount, it is Christ himself who is proclaimed, not this or that truth or doctrine about him or some particular action he performed. . . . The testimony is given to "the Christ, the whole Christ, and nothing but the Christ." . . . This is the common denominator of the New Testament as a whole, This is the one fact to which the whole New Testament bears witness.[82]

Some may wonder at Bonhoeffer's christocentric interpretation, especially other theologians. Bonhoeffer, after all, had written an habilitation thesis. Though his work was in systematic theology, and he did much research especially on the doctrine of ecclesiology, some would say his biblical exposition lacks exegetical and critical methodologies. Another passage in which one gains insight into Bonhoeffer's opinion of Scripture is the following:

. . . . in the cross of Jesus the Scripture, that is, the Old Testament is fulfilled. Thus the whole Bible is permeated by the divine intention of being that word in which God wants to be found by us. No place that

---

[81] Dietrich Bonhoeffer, *Life Together* (New York: Harper & Row Publishers, 1978), 50-51.
[82] Dietrich Bonhoeffer, *Reflections on the Bible* (Peabody, MA: Hendrickson Publishers, 2004), 98.

seems pleasant to us, or that at first even seems reasonable to us, but a place in every way strange to us, totally alien to us. Precisely there is the place God has chosen to meet us. This is the way I now read the Bible. I ask of every passage, "What does God have to say to us here?" And I ask God what he wants to say. . . . Is it then also conceiv- able that I am now more prepared for a *sacrificiium intellectus* (offering my intellect as a sacrifice [to God])--. . . . I would rather do this than to go ahead and say at my own discretion, "This is divine, that is merely human!"[83]

Unlike Bultmann, the majority of Bonhoeffer's writings were not done in an academic setting. He was constantly involved in ecclesiastical matters, and from the late 1930's until his death in 1945, he was literally a hunted man. His life experiences would not allow him the time to delve more deeply into many of the issues of which he wrote. Some might say at times he wrote more from the heart than the mind, though this certainly would be too critical an assessment. He has great capacity for scholarship, and this is seen more in his two works, *Sanctorum Communio* and *Akt und Sein*. Karl Barth even referred to the former as a "theological miracle." But his situation led him to search constantly the scriptures, and with the resources which he had at hand, he was able to interpret the Old and New Testaments—his preaching led him to engage in exegesis. Harrelson states concerning Bonhoeffer's method in the writing of *The Cost of Discipleship*:

> Bonhoeffer only occasionally makes explicit use of the findings of critical scholars. He goes his own way in the interpretation of the Gospels. Only rarely does he indicate that we may not have Jesus' own words in the Gospel records. Seldom does he distinguish between the Synoptic and Johannine Gospels; both are used as equally reliable records of Jesus' words and deeds. A church theologian is here writing for the Church. Much knowledge of critical issues is presupposed on the part of his readers, much goes unsaid, in the interest of calling the Church of Jesus Christ to concrete acts of obedience to its Lord.[84]

b. *Nachfolge* (*The Cost of Discipleship*)

Jean Lasserre gave to Bonhoeffer the initial impetus to write *The Cost of Discipleship* when he inquired of Bonhoeffer concerning the connection between the Word of God and Christians who are attempting to live out their faith in the modern world.[85] In 1944, Bonhoeffer writes that he can

---

[83] Bonhoeffer, *Reflections on the Bible*, 109-10.
[84] Walter Harrelson, "Bonhoeffer and the Bible," in *The Place of Bonhoeffer*, 123.
[85] Bethge, *Dietrich Bonhoeffer: A Biography*, 153-54.

see the "dangers" of *The Cost of Discipleship*, but that he still stands by what he wrote.[86]

Bethge believes that the thesis of *The Cost of Discipleship* is as follows:

> Basically what Bonhoeffer was seeking to do in this book was to reaffirm the elusive concept of "faith" in all its complications. Ultimately his tireless search since the time of *Sanctorum Communio* for the concrete social nature of the Body of Christ was bound to make him reexamine the Reformers' general condemnation of faith as a *"habitus."* Did this rejection really mean that any interest in its dimension of existence was rooted by definition in evil? This is what Bonhoeffer himself had been taught and passed on to others. Yet Bonhoeffer had always been inclined to add a third note, that of earthly comnunity, to the two classic ecclesial notes, word and sacrament.[87]

To Bonhoeffer, then, the Church is the real body of Christ on earth. Discipleship is of paramount importance to Bonhoeffer, and he combines the doctrines of justification and sanctification under the category of discipleship. Bethge says: "Yet with his key formula, 'only the believer is obedient, and those who are obedient believe,' he did not mean to question the complete validity of Luther's *sola fide* and *sola gratia,* but to assert their validity by restoring to them their concreteness here on earth."[88]

Another major theme in *The Cost of Discipleship* is the communal nature of the Church, a body composed of individual Christians, each living in relationship to one another. There is no room for an individualistic spirit in the Body of Christ—each one is in a sense dependent upon the other. In fact, in later years Bonhoeffer alludes to religion as "individualism," and this understanding is a negative connotation with him. Discipleship means that one is there for the other, and the following after Christ is never a life which is to be lived in a selfish and egocentric manner. Bonhoeffer states:

> No one can become a new man except by entering the Church, and becoming a member of the Body of Christ. It is impossible to become a new man as a solitary individual. The new man means more than the

---

[86] Ibid., 460.
[87] Ibid., 454.
[88] Bethge, *Dietrich Bonhoeffer: A Biography,* 454.

individual believer after he has been justified and sanctified. It means the Church, the Body of Christ, in fact it means Christ himself.[89]

Bonhoeffer hopes that by defining with clarity the Christian's and the Church's responsibility, the promethean chain which bound the German Church to the control of the National Socialist Party would be broken. He believes that the doctrine of cheap grace characterizes the church in Germany during his time; such a lack of understanding true grace had cheapened the Gospel, and gradually transformed the Church into the image of the demonic rather than the divine.

As he views the present-day Church, he is aware that many look at grace as that which can absolve their willful sinning. This is grace which justifies the sin and not necessarily the sinner—it is grace which covers everything in order that all can stay the same. He clearly states the character of this enemy of the Church:

> Cheap grace means the justification of sin without the justification of the sinner. Grace alone does everything, they say, and so everything can remain as it was before. . . . The world goes on in the same old way, and we are still sinners. . . . Cheap grace is the preaching of forgiveness without requiring repentance, baptism without church discipline, Communion without confession, absolution without personal confession. Cheap grace is grace without discipleship, grace without the cross, grace without Jesus Christ, living and incarnate.[90]

Bonhoeffer believes that this kind of grace actually was not grace, and this twisted doctrine threatened to destroy the German Church. To Bonhoeffer, it seems that the majority had become secularized; though baptized, there was no true Christian substance to their lives, and many had a false sense of security. Their spiritual lives were mediocre at best, and perhaps even the majority was living in disobedience to the claims of the Gospel. Bonhoeffer lamentingly writes: "We must undertake this task because we are not ready to admit that we no longer stand in the path of true discipleship. We confess that. . . we are no longer sure that we are members of a Church which follows its Lord."[91]

The problem which Bonhoeffer addresses is the state of the church in Germany before the rise of the German Christians and the establishment of the Reich Church; therefore, Bonhoeffer's *The Cost of Discipleship* goes

---

[89] Dietrich Bonhoeffer, *The Cost of Discipleship* (New York: Simon & Schuster, 1995), 242.
[90] Bonhoeffer, *The Cost of Discipleshp*, 44-45.
[91] Ibid., 55.

beyond being a response to the events of 1933. The work was a challenge to the spiritual lethargy of traditional Lutheranism which had been used by the German Christians to fit into the agenda of National Socialism. Bonhoeffer at an early age had been influenced by the thought of Martin Luther. However, many contemporary Lutheran theologians had either ignored or demeaned Luther's doctrine of justification through faith; thus, many had interpreted the doctrine to justify a life without good works. Bonhoeffer believes that such a doctrine desecrates the Gospel, and to him the life of true grace is found in following the mandate to follow Christ as closely as possible. He warns his fellow churchmen:

> We Lutherans have gathered like eagles round the carcase of cheap grace, and there we have drunk of the poison which has killed the life of following Christ. It is true, of course, that we have paid the doctrine of pure grace divine honours unparalleled in Christendom, in fact we have exalted that doctrine to the position of God himself. Everywhere Luther's formula has been repeated, but its truth perverted into self-deception. So long as our Church holds the correct doctrine of justification, there is no doubt whatever that she is a justified church! So they said, thinking that we must vindicate our Lutheran heritage by making this grace available on the cheapest and easiest terms. To be "Lutheran" must mean that we leave the following of Christ to the legalists, Calvinists and enthusiasts—and all this for the sake of grace. We justified the world, and condemned as heretics those who tried to follow Christ. The result was that a nation became Christian and Lutheran, but at the cost of true discipleship. The price it was called upon to pay was all too cheap. Cheap grace won the day.[92]

Bethge explains, "For the newcomers the first classes in Zingst were a breathtaking surprise. They suddenly realized that they were not there simply to learn new techniques of preaching and instruction, but would be initiated into something that would radically change the prerequisites for those activities."[93] These lectures, of course, formed the basis for *The Cost of Discipleship*. At Finkenwalde, Bonhoeffer wrote the book and lived out the central thesis; thus, the book became the seminary's 'badge of honor.' Interestingly, some have claimed that the book has an angry tone to it, and that the book mirrors the angry and violent times in which it was written.[94]

---

[92] Bonhoeffer, *The Cost of Discipleship*, 53.
[93] Bethge, *Bonhoeffer; A Biography*, 450.
[94] William Kuhns, *In Pursuit of Dietrich Bonhoeffer*, Foreward by Eberhard Bethge (Dayton: Pflaum Press, 1967), 81. Kuhns characterizes the book as, ". . . entirely serious, rarely speculative, often rhetorically powerful—but always angry."

Bonhoeffer desires to put grace back into a context where it belongs, and that is in the incarnation. From this perspective grace is costly—costly to both the Father and the Son; the Father had to relinquish the Son and the latter experienced humiliation and death. This grace is freely offered to the Christian, but it will still cost him. This grace condemns sin and requires the Christian to follow Christ and summons the Christian to complete loyalty to Christ. Only those who wholeheartedly follow Christ are able to claim that they have been justified by faith, and thus Bonhoeffer believes:

> The only man who has the right to say that he is justified by grace alone is the man who has left all to follow Christ. Such a man knows that the call to discipleship is a gift of grace, and that the call is inseparable from the grace. But those who try to use this grace as a dispensation from following Christ are simply deceiving themselves.[95]

One cannot simply state that he is a disciple and then live as one desires. One must attempt to follow Christ as closely as possible.

Bonhoeffer is concerned about the relationship between faith and obedience. Lutherans traditionally had viewed faith's priority over obedience. However, his followers left out the obligation of discipleship to the extent that, "... justification of the sinner in the world degenerated into the justification of sin and the world. Costly grace was turned into cheap grace without discipleship."[96] Bonhoeffer desires to align the relationship of faith and obedience; salvation by faith must be seen as concrete and interpreted in a responsible manner. The belief that faith exists connected to obedience is proposed in two propositions which must be held together: "... *only he who believes is obedient, and only he who is obedient believes.*"[97] These two, then, must not be separated from one another.

Bonhoeffer does not go into much detail about the distinction between faith and obedience. However, he does continue to emphasize that obedience is the first step of discipleship, and this is the only way one can be a true follower of Christ. When one hears the call of Christ through the Word or the sacrament, he must follow. By trusting Christ totally, one learns the meaning of faith. Bonhoeffer is very forceful in his emphasis upon obedience: "The road to faith passes through obedience to the call of Jesus. Unless a definite step is demanded, the call vanishes in the air, and if men imagine that they can follow Christ without taking this step, they

---

[95] Bonhoeffer, *The Cost of Discipleship*, 53.
[96] Ibid., 50.
[97] Bonhoeffer, *The Cost of Discipleship*, 63.

are deluding themselves like fanatics."[98] The book is a warning to all who claim to be disciples of Jesus Christ, but they will not follow him totally. Woelfel even emphasizes an eschatological meaning to *The Cost of Discipleship,* describing the book as ". . . a trumpet call to the church in the midst of her last days."[99] Though Bonhoeffer would have a different opinion about the world in later years, at the point of writing *The Cost of Discipleship,* he believes that the cross placed the world and the church in polar extremes to one another. In the hour of the church's crisis, Bonhoeffer shared with his students messages from the Sermon on the Mount which were to encourage those who were preparing for ministry to understand the desperate situation in their country at that particular period.

It seems that Bonhoeffer went through various stages in his theological thought, and this is one reason why many find his theological thinking challenging. Bonhoeffer changes emphases, depending on the particular period of his life. Early in his career, he views the church in a concrete manner, whereas in the 1930s he views the church in a sectarian manner, and sees it as not only distinct form the world, but over against it. In his prison letters written between 1943 and 1945, he identifies the church with the world and has a positive view concerning the latter. He also had a tendency to be interested in a particular topic and then to abandon it. The Sermon on the Mount is such an example because before the late 1930s he was interested in the topic, but in later years he made little reference to it. Concerning this issue Barth explains:

> As always with Bonhoeffer, one is faced by a peculiar difficulty. He was—how shall I put it?—an impulsive visionary thinker who was suddenly seized by an idea to which he gave lively form, and then after a time he called a halt (one never knew whether it was final or temporary) with some provisional last point or other. Was this not the case with *The Cost of Discipleship?*[100]

Eberhard Bethge even said of Bonhoeffer: "He was never the convenient analyst who addressed people from an easy chair. He was not the comfortable contemporary. He was usually moving on to a new playing

---

[98] Ibid., 63.
[99] Woelfel, *Bonhoeffer's Theology,* 243.
[100] John A. Phillips, *Christ for us in the Theology of Dietrich Bonhoeffer,* 251, quoted in David H. Hopper, *A Dissent on Bonhoeffer* (Philadelphia: The Westminster Press, 1975), 27.

field just when others turned up for the game."[101] Nevertheless, one can reasonably state that the major theme of *The Cost of Discipleship* is indeed that of discipleship and an explanation of what that commitment means.

The Cost of Discipleship consists of four parts as follows: "Grace and Discipleship," "The Sermon on the Mount," "The Messengers," and "The Church of Jesus Christ and the Life of Discipleship." Though the original manuscript has been lost, Bethge claims that the second part is from the Finkenwalde lectures from winter of 1935 through summer of 1937. He describes the third part as ". . . an abridged and rearranged version of Bonhoeffer's main series of lectures on the New Testament, which he delivered to all the Finkenwalde groups but the first."[102]

In 1929 Bonhoeffer's interest in ethics led him to consider the Sermon on the Mount as the ultimate expression of the ethical commands of Jesus. Bonhoeffer's interpretation of the Sermon on the Mount is a traditional Lutheran interpretation, stating that a literal understanding of the Sermon makes it law. However, the law has been abolished in Christ; therefore, its primary value is that it demonstrates what God's will can be for the modern man. While in Barcelona, Bonhoeffer preached:

> It is the greatest of misunderstandings to make the commandments of the sermon on the Mount into laws once again by referring them literally to the present. This is not only senseless because it is impractical, but still more, it is against the spirit of Christ, who brought freedom from the law. The whole life of say, Count Tolstoy and so many others has been lived under this misunderstanding.[103]

It appears that when Bonhoeffer discovered the social gospel in New York City, he is encouraged to reconsider this opinion; however, there is no evidence of a change until his experience in London from 1933-1935. In 1934 as a pastor in London, he wrote to Erwin Lutz:

> Please write and tell me some time what you say when you preach about the Sermon on the Mount. I am working on this now—trying to keep it extremely simple and straightforward, but it always comes back to keeping the commandment and not evading it. Discipleship of Christ—I'd like to know what that is—it is not exhausting in our concept of faith. I am setting

---

[101] Eberhard Bethge, "The Challenge of Dietrich Bonhoeffer's Life and Theology," in *World come of Age*, ed., Ronald Gregor Smith (Philadelphia: Fortress Press, 1967), 23.
[102] Bethge, *Dietrich Bonhoeffer*, 451.
[103] Dietrich Bonhoeffer, *No Rusty Swords*, ed. E.H. Robertson and (New York: William Collins Sons, 1977), 41.

to work on something that I might describe as an exercise—this is the first step.[104]

It was during these years that Bonhoeffer studied with great interest the Sermon on the Mount as well as the subject of discipleship. Bethge does believe that Bonhoeffer could be demanding, and that his sermons even had a strong eschatological tone to them which emphasize in particular the kingdom of heaven.[105]

It was from 1935-1937 that his interest in the Sermon on the Mount is most evident, and these were the years of his involvement with a seminary at both Zingst and Finkenwalde. He sees that the Sermon is most valuable as a message against the agenda of the German Christians and especially against what he saw as the false doctrine of cheap grace. Writing to his brother Karl-Friedrich, he states:

> I think I am right in saying that I would only achieve true inner clarity and sincerity by really starting to take the Sermon on the Mount seriously. This is the only source of strength that can blow all this stuff and nonsense sky-high, in a fireworks display that will leave nothing behind but one or two charred remains. The restoration of the church will surely come from a new kind of monasticism, which will have nothing in common with the old but a life of uncompromising adherence to the Sermon on the Mount in imitation of Christ. I believe the time has come to rally people together for this.[106]

Some members in the Confessing Church became weary with Bonhoeffer's continually emphasizing the Sermon on the Mount. Historically, the Sermon had been seen in a somewhat abstract manner. However, Bonhoeffer believes in a concrete interpretation, and that this particular Word has a compelling hold on Christians today. He argues: "The Sermon on the Mount is not a statement to be treated in a cavalier fashion—by saying this or that isn't right or that here we find an inconsistency. Its validity depends on its being obeyed. This is not a statement that we can freely choose to take or leave. It is a compelling, lordly statement."[107] Bonhoeffer believes that the Church must not only know in an academic way the teachings of the Sermon, but the message

---

[104] Dietrich Bonhoeffer, Letter to Erwin Lutz, April 1934, from *DBW* 13: 129, quoted in Bethge, *Dietrich Bonhoeffer,* 458.
[105] Bethge, *Dietrich Bonhoeffer,* 331.
[106] Dietrich Bonhoeffer, Letter to Karl-Friedrich Bonhoeffer, January 14, 1935, from *DBW* 13: 272-73, quoted in Bethge, *Dietrich Bonhoeffer,* 462.
[107] Dietrich Bonhoeffer, from *CD,* [cf. *DBW* 4:191, n. 28], quoted in Bethge, *Dietrich Bonhoeffer,* 450-451.

itself must be put into continuous practice; through living out the message, this is one major antidote against cheap grace.

To the dismay of the Confessing Church, The Reich Bishop also referred to the Sermon on the Mount as a standard under which the German Christians were to live their lives. In the foreward to the *Deutsche Gottesworte,* he writes: "'For you, my comrades in the Third Reich, I have not translated the Sermon on the Mount but Germanized it. . . . Your Reich Bishop.' The blessedness promised to the meek, he interprets as: 'Happy is he who always observes good comradeship. He will get on well in the world'; the cross is interpreted: 'Take pains to maintain a noble, calm attitude, even to one who insults or persecutes you'"[108] To Bonhoeffer and members of the Confessing Church, this type of interpretation does nothing for the cause of evangelization, and he maintains that there must not be closeness between the Gospel and those who endorsed "German awakening."[109]

In order to understand Bonhoeffer's interpretation of the Sermon on the Mount, one must have a better understanding of his method of interpretation. Basic issues such as his view of scripture, exegetical methodology, understanding of the original passage, as well as the application of the Sermon on the Mount are all important.

His studies for advanced degree were at both Tübingen and Berlin—two schools which during the period of his studies accepted higher critical methodologies. Bonhoeffer does not hold to a verbal inspiration view of the composition of the scriptures. Bonhoeffer has an existential methodology which appears to be close to Karl Barth in that he believes the words of scripture are fallible. However, it is still possible for the Holy Spirit to witness to the resurrected Christ through the total corpus of Scripture; this word is for the believer in his present situation. Bonhoeffer does not look at the minutiae of exegesis. For example, he does not give Greek renditions of various words, or look at the tenses of the verbs. His exegesis is not textual, but more theological. He does state that scripture witnesses to Christ, "Finally, even the commandments and the parenthetic material of the New Testament are strictly to be regarded as a witness to Christ, as the crucified and risen Lord. . . . Thus the commandments of the Sermon or the Pauline material must be understood as witnesses to the Lord, the Crucified and Risen One."[110] Bonhoeffer believes that exegesis will lead one to Christ, whether in the Old Testament or the New

---

[108] Ludwig Müller, *Deutsche Gotteswort* (1936), 9, 17. quoted in Bethge, *Dietrich Bonhoeffer,* 542.
[109] Bethge, *Dietrich Bonhoeffer,* 542.
[110] Bonhoeffer, *No Rusty Swords,* 315.

Testament. He says: "... exegesis is the certainty that Christ is the subject of the interpretation."[111] He does speak in exuberant tones about an allegorical method of interpretation, though he is careful to state that neither a literal nor an allegorical method of interpretation alone is sufficient.[112]

His christological interpretation, it can be argued, leaves out much of which is contained in Scripture such as the distinctions between Israel and the Church, the covenants, apocalypticism and various themes which one can find in or through both testaments. The philological, archaeological and historical backgrounds are missing, and the novice who looks at Bonhoeffer may quickly conclude that he is somewhat naïve in his biblical interpretation. But of course this is not the situation.

Bonhoeffer is most interested in the application of the message of discipleship. It is as if he is asking, how can one put what one reads and meditates upon into practice? The Christian must so live before the world that the latter will have to acknowledge that there is a better standard by which to live life. Bonhoeffer admits that there are many different interpretations of the Sermon on the Mount, but application is the proof that one has truly comprehended the message. He believes:

> Humanly speaking, we could understand and interpret the Sermon on the Mount in a thousand different ways. Jesus knows only one possibility: simple surrender and obedience, not interpreting it or applying it, but doing and obeying it. That is the only way to hear his word. But again he does not mean that it is to be discussed as an ideal, he really means us to get on with it. . . . The only proper response to this word which Jesus brings with him from eternity is simply to do it. Jesus has spoken: his is the word, ours the obedience. Only in the doing of it does the word of Jesus retain its honor, might and power among us. Now the storm can rage over the house, but it cannot shatter the union with him, which his word has created. . . . If we start asking questions, posing problems, and offering interpretations, we are not doing his word.[113]

The conditions and demands of the Sermon on the Mount are extremely severe, and it is impossible for one to keep them literally. Bonhoeffer is not necessarily stating that one must rigidly keep each one; rather, one must be obedient to the word of Christ which is seen in the text. This obedience manifests itself in obedience to Christ.

---

[111] Ibid.
[112] Bonhoeffer, *No Rusty Swords,* 316.
[113] Bonhoeffer, *The Cost of Discipleship,* 196-97.

One might wish that Bonhoeffer had given more of the *Sitz im Leben* of the text—the following basic questions are significant: Who are the recipients of the message, and what is the cultural milieu? What is the kingdom of which Jesus preached? Since Bonhoeffer's interpretation is more theological than textual, and his orientation is toward existentialism, these kinds of questions are not addressed fully.

He does present Jesus on the mountain giving forth a message, and there is a mass of people out of which comes the disciples. The masses Bonhoeffer compares to the German National Church who have not been obedient to the call, but the disciples hear and follow. Bonhoeffer states the aim of the Beatitudes: "Hence the aim of this Beatitude is to bring all who hear it to decision and salvation. All are called to be what in the reality of God they are already. The disciples are called blessed because they have obeyed the call of Jesus, and the people as a whole because they are heirs of the promise."[114]

Jesus fulfills the law, and his fulfillment of it expresses the law's intended interpretation. Bonhoeffer believes: "Jesus, however, takes the law of God in his own hands and expounds its true meaning. The will of God, to which the law gives expression, is that men should defeat their enemies by loving them."[115] Jesus contradicts all the false interpretations of the law; the Old Testament law is still important, but the Christian is no longer under its demands.

Bonhoeffer appears to be an amillennialist, that is, the kingdom was initiated with the incarnation of Jesus, and in the Beatitudes the disciples, and thus the Church, had the offer of the kingdom. Jesus' death and resurrection compels the kingdom to continue to enlarge and will continue to do so until the coming of Christ. He believes:

> . . . when the kingdom of heaven descends, the face of the earth will be renewed, and it will belong to the flock of Jesus. God does not forsake the earth: he made it, he sent his Son to it, and on it he built his Church. Thus a beginning has already been made in this present age. A sign has been given. The powerless have here and now received a plot of earth, for they have the Church and its fellowship, it goods, its brothers and sisters, in the midst of persecutions even to the length of the cross. The renewal of the earth begins at Golgotha, where the meek One died, and from thence it will spread. When the kingdom finally comes, the meek possess the earth.[116]

---

[114] Bonhoeffer, *The Cost of Discipleship*, 107.
[115] Bonhoeffer, *The Cost of Discipleship*, 147.
[116] Ibid., 110.

Bonhoeffer devotes more discussion to chapter two, the Sermon on the Mount, than to any of the other four chapters. His exposition contains fifteen homilies from Matthew 5-7, and these various homilies are divided according to the divisions in the book of Matthew. He commences by giving the title of Matthew 5, "Of the Extraordinariness of the Christian Life." Bonhoeffer summarizes what he believes is the essence of the fifth chapter of Matthew: "In chapter 5 we were told how the disciple community is essentially visible in character. . . . We saw that the hallmark of Christianity is our separation from the world, our transcendence of its standards, and our extraordinariness."[117] The disciple is to be characterized by separation from the world and a character which is extraordinary.

He entitles the sixth chapter of Matthew, "Of the Hidden Character of the Christian Life." In this subdivision, Bonhoeffer emphasizes that the "extraordinariness" of the disciples is found in their devotion and righteousness. He also speaks against any type of self-aggrandizement when he writes: "All that the follower of Jesus has to do is to make sure that his obedience, following and love are entirely spontaneous. If you do good, you must not let your left hand know what your right hand is doing, you must be quite unconscious of it."[118] These two sections of Bonhoeffer's exposition portray that the disciples of Jesus are truly unique—they are not like those who are not disciples of Christ. Their character is different; their thoughts are centered upon what it means to be continually a kingdom-bound person. His final chapter which discusses the Sermon on the Mount is entitled, "The Separation of the Disciple Community," and this subdivision admonishes followers of Jesus not to judge others, for Jesus will one day judge equitably all, especially those who have rejected him. The three sections, then, are Bonhoeffer's understanding and exposition of the Sermon on the Mount.

Bonhoeffer first discusses Matthew 5:1-12, and titles this, "The Beatitudes." He portrays Jesus speaking to the multitude, and his disciples are present. "The disciples will be his messengers and here and there they will find men to hear and believe their message. Yet there will be enmity between them right to the bitter end. . . . Christ, the disciples, and the people, the stage is already set for the passion of Jesus and the Church."[119] To suffer for righteousness, Bonhoeffer, believes, refers to suffering for any just cause, and those who undergo such persecution receive a special commendation from Jesus. He relates this message to the present situation

---

[117] Bonhoeffer, *The Cost of Discipleship*, 155.
[118] Ibid., 159.
[119] Bonhoeffer, *The Cost of Discipleship*, 106.

of all true disciples. He writes of an eschatological promise when he declares: ". . . the world cries 'Away with them, away with them!' Yes, but wither? To the kingdom of heaven. 'Rejoice and be exceedingly glad: for great is your reward in heaven.' There shall the poor be seen in the halls of joy."[120] Prophetically, these words would prove to be especially valuable to the members of the Confessing Church.

Bonhoeffer then discusses "The Visible Community" which is from Matthew 5:13-16. He writes of the necessity for disciples to be the "salt" of the earth, that is, they are to represent the highest good. Though they are disciples who will realize an heavenly destiny, they are to live on earth in such a manner that they bring honor to God. He also uses the metaphor of light to a world which is lost. Bonhoeffer constantly reminds one that he is to glorify God and not be concerned about human recognition. "But there is nothing for us to glorify in the disciple who bears the cross, or in the community whose light so shines because it stands visibly on a hill—only the Father which is in heaven can be praised for the 'good works.'"[121]

In Matthew 5:17-20, he discusses "The Righteousness of Christ." Christ fulfilled the law, and disciples by their relationship to him are able to exceed the Pharisees' righteousness. The disciples are still to be obedient to the law, and not simply discuss its demands.

In the section, "The Brother" (Matthew 5:21-26), Bonhoeffer emphasizes that the Pharisees did not understand Jesus' relation to the law. He even refers to the "heresy" of the Pharisees! A brother is not only a fellow Christian, but it is one who is his neighbor, or one who is in close proximity to him, and against such a person anger is forbidden. Bonhoeffer believes: "Anger is always an attack on the brother's life, for it refuses to let him live and aims at his destruction. Jesus will not accept the common distinction between righteous indignation and unjustifiable anger. . . . A deliberate insult is even worse, for we are openly disgracing our brother in the eyes of the world. . . ."[122]

Bonhoeffer then moves to the discussion of "Woman" (Matthew 5:27-32). He believes that "momentary desire" is a hindrance to truly following Christ. The issue of whether the commands are to be understood in a literal fashion or not portrays Bonhoeffer's serious attempt to understand the demands of this text:

---

[120] Ibid., 114.
[121] Ibid., 119.
[122] Bonhoeffer, *The Cost of Discipleship*. 127. Bonhoeffer does refer to the Greek word translated "without a cause," and that the word is not contained in two manuscripts, but is found in the majority of manuscripts.

Our natural inclination is to avoid a definite decision over this crucial question. But the question is itself both wrong and wicked, and it does not admit of an answer. If we decide not to take it literally, we should be evading the seriousness of the commandment, and if on the other hand we should decide it was to be taken literally, we should at once reveal the absurdity of the Christian position, and thereby invalidate the commandment. The fact that we receive no answer to this question only makes the commandment even more inescapable. We cannot evade the issue either way; we are placed in a position where there is no alternative but to obey.[123]

Bonhoeffer believes that Jesus' teaching is an assist against any sexual impurity among those who would be true disciples of Jesus.

"Truthfulness" (Matthew 5:33-37), is the next topic which Bonhoeffer discusses. He surveys the historical views of a Christian taking an oath. The existence of oaths is but an attestation to the fact that lies occur. He emphasizes that a true disciple is always to speak the truth; one is to be very careful when giving an oath, especially if the issue is something which is future.

"Revenge" (Matthew 5:38-42), is another topic which Bonhoeffer surveys. Some have questioned Bonhoeffer's discussion of this topic since he was involved in conspiracy against the government; thus, he does not hold to an absolute interpretation of this pericope. This section is connected to the Beatitudes and displays that the disciple has given up all rights in order to be a genuine disciple. He believes: "There is no deed on earth so outrageous as to justify a different attitude. The worse the evil, the readier must the Christian be to suffer; he must let the evil person fall into Jesus' hands."[124]

Bonhoeffer moves on to discuss "The Enemy—The Extraordinary" (Matthew 5:43-48). He places an emphasis upon the fact that for the first time in the Sermon on the Mount, the word "love" is used. Loving one's enemy is not an abstract concept for followers of Jesus, for all who are disciples are aware that they are and will be despised by some for living a separate life. The one who follows Christ has a life which is marked by "extraordinariness," that is, he lives a life marked by total obedience. Bonhoeffer believes that only in the Old Testament is there found to be true holy wars; the Church today is not involved in such a war, nor can she justify such. The person who lives out and obeys the law, and does as

---

[123] Ibid., 132.
[124] Bonhoeffer, *The Cost of Discipleship*, 142.

Christ has commanded, understands the meaning of Matthew 5:48: "The perfect are none other than the blessed of the beatitudes."[125]

Bonhoeffer commences the sixth chapter of Matthew with the explanation that the visible Christian life is also a hidden life, and he calls this "The Hidden Righteousness," and the exposition is taken from Matthew 6:1-4. Bonhoeffer claims disciples are confronted with a paradox—they are to perform deeds which are visible, but they are never to be done with the intention of making them visible. From whom should they hide their good works? He suggests not from others, but from themselves! He believes: "Our task is simply to keep on following, looking only to our Leader who goes on before, taking no notice of ourselves or of what we are doing. We must be unaware of our own righteousness, and see it only so far as we look unto Jesus."[126] The issue of the motive for why one engages in a given activity is of paramount importance. He reiterates the importance of love: "Love, in the sense of spontaneous, unreflective action, spells the death of the old man. For man recovers his true nature in the righteousness of Christ and in his fellow man."[127] In this section he is writing of the sanctified life.

Matthew 6:5-15 Bonhoeffer calls "Hiddenness of Prayer." Even if one engages in lengthy prayer, the time spent can be fruitless unless Jesus is recognized as the mediator. It does not matter where or when we pray, ". . . what matters is the faith which lays hold on God and touches the heart of the Father who knew us long before we came to him."[128] One must surrender his will completely to Christ, and live in fellowship with him. Bonhoeffer compares the relationship of the one who prays to the Father as a child and earthly father relationship. The prayer is to be done in secret and not in such a manner as to draw attention to the person engaging in prayer. Bonhoeffer writes encouragingly, "Christians ask God not to put their puny faith to the test, but to preserve them in the hour of temptation."[129]

Bonhoeffer calls his next section, "The Hiddenness of the Devout Life" (Matthew 6:16-18). He begins by referring to the benefits of fasting: "Fasting helps to discipline the self-indulgent and slothful will which is so reluctant to serve the Lord, and it helps to humiliate and chasten the flesh."[130] He believes that fasting and a life which is characterized by

---

[125] Ibid., 154.
[126] Bonhoeffer, *The Cost of Discipleship*, 158.
[127] Ibid., 160.
[128] Ibid., 163.
[129] Bonhoeffer, *The Cost of Discipleship*, 167.
[130] Ibid., 169.

abstinence will display how different the Christian lives from those who are outside of the faith. Those who mortify the flesh, he believes, are actually more aware of the dangers of pride, and they are constantly vigilant against inroads which pride can make in their lives. He believes that sometimes Christians will even use the excuse of "evangelical liberty," but in reality this too is nothing but cheap grace. Personal asceticism, Bonhoeffer believes, is important.

The final section in the sixth chapter, verses 19-34, which Bonhoeffer considers he calls, "The Simplicity of the Carefree Life." One must look only to Christ in order to truly follow him; if there is a division of allegiance, the disciple can no longer be a genuine disciple of Jesus Christ. He believes, "Worldly possessions tend to turn the hearts of the disciples away from Jesus. What are we really devoted to? That is the question."[131] Bonhoeffer believes that any type of hoarding material possessions is idolatry.

He gives the title, "The Separation of the Disciple Community" for the seventh chapter of Matthew, and titling the first section, "The Disciple and Unbelievers," he discusses verses 1-12. He believes that the disciple must break his ties to old relationships, and he addresses the issue of how one relates to non-Christians. He strongly recommends that the disciple not possess a superior attitude and act in a condescending manner to those who are not followers of Christ. Such an attitude could disqualify them from being a disciple: "If they do so, they will themselves be judged by God. The sword wherewith they judge their brethren will fall upon their own heads. Instead of cutting themselves off from their brother as the just from the unjust, they find themselves cut off from Jesus."[132] A true disciple is not interested in attacking others, rather, such a person loves unconditionally and seeks the best in others' lives.

He entitles the next section in the seventh chapter of Matthew, "The Great Divide" (Matthew 7:13-23). Bonhoeffer said as the original followers of Jesus were few in number, so today the number who follow him is not great. He admits that this life of following Jesus is not easy, and at times there will be great difficulty: "The path of discipleship is narrow, and it is fatally easy to miss one's way and stray from the path, even after years of discipleship. And it is hard to find. On either side of the narrow path deep chasms yawn. To be called to a life of extraordinary quality, to live up to it, and yet to be unconscious of it is indeed a narrow way."[133] He believes that followers of Christ cannot simply leave the world completely

---

[131] Ibid. 174.
[132] Bonhoeffer, *The Cost of Discipleship*, 183.
[133] Ibid., 190.

and cling to one another for emotional support. He also warns against false prophets, even within their own midst; thus, a true disciple must be able to genuinely distinguish themselves from "pseudo-Christians." Bonhoeffer concludes, "If we follow Christ, cling to his word, and let everything else go, it will see us through the day of judgment. His word is his grace."[134]

The final section on the Bonhoeffer's exposition of the Sermon on the Mount is simply entitled, "The Conclusion," (Matthew 7:24-29). He admits that there could be many different interpretations of the Sermon on the Mount, but that Jesus accepts only one—"Simple surrender and obedience, not interpreting it or applying it, but doing and obeying it. This is the only way to hear his word. But again he does not mean that it be discussed as an ideal, he really means us to get on with it."[135] To fail to do what Jesus has commanded is to live a lie and not to builds one's house upon a rock according to Bonhoeffer, and he forcefully ends his argument against cheap grace.

Bonhoeffer acknowledges that there are several different interpretations of the Sermon on the Mount, and he is concerned that those who read *The Cost of Discipleship* be aware of some basic questions as one reads the biblical text: "What did Jesus mean to say to us? What is his will for us today? How can he help us to be good Christians in a modern world? In the last resort, what we want to know is not, what would this or that man, or this or that Church, have of us, but what Jesus Christ himself wants of us."[136]

Thus, it appears that Bonhoeffer's interpretation of the Sermon on the Mount is absolutist, that is, the mandates are to be obeyed. However, at times it appears that Bonhoeffer is somewhat inconsistent in his methodology of interpretation. For example, he believes that Jesus grants no exceptions for the swearing of oaths, but then states that when various conditions have been fulfilled, it is acceptable to swear an oath.[137] Another example is Matthew 5:29, which text states that the eye should be gouged out and thrown away if the eye causes one to sin. He has been writing of the rigorous demands of Jesus' words, and that they are to be taken literally and seriously, but also states that we must determine if the passage is to be taken literally or figuratively; if one takes the command literally, this is absurd according to Bonhoeffer.[138] Finally, there are some who would argue that though Bonhoeffer preaches pacifism and resisting

---

[134] Bonhoeffer, *The Cost of Discipleship*, 195.
[135] Ibid., 196-97.
[136] Ibid., 35.
[137] Bonhoeffer, *The Cost of Discipleship*, 137.
[138] Ibid., 132.

evil in a gentle spirit, his latter years display an about face concerning how one should overcome evil and oppression.

Bonhoeffer's method of interpretation is strongly influenced by existentialism, and if it is necessary to place him in a theological category, he would possibly be called a Neo-orthodox. He has a high view of scripture, but it cannot be said that he was a literalist in his understanding of scriptural interpretation. He appreciates the text's immediate application to the reader and his life. Bonhoeffer is not an exegete in the Reformed tradition; that is, he does not delve into the various meanings and nuances of words, though at times he will refer to variant readings in manuscripts. Bonhoeffer's training as a theologian is more conducive to understanding the text as applying to the person's situation currently; thus, a detached objectivity is not of interest to him. His situation as a professor in a free-standing seminary forces him to search the scriptures in order to determine how one should live authentically in a political situation in which he felt many were veering from the true teachings of the Church and Scripture. Bonhoeffer is aware that a simple historical-grammatical method of interpretation is not sufficient—one must also understand the *Sitz im Leben* as well.

The reader is impressed with Bonhoeffer's immediate application of the biblical text in *The Cost of Discipleship*. Interestingly, he quotes a variety of individuals such as Luther, Kierkegaard, Kohlbrugge, and even Faust. He quotes a Psalm as well to substantiate a point which he is making about a particular New Testament theme.[139] He places an emphasis upon application of scripture as well. Bonhoeffer states: "By eliminating simple obedience on principle, we drift into an unevangelical interpretation of the Bible."[140] He continues:

> We take it for granted as we open the Bible that we have a key to its interpretation. But then the key we use would not be the living Christ, who is both Judge and Saviour, and our use of this key no longer depends on the will of the living Holy Spirit alone. The key we use is a general doctrine of grace which we can apply as we will.[141]

He writes about the fact that if one's exegesis is truly "evangelical," the interpreter will not completely identify with those whom Jesus personally called. He believes, "It would be a false exegesis if we tried to behave in our discipleship as though we were the immediate contemporaries

---

[139] Bonhoeffer, *The Cost of Discipleship*, 59. Cf., 98-99, 147, 246.
[140] Ibid., 83.
[141] Ibid., 83-84.

of the men Jesus called. . . . It is neither possible nor right for us to try to get behind the Word of the Scriptures to the events as they actually occurred. Rather the whole Word of the Scriptures summons us to follow Jesus."[142]

Bonhoeffer's method is indebted to existentialism, and the application of the mandate of scripture is to live obediently and follow Christ, that is, to have a character patterned after Jesus. He argues for an active Christian experience and certainly passivity is never an option.

C. Reconstruction of Bonhoeffer's Hermeneutical Principles

One is impressed that Bonhoeffer's christocentrism expresses itself in a life which is lived out in a Christian manner; he never was a spectator, but an innovator and caught up with the biblical mandate to follow Christ. At times he does appear to accept almost a naïve biblicism, and upon first acquaintance with him, one could quickly come to a wrong conclusion concerning his method and even conclusions. He believes: "The criterion for a decision must be sought in scripture."[143] However, what was his method of hermeneutics?

His life, especially after the year 1933, was unsettled and he did not have the convenience of researching and writing under the auspices of a major university and chair of theology. His personality was such that even though he was experiencing difficulties and his life was very unsettled, he was able to research and write under conditions which perhaps most would not be able to produce material of lasting worth. His life's work and mission forced him back into the scriptures in order to find personal meaning and also meaning for the political upheaval which was occurring in the latter years of his life. Bethge writes: "Those who met him after 1931 were impressed by his breadth of knowledge, his concentrated energy, analytical and critical acumen, as well as his personal commitment that engaged his entire personality and his behavior in innumerable ways."[144] Bethge also cites an observation by Paul Lehmann who noted a difference in Bonhoeffer which apparently had happened in Bonhoeffer during the span of several years in which they had not seen one another: "He [Bonhoeffer] practiced a meditative approach to the Bible that was

---

[142] Ibid., 84.
[143] Dietrich Bonhoeffer, *Christ the Center*, intro., Edwin Robinson, Trans., John Bowden (New York: Harper and Row, 1966), 96.
[144] Bethge, *Bonhoeffer: A Biography,* 203

obviously very different from the exegetical or homiletical use of it."[145] This was said of Bonhoeffer in 1933. Bethge gives more insight into Bonhoeffer's method during this period:

> He alluded increasingly to a communal life of obedience and prayer, which could perhaps renew the credibility of the individually isolated and privileged ministry. He viewed all this not as a counter to reformed theology but as based upon it. More and more frequently he quoted the Sermon on the Mount as a statement to be acted upon, not merely used as a mirror. He began taking a stand for Christian pacifism among his students and fellow clergy, although hardly anyone noticed at the time. To his students his piety sometimes appeared too fervent, and was impressive only because it was accompanied by theological rigor and a broad cultural background.[146]

Bonhoeffer says very little about historical criticism, and his remarks are somewhat general on this topic. For example, he states: "We have in the first place to do with a book, which we find in the secular sphere. . . . It is meant to be read with the means of historical and philological criticism."[147] Thus, at times Bonhoeffer appears to be enigmatic in that in many of his biblical writings there is a lack of historical critical methodology. On the other hand, he expresses a positive attitude toward historical criticism:

> We must be ready to admit the concealment of history and thus accept the course of historical criticism. But the Risen One encounters us right through the Bible with all of its flaws. We must encounter the straits of historical criticism. Its importance is not absolute, but at the same time it is not a matter of indifference. In fact it never leads to a weakening of the faith but rather to its strengthening, as concealment in historicity is part of Christ's humiliation.[148]

Woelfel, however, believes that Bonhoeffer is somewhat conservative in his biblical methodology:

---

[145] Ibid., 204
[146] Ibid.
[147] Bonhoeffer, *Christ the Center,* intro., Edwin Robertson, Trans., John Bowden (New York: Harper and Row, 1966), 75, quoted in Woelfel, *Bonhoeffer's Theology,* 213.
[148] Bonhoeffer, *Christ the Center,* 76, quoted in Woelfel, *Bonhoeffer's Theology,* 76. Cf., Bethge, *Bonhoeffer, A Biography.* The author writes: "At the University in Berlin he was confronted with the historical-critical method, early Christianity, Luther and Lutheranism, and the nineteenth century," 88.

Bonhoeffer's biblical exegesis, viewed from a strictly historical point of view, came down rather consistently on the conservative side. Yet, as the issue of the Virgin Birth shows, he combined a fully christocentric dogmatic theology with a reverent openness and reticence about matters which the Bible only hints or leaves to one side. His close attention to the actual words and situations of Scripture and to the priorities—the "degrees of knowledge and degrees of significance"—which biblical faith itself recognizes, gave his interpretation of Christianity modernity, freshness, and life. . . . Bonhoeffer was moving decidedly away from system building, from that intense preoccupation with the internal problems of dogmatics. . . . [149]

Bonhoeffer wanted to write a work concerning hermeneutics specifically, but he never did so. Bethge says that in 1936 Bonhoeffer had planned to write a work on hermeneutics, but for some reason he never did follow through with this writing.[150] What is extant is Bonhoeffer's lecture which he gave on August 23, 1935, entitled, "The Presentation of New Testament Texts." He gave this message to preachers and curates of the Saxony province of the Confessing Church in Hauteroda. Bonhoeffer believed that those within the church who support Nazism either blatantly or unknowingly misinterpreted scripture; thus, this lecture was given to enable members of the Confessing Church to understand a method for correctly interpreting scripture. He believed that the German Christians were using scripture for their own agenda, and were engaging in eisegesis, that is, finding support for their own opinions and desires from scripture. Bonhoeffer believed that the German Christians were "Germanizing" Christianity, and that ultimately they were sacrificing truth to a pagan ideology. He is adamant that the present age must justify itself before Christianity and not vice versa.

Bonhoeffer begins by stating: "In principle, it is possible to explain the interpretation of the New Testament message in two ways. Either the biblical message must justify itself in the present age and must therefore show itself capable of interpretation or the present age must justify itself before the biblical message and therefore the message must become real."[151] He gives a short history of Rationalism as expressed in the eighteenth, nineteenth and twentieth centuries. Bonhoeffer believes that the central question is, "Can Christianity make itself real to us, just as we

---

[149] Woelfel, *Bonhoeffer's Theology,* 222.
[150] Bethge, *Bonhoffer: A Biography,* 528.
[151] Bonhoeffer, "The Presentation of the New Testament Texts," in *No Rusty Swords,* 302-03.

are?"[152] We see that he is not speaking about "correct" exegesis or even a particular hermeneutic, thus, his existential orientation is manifesting itself. He is not interested in understanding the cultural background of a given text, at least in this speech; rather, he concerns himself with the human situation, or the person who is involved with choices and issues germane to life. He says that the tendency for many is simply to sift the Christian message through the sieve of reason, culture and politics, and he believes, "*This presentation* of the Christian message leads directly to paganism. It therefore follows that the only difference between the German Christians and the so-called neo-pagans is one of *honesty*."[153] He says that also there is a cry for relevance of the Christian message, which was especially important to the German Christians; he believes that their outcry of relevance is not to be taken too seriously since ". . . it was at best the terror-stricken shout of those who saw the gulf between Christianity and the world opening up beneath them, who, conscious of their complete conformity to the world. . . pulled down Christianity with themselves in their fall into the world."[154] He mentions that even theologians who are "from our side" such as Heim, Schlatter, and Althaus, all seem overly concerned with the issue of relevance and presentation. Speaking concerning the issue of relevance, he says: "Anyone who is thirsty has always found living water in the Bible itself or in a sermon *in fact* based on the Bible, even if it were a little out-of-date."[155] He believes that if the question of relevance of the Christian message is emphasized too much, that this outcry is a symptom of an eroding faith. Bonhoeffer believes that Luther's version of the Bible should fulfill anyone's need of a Gospel presentation in a German way.

Bonhoeffer's in this lecture emphasizes that where Christ is mentioned in the New Testament, there is relevance. He also places a significant emphasis upon the Holy Spirit:

> *The most concrete element of the Christian message* and of textual exposition is not a human act of presentation but is always God himself, it is the Holy Spirit. Because the 'content' of the New Testament is this, that Christ speaks to us through his Holy Spirit, and because this does not happen outside or alongside, but solely and exclusively *through the word* of Scripture, keeping to the content, i.e. the adherence of preaching to the Scriptures, is itself presentation—'keeping to the content' both as a

---

[152] Ibid., 303.
[153] Ibid., 304.
[154] Bonhoeffer, "The Presentation of the New Testament Texts," in *No Rusty Swords*, 304.
[155] Ibid., 305.

method. . . and as obedience and trust towards the fact of the Holy Spirit. For the matter of this content is the Holy Spirit himself, and he is the presence of both God and Christ.[156]

Thus, Bonhoeffer's pneumatological emphasis is strong, though he does not give much detail or even scriptural references for this belief. One would think that he would at least give some Pauline support for his statements concerning the work of the Holy Spirit.

Interestingly, Bonhoeffer does speak a great deal about the significance of exegesis, though because of his life experiences, he would approach exegesis out of the context of living out his scriptural view of discipleship. Especially is this the situation toward the end of his life, in particular when he finds himself in prison. In his lecture, "The Presentation of New Testament Texts," Bonhoeffer writes concerning exegesis:

> If we have learnt that correct presentation lies in our coming to the content and expressing that content in words, as far as method is concerned it will mean that preaching which is relevant to the present age must be essentially *exegesis*, exegesis of the Word that alone has power to make itself present, exegesis of Scripture. The act of presentation, insofar as it can be achieved by us through any method at all, is strict and exclusive reference to the word of scripture. *Thus the movement is not from the word of Scripture to the present; it goes from the present to the word of scripture and remains there.* (Italics mine). It is thus apparently away from the present, but it is away from the false present in order to come to the true present. If this seems incomprehensible to anyone, it is because he has not yet grasped the basic supposition that there is only 'present' where Christ speaks with the Holy Spirit. This backward movement towards the Scripture closely corresponds to the backward movement of Christian faith and Christian hope, namely toward the cross of Christ; and it is the historicity of the revelation of Christ which is expressed.[157]

By using the word "Presentation *(Vergegenwärtigung)*, Bonhoeffer references the discovering of the eternal. He believes that there is something eternal in history; thus, he believes: "In our case it means *discovering* the eternal doctrine, or the general ethical norms, or the myth, contained in Holy Scripture and the application of this general element to the present situation of each person today."[158] This discovering he

---

[156] Ibid., 306.
[157] Bonhoeffer, "The Presentation of New Testament Texts," in *No Rusty Swords,* 307.
[158] Bonhoeffer, "The Presentation of New Testament Texts," in *No Rusty Swords,* 308

concedes is only possible by the individual. But how is this possible? Bonhoeffer believes: "Because like can only be recognized by like, the interpreter of Holy Scripture can on the basis of the general ideas and standards which he has within him recognize these again in Scripture and discover them."[159] To Bonhoeffer, the person is the subject of presentation, and he claims: "Here Scriptural exegesis means the referring of Scripture to the eternal truths which I already know—be it an intellectual truth, an ethical principle, a general human insight, or a myth. In other words, the truth is already established before I expound Scripture."[160]

He believes that the interpreter can distinguish the word of God from the word of man in scripture. As in secular literature, one can distinguish the writing of the author from that which is spurious, so the interpreter can separate that which is genuine from the false. God, according to Bonhoeffer, speaks his word through the word of man. But in the final analysis, "God alone says where his word is, and that means that God alone presents his Word, that the Holy Ghost is the principle of interpretation. . . . The only method of presentation is therefore the exegesis of the content of the text as the witness of Christ, and such exegesis has the promise of the presence of Christ."[161] He claims that the most concrete form of the sermon is not the application which he will have for the sermon, that is, how the message which has been preached can be lived out in the daily lives of the congregants, but the Holy Spirit who speaks through the text of the Bible. To Bonhoeffer, "Even the clearest application, the most distinct appeal to the congregation, is irrelevant so long as the Holy Spirit himself does not create the *concretissimum*, the present."[162] Bonhoeffer's writings in comparison to Bultmann's are not as exegetical, and it is obvious that he does not concern himself with the original languages as much as did Bultmann. Bonhoeffer emphasizes more pneumatological enablement and practical application. Bonhoeffer repeatedly refers to the New Testament as a "witness" to Christ, and the New Testament is the fulfillment of the promise which is found in the Old Testament. He believes that all texts in the New Testament witness equally to Christ, that is, there is no difference of validity in the sayings of Jesus or the writings of Paul.

---

[159] Ibid.
[160] Ibid.
[161] Ibid., 310
[162] Bonhoeffer, "The Presentation of New Testament Texts," in *No Rusty Swords,* 310.

Bonhoeffer does not exclude the possibility of an allegorical interpretation of scripture, though he does believe that there must be caution exercised. He gives his conclusion on the matter by asserting:

> That neither a literal exegesis nor an allegorical exegesis of Holy Scripture proves the character of Holy Scripture as witness; this is done by God alone, who professes his witness in his own time. . . . The right to use allegorical exegesis lies in the recognition of the possibility that God does not allow his Word to be exhausted in its historical-logical-unequivocal sense, but that the Word has still other perspectives and can be put to the service of a better knowledge. Luther emphatically held out for the *unequivocal sense of Scripture* as opposed to the fourfold or sevenfold sense of Scripture—clarity, truth . . . he himself allegorized in his lectures on the Psalms! The sole decisive criterion is only whether what is revealed here is Christ himself. Thus the important things are 1 the *content* of allegorical and symbolic typological exegesis, and 2 that this power of allegor- izing, symbolic witness to Christ, this transparency is applied *only to the Word of Scripture. Within these two limits it seems to me that the allegorical, etc., exegesis must find a place*; the New Testament itself has made use of it within these limits. Why should we consider it impossible? The allegorical exposition of Scripture remains a splendid freedom of the church's exegesis, not as a false means of proof, but as a celebration of the fullness of the witness to Christ in Scripture.[163]

Bonhoeffer states that the Christian's witness has limits; however, within this limitation, there is a measure of freedom. He believes that it is only the original text which is inspired, and that a translation is always fatal to any theory of verbal inspiration. However, he is open to use of a legitimate translation.

He discusses the second major freedom of the preacher, and that is the freedom of the text which will be preached. Bonhoeffer asserts:

> Although the preaching of any text must be a preaching of Christ and each time it must be the whole Christ who is preached, *the choice of the text remains* (relatively!—we do not discuss the use of a lectionary here!) *free.* Now how is this freedom to be used appropriately? Shall I ask, "What does the congregation want to hear today? What is it asking about? What has happened in the last week? These questions are right and necessary for a responsible pastor. But they need a presupposition. The presupposition is that the pastor knows that a congregation does not really ask about this or that thing which is in the foreground; whether it knows it or not, it asks about what is in the background, always about the *whole Christ,* and he knows that only the preaching of the whole Christ can answer any

---

[163] Bonhoeffer, "The Presentation of New Testament Texts," 316

particular questions which happen to be in the fore-ground. . . . but where Christ is preached and not this or that truth, error can be avoided. The freedom of presentation serves the totality of the witness to Christ.[164]

One cannot help but notice, then, the christocentric emphasis in Bonhoeffer's hermeneutical presuppositions. For him, all of Scripture points to Christ, and this strong accentuation of Christ is especially seen in his *The Cost of Discipleship.*

He believes that the person is related to "community" and to Christ. This emphasis is also evident is his work *Life Together.* This work was published in 1939 and was the most widely read of all of Bonhoeffer's works during his lifetime. Bethge believes:

> The publication of *Life Together* caused quite a sensation, for this was something entirely new in Protestant Germany. Although short-lived, Finkenwalde had revealed a weak spot within Protestantism and, moreover, had sought practical solutions where others felt helpless. It seemed as though something had been restored to the church which had long been confined to conventicles or sects, and had been sought by group movements or brotherhoods such as those of St. Michael's and Sydow. Here were the outlines of a living Protestant community, not revived in opposition to or outside the churches of the Reformation (as had happened in Herrnhut), but within the church itself, undertaken and upheld out of a renewed understanding of the church. In the midst of the great crisis and weakness besieging the privileged ministry of the *Volkskirche,* Finkenwalde offered an alternative with its new forms of service. . . . [165]

In this short work of five chapters, Bonhoeffer outlines what it means to live in community with other Christians. He believes that it is sheer joy and provides strength for living when one is in the presence of Christians; they can receive the sacrament with thanksgiving and the realization that one day the promise of redemption will occur. "Therefore, let him who until now has had the privilege of living a common Christian life with other Christians praise God's grace from the bottom of his heart. Let him thank God on his knees and declare: It is grace, nothing but grace, that we are allowed to live in community with Christian brethren."[166] Repeatedly throughout this work, Bonhoeffer states that Christianity is community in and through Jesus Christ. During these years, Bonhoeffer was experiencing a measure of estrangement ecclesiastically and politically,

---

[164] Ibid., 317-18.
[165] Bethge, *Bonhoeffer; A Biography,* 469-70.
[166] Dietrich Bonhoeffer, *Life Together*, Trans., John W. Doberstein (New York: Harper & Row Publishers, 2003), 20.

and the concept of community during these very difficult years was all the more meaningful for him because of his outward circumstances and challenges. He explains what Christian community means by writing: "It means, first, that a Christian needs others because of Jesus Christ. It means, second, that a Christian comes to others only through Jesus Christ. It means, third, that in Jesus Christ we have been chosen from eternity, accepted in time, and united for eternity."[167]

He writes about how the Reformers spoke of righteousness, that is, an "alien righteousness," or that which comes from without the person. Bonhoeffer repeatedly speaks about the sufficiency of the Word, and that Jesus is the ultimate expression of this Word.

Christian community to him does not mean sectarianism, an accusation that Bonhoeffer surely heard repeatedly. "In other words, life together under the Word will remain sound and healthy only where it does not form itself into a movement, an order, a society, a *collegium pietatis,* but rather where it understands itself as being a part of the one, holy, catholic, Christian Church, where it shares . . . in the sufferings and struggles and promise of the whole Church."[168]

He is adamant in believing that those who appear insignificant must not be excluded from the fellowship of the community, for this could in reality mean the exclusion of Christ. At the center of every relationship stands Christ. The concept of community is most significant to Bonhoeffer. He articulates:

> There is probably no Christian to whom God has not given the uplifting *experience* of genuine Christian community at least once in his life. But in this world such experience can be no more than a gracious extra beyond the daily bread of Christian community life. We have not claim upon such experiences, and we do not live with other Christians for the sake of acquiring them. It is not the experience of Christian brotherhood, but solid and certain faith in brotherhood that holds us together. That God has acted and wants to act upon us all, this we see in faith as God's greatest gift, this makes us happy, but it also makes us ready to forego all such experiences when God at times does not grant them. We are bound together by faith, not by experience.[169]

He sees an interplay between speech and silence. Both are needed. He sounds a warning that one should be aware if he cannot be in community, but likewise be alarmed if he cannot be alone. Speech is important for

---

[167] Bonhoeffer, *Life Together,* 21.
[168] Ibid., 37.
[169] Bonhoeffer, *Life Together*, 39.

community, but so is silence. "The Word comes not to the chatterer but to him who holds his tongue. The stillness of the temple is the sign of the holy presence of God in His Word."[170] To Bonhoeffer, then, silence is waiting for God in an active manner, not passive, to discern what is being said to the individual, and to Bonhoeffer this may include a blessing. The method of silence impacts one's entire day as one determines how and when to speak with others and it develops into a community relationship. Silence before the Word, Bonhoeffer believes leads to correct hearing and speaking. We see a subjective, somewhat existential approach in Bonhoeffer's method at times. He advises:

> We shall not discuss here all the wonderful benefits that can accrue to the Christian in solitude and silence. It is all too easy to go astray at this point. We could probably cite many a bad experience that has come from silence. Silence can be a dreadful ordeal with all its desolation and terrors. It can also be a false paradise of self-deception; the latter is no better than the former. Be that as it may, let none expect from silence anything but a direct encounter with the Word of God, for the sake of which he has entered into silence. But this encounter will be given to him. The Christian cannot lay down any conditions as to what he expects or hopes to get from this encounter. If he will simply accept it, his silence will be richly rewarded.[171]

He emphasizes meditation repeatedly throughout *Life Together*. He says that the precedent for meditation is from the period of the ancient church and the Reformation.

Bonhoeffer believes that the text must "speak" to the preacher first before he can speak to others. He believes that one must understand the content of the verse and context first, and at this step one is not concerned about conducting a Bible study or preparing for a sermon. One must attempt to clear his mind of distractions. He believes that it may take some time, but God's Word will come in an intimate way for the one who is sincerely seeking. He says about the Word: "But it will surely come, just as surely as God Himself has come to men and will come again. This is the very reason why we begin our meditation with prayer that God may send His Holy Spirit to us through His Word and reveal His Word to us and enlighten us."[172]

One finds many themes from his "The Presentation of the New Testament Texts," and *Life Together* in Bonhoeffer's *The Cost of*

---

[170] Ibid., 79.
[171] Ibid., 80-81.
[172] Bonhoeffer, *Life Together,* 82-83.

Discipleship. The theme of the Gospel mandate to follow Christ wholeheartedly is found as well as that of the inherent relevance of Scripture. The pneumatological emphases are also obvious in all, but are subordinate to the christological. His approach is somewhat existential in that we find him speaking about discerning the Word of God in a subjective manner. He believes that Scripture contains the word of man and the Word of God, and it is possible to distinguish the two.

The hermeneutical program we find in *The Cost of Discipleship* revolves around the essential theme of discipleship. One is in community with other Christians in the journey of following Christ. Godsey insightfully writes concerning the issue of living out the Gospel:

> Bonhoeffer does not believe that words alone, even words informed by a theology of revelation, will have much impact upon a mature world. What is needed is a church that takes seriously its call to participate in the being of Christ in the world, a church that loves the world so much that it does not try to impose upon it some absolute, but rather shares willingly and joyously in its immediate, relative realities. Only a community that is willing to live and suffer in, for, and with the world in its common life will be able to speak God's reconciling word.[173]

We find in *The Cost of Discipleship* a view of the world which is not as conciliatory as in *Letters and Papers form Prison.* However, the strong emphasis on community is seen especially in his earlier writings.

Bonhoeffer emphasizes both the solitary individual and his following Christ wholeheartedly; one must renounce all in order to be a genuine disciple: "Peter had to leave the ship and risk his life on the sea, in order to learn both his own weakness and the almighty power of his Lord. If Peter had not taken the risk, he would never have learnt the meaning of faith."[174] Bonhoeffer also gives negative examples of those who would not renounce their earthly goods and thus follow Christ with enthusiasm and sincerity. The rich young ruler is such a person as well as the lawyer recorded in Luke 10:25-29. These two individual are not willing to count the cost and believe that Jesus is who he said that he is. Pride and the cares of temporal matters consume them. He continues his emphasis upon the individual's responsibility to follow Christ:

> The cross is laid upon every Christian. The first Christ-suffering which every man must experience is the call to abandon the attachments of this

---

[173] John D. Godsey, *The Theology of Dietrich Bonhoeffer* (Philadelphia: The Westminister Press, 1960), 276-77.
[174] Bonhoeffer, *The Cost of Discipleship,* 63.

world. It is that dying of the old man which is the result of his encounter with Christ. . . . When Christ calls a man, he bids him come and die. It may be a death like that of the first disciples who had to leave home and work and follow him, or it may be a death like Luther's, who had to leave the monastery and go out into the world. But it is the same death every time— death in Jesus Christ, the death of the old man at his call.[175]

In his chapter, "Discipleship and the Individual," Bonhoeffer believes that every person is called individually and individual calling connotes that there will be loneliness and solitude. "By calling us he has cut us off from all immediacy with the things of the world. He wants to be the centre, through him alone all things shall come to pass. He stands between us and God, and for that very reason he stands between us and all other men and things. *He is the Mediator*, not only between God and man, but between man and reality."[176] In relationship with Christ, the individual is able to draw strength for the spiritual journey which is to be faced with courage and the certitude that God is near at hand.

In Bonhoeffer's concluding chapter in *The Cost of Discipleship*, he discusses the community relationship which the follower of Christ possesses. He reminds his readers that Jesus Christ is alive and he is speaking directly from the Scriptures: "He comes to us to-day, and is present with us in bodily form and in his word. If we would hear his call to follow, we must listen where he is to be found, that is, in the church through the ministry of Word and Sacrament. The preaching of the Church and the administration of the sacraments is the place where Jesus Christ is present."[177] He believes that Jesus speaks to us today as he did to his first disciples. If one is close to him, Bonhoeffer claims, it is possible to hear the command to follow.

Bonhoeffer places a significant emphasis upon the sacrament of baptism. He believes that when the name of Christ is spoken over the one who is to be baptized, that individual becomes a partaker of the name, and the person is baptized "into" Christ. He describes the spiritual movement which occurs in a dramatic manner:

> Baptism therefore betokens a *breach*. Christ invades the realm of Satan, lays hands on his own, and creates for himself his Church. By this act past and present are rent asunder. The old order is passed away, and all things have become new. This breach is not affected by man's tearing off his own chains through some unquenchable longing for a new life of freedom.

---

[175] Ibid., 89-90.
[176] Bonhoeffer, *The Cost of Discipleship*, 95.
[177] Ibid., 225-26.

The breach has been affected by Christ long since, and in baptism it is effected in our own lives. . . . Christ the Mediator has stepped in between us and them. The baptized Christian has ceased to belong to the world and is no longer its slave. He belongs to Christ alone, and his relationship with the world is mediated through him.[178]

He believes that in baptism one dies to the world and to his old self. But the person is placed in fellowship with Christ and the Christian community. He believes that baptism is a public act, since it is a means by which one is engrafted into the body of Christ. Baptism is never to be repeated, thus, there is a certain finality about the event. He emphasizes the community aspect of baptism: "As far as infant baptism is concerned, it must be insisted that the sacrament should be administered only where there is a firm faith present which remembers Christ's deed of salvation wrought for us once and for all. That can only happen in a living Christian community."[179]

In the section entitled "The Body of Christ," Bonhoeffer commences by stating that the first disciples lived in the presence and communion with Jesus. Though Jesus is no longer visibly present, followers of the Christ can enjoy the same fellowship with Christ as did the original followers. Bonhoeffer even states that the present disciples can have a closer relationship with Jesus! "The disciples enjoyed exactly the same bodily communion as is available for us to-day, nay rather, our communion with him is richer and more assured than it was for them, for the communion and presence which we have is that of the glorified Lord."[180] Bonhoeffer clearly states that Jesus took on human flesh and that he was not merely a prophet or charismatic person, but is the incarnate Son of God. The disciples are dependent upon him: "The disciples have communion and fellowship in the Body of Christ. They live and suffer in bodily communion with him. That is why they must bear the burden of the cross. In him they are borne and taken up."[181] He asks the question, how do we participate in the Body of Christ? His sacramental theology is pronounced here in that he believes that the preaching of the Word is not sufficient to make one a member of the Body of Christ, but baptism is most important as this sacrament incorporates one into Christ's Body. The Lord's Supper nourishes and sustains one's fellowship and faith as he continues to experience growth and continued sanctification. "The sacraments begin

---

[178] Bonhoeffer, *The Cost of Disciplehsip*, 231.
[179] Ibid., 235.
[180] Bonhoeffer, *The Cost of Discipleship*, 236.
[181] Ibid., 238.

and end in the Body of Christ, and it is only the presence of that Body which makes them what they are."[182] He believes that all people are in a degree related to Christ because of the Incarnation, but it is only the Christians who are "with Christ" in a special sense. "For the rest of mankind to be with Christ means death, but for Christians it is a means of grace."[183]

Since the ascension of Christ, the Church, the Body of Christ, is the real presence of Christ on earth. He warns that one should not think of the Church as an institution, and that salvation is connected with belonging to what he considers the true Church:

> No one can become a new man except by entering the Church, and becoming a member of the Body of Christ. It is impossible to become a new man as a solitary individual. The new man means more than the individual believer after he has been justified and sanctified. It means the Church, the Body of Christ, in fact it means Christ himself.[184]

He writes of the Church being of one entity but consisting of a fellowship of believers. He continues to have a strong emphasis upon pneumatology—the Spirit works to bring Christ to each member. "The Church of Christ is the presence of Christ through the Holy Spirit. In this way the life of the Body of Christ becomes our own life. In Christ we no longer live our own lives, but he lives his life in us. The life of the faithful in the Church is indeed the *life of Christ within them* (Gal. 2.20; Rom. 8.10; II Cor. 13.5; I John 4.15)."[185]

In the section "The Visible Community," Bonhoeffer goes into great detail about Christ's physical body, and that he believes the body of the exalted Lord is now a visible body in the shape of the Church on earth. He gives a clear statement concerning his belief of the connection of the individual and community of believers to Christ:

> The fellowship between Jesus and his disciples covered every aspect of their daily life. Within the fellowship of Christ's disciples the life of each individual was part of the life of the brotherhood. The common life bears living testimony to the concrete humanity of the Son of God. The bodily presence of God demands that for him and with him man should stake his own life in his daily existence. With all the concreteness of his bodily existence, man belongs to him who for his sake took upon him the human

---

[182] Ibid., 239.
[183] Ibid., 240.
[184] Bonhoeffer, *The Cost of Discipleship,* 242.
[185] Ibid., 244.

body. In the Christian life the individual disciple and the body of Jesus Christ belong inseparably together.[186]

Throughout these latter sections, Bonhoeffer uses many New Testament Greek words. One wishes perhaps that he had gone into greater detail concerning the various words, perhaps citing other scriptural passages where the particular word is found, but he does not engage in this.

He also uses the example of Onesimus, and as a baptized person, Paul argues that his master should receive him back without punishment. He as an individual is a member of the Christian community—related to Christ he is deserving of compassion and forgiveness. He also emphasizes that if one Christian is wronged by those in the world, another brother should comfort and encourage that person who is experiencing dishonoring by the world. "For the Christian serves the fellowship of the Body of Christ, and he cannot hide it from the world. He is called out of the world to follow Christ."[187] At times it appears that Bonhoeffer is encouraging the disciple not to distain the world, but to witness to it through a righteous life: "To stay in the world with God means simply to live in the rough and tumble of the world and at the same time remain in the Body of Christ, the visible Church, to take part in its worship and to live the life of discipleship. In so doing we bear testimony to the defeat of the world."[188] As individuals related to Christ, each one is also related to the community. Bonhoeffer says:

> In the world the Christians are a colony of the true home, they are strangers and aliens in a foreign land, enjoying the hospitality of that land, obeying its laws and honoring its government. They receive with gratitude the requirements of their bodily life, and in all things prove themselves honest, just, chaste, gentle, peaceable, and ready to serve. They show the love of God to all men, "but especially to them that are of the household of faith" (Gal. 6.10; II Pet. 1.7). . . . At any moment they may receive the signal to move on. They will strike their tents, leaving behind them all their worldly friends and connections, and following only the voice of their Lord who calls. They leave the land of exile, and start their homeward trek to heaven.[189]

In his second to the final section "The Saints," Bonhoeffer emphasizes that Christians partake in Christ's righteousness: "By sharing in his death we too become partakers of his righteousness. For it was *our* flesh Christ

---

[186] Ibid., 254.
[187] Ibid., 258.
[188] Ibid., 260.
[189] Bonhoeffer, *The Cost of Discipleship,* 270.

took upon him, and our sins which he bore bodily on the tree (I Pet. 2.24). What happened there to him happened to us all. He shared our life and death, that we might partake of his life and death."[190] He then goes into great detail about sanctification, comparing the community of saints as a train traveling through enemy territory. He even uses the analogy of the ark which was sealed with pitch in order that it might withstand the assaults of the destructive floods. He clearly states that "The community of saints is not an 'ideal' community consisting of perfect and sinless men and women, where there is no need of further repentance. No, it is a community which proves that it is worthy of forgiveness by constantly and sincerely proclaiming *God's* forgiveness (which has nothing to do with self-forgiveness)."[191] He speaks against any form of pride—especially spiritual pride. "The moment we begin to feel satisfied that we are making some progress along the road of sanctification, it is all the more necessary to repent and confess that all our righteousnesses are as filthy rags. Yet the Christian life is not one of gloom, but of ever increasing joy in the Lord. God alone knows our good works."[192]

In Bonhoeffer's final section "The Image of Christ," he commences with quoting Romans 8:29, acknowledging that the verse is a mystery to him. He believes that the passage is teaching that the goal is to take on the image of Christ. He continues to emphasize that the solitary Christian takes on the character of Christ, that "The form of Christ incarnate makes the Church into the Body of Christ. All the sorrows of mankind fall upon that form, and only through that form can they be borne."[193]

D. View on the Prison Letters and the Hermeneutical Program Formulated from within the Prison Cell

Bonhoeffer's personally written letters as recorded in *Letters and Papers from Prison* extend from April 5, 1943, until January 17, 1945. The prison letters of Dietrich Bonhoeffer are either loathed or loved as there are a variety of opinions concerning their meaning, and exactly what it is that Bonhoeffer is attempting to convey. Rene Marle states that he desires to understand the letters in their context, and he is not interested in ascertaining if themes can be found in previous writings. Marle believes:

---

[190] Ibid., 274.
[191] Ibid., 286.
[192] Ibid., 297.
[193] Bonhoeffer, *The Cost of Discipleship,* 302.

In describing Bonhoeffer in this final stage of his life as a 'man of disturbing vision', I want to suggest that some of the trains of thought he sketches here could easily lead to disastrous consequences. Some rash people have made him their authority for putting forward an attack on traditional Christianity which practically amounts to destroying it altogether. He himself, as we shall see, was aware of the dangers inherent in any study of obviously incomplete and one-sided reflections. . . . But I use the term 'disturbing' in a positive sense as well. These penetrating insights, rising out of an extraordinary inner experience and inspired wholly by the Church's mission and an unconditional fidelity to Jesus Christ, can hardly leave us cold. Though we have every right—indeed a positive duty—to react with certain criticisms, to fill in certain gaps, it can do nothing but good to let ourselves be disturbed by them.[194]

Marle writes about the "apocalyptic atmosphere" under which Bonhoffer wrote, and he gives considerably weight to the fact that Bonhoeffer knew he could be facing death.[195]

But there are other interpretations of what Bonhoeffer is attempting to convey in his prison letters. E. H. Robertson believes that the doctrine of ecclesiology is heavily emphasized in Bonhoeffer's letters. Many have interpreted Bonhoeffer to imply that the Church is or will eventually no longer be viable in an increasingly secularized world. However, Robertson claims that Bonhoeffer is stating that the Church is the expression of Christ in the world.[196] After surveying several of the prison letters, Hopper concludes: "At the end, Bonhoeffer's statement of faith and his humanity were not very different from the faith and humanity of the long nineteen hundred years of Christian history. And it is this Bonhoeffer—not the restless, provocative theologian—who is likely to strengthen and nurture the faith of the church."[197] Hopper also alludes to the ". . . inner tensions that emerge from his fragmentary theological statements. . . ."[198] Woelfel, on the other hand, writes about the "radical expression" of the prison letters. He also believes that the word "penultimate" is highly significant in the prison letters: "In the prison letters Bonhoeffer affirmed even more decisively the importance of living in the penultimate, of loving this earth in all of its brokenness. His positive evaluation of secularity must be seen

---

[194] Rene Marle, *Bonhoeffer: The Man and His Work* (New York: Newman Press, 1967), 107-08.
[195] Ibid., 108.
[196] E. H. Robertson, *Dietrich Bonhoeffer* (Richmond: John Knox Press, 1969), 34.
[197] David H. Hopper, *A Dissent on Bonhoeffer* (Philadelphia: The Westminster Press, 1975), 144.
[198] Ibid., 140.

in large part as a manifestation of this appreciation of the penultimate, the natural."[199] It is seen, then, that there are a variety of conclusions concerning what it was that Bonhoeffer is attempting to convey in his prison letters. Eberhard Bethge is perhaps the person who gives the most even-handed interpretation of the letters since many of them were addressed to him, and he had been associated with Bonhoeffer for so many years.

Bethge says that "the nonreligious interpretation of biblical terms in a world come of age" is still not fully understood and has either been accepted or rejected since his letters first appear in 1951-1952.[200] There are several other key words, however, which Bonhoeffer uses that have created much interest in his imprisonment from 1943-1945.

His letters are not lengthy, and the first one which is recorded on April 14, 1943, was written to his parents. In this letter he desires to reassure his parents that he is doing well, and that he is surprisingly comfortable in his surroundings. He is concerned that his imprisonment is causing them duress, and he does not want them to worry. Bonhoeffer tells them that he has his Bible and also that he is reading Paul Gerhardt's hymns and is memorizing them. He writes about his fiancée, and that these days must be difficult for her, especially since she has lost her father and brother in the war.

These initial letters from Tegel Prison are almost light hearted. He writes about his reading, being out of his cell for a half hour daily, loved-one's birthdays—the general tone of his letters is that he is thankful even though he is in difficult circumstances. He remarks in his Easter Day 1943 letter how quickly time passes, but that he is memorizing scripture is reading from the Psalms. In his April 5, 1943 letter to Hans von Dohnanyi, Bonhoeffer writes that he has been engaged to Maria von Wedemeyer since January. In this letter he says that he is reading a great deal and is systematically having a quiet time in the morning and evening. In his May 15, 1943 letter addressed to his parents, Bohoeffer quotes several times from the Psalms which allude to time. He also tells them that he is reading the Bible from cover to cover.

There is a change in the tone of his letters beginning with the June 14, 1943 letter. He writes: "When the bells rang this morning, I longed to go to church, but instead I did as John did on the island of Patmos, and had such a splendid service of my own that I did not feel lonely at all, for you were all with me, every one of you, and so were the congregations in

---

[199] James W. Woelfel, *Bonhoeffer's Theology* (New York: Abingdon Press, 1970), 249.
[200] Eberhard Bethge, *Dietrich Bonhoeffer,* 853-54.

whose company I have kept Whitsuntide."[201] He continues: "One hears nothing but the tramp of prisoners pacing up and down in their cells. How many comfortless and un-Whitsun-like thoughts there must be in their minds! If I were the prison chaplain here, I should spend the whole time from morning till night on days like this, going through the cells; a good deal would happen."[202] He mentions that he had thought that he would have been released by now, but that overall he is confident about the future. With affection, he mentions Maria and says that he pictures both of them together in the future.

In his June 24, 1943 letter we see a hint of melancholy. "You father, know all this quite well from your long experience of prisoners. I am not yet sure what the so-called prison psychosis is, though I am getting a pretty good idea."[203] Apparently, he left off writing this letter since he writes, "I have just come back and have seen Maria—an indescribable surprise and joy. I knew about it only a minute beforehand. It's still like a dream—really an almost unimaginable situation—what will we think of it one day? What one can say at such a time is so trivial. . . . It was so brave of her to come.[204] The tone of this letter is one of quiet resignation as he quotes Professor Schlatter's words about how Christians must be patient when being held for investigation.

His letters from July 3, 1943, until November 17, 1943, are filled with concern for family members, words of affection for Maria, reports of what he has been reading, and reminders especially to his parents not to worry about him. His letter of November 18, 1943, is addressed to Bethge, and Bonhoeffer relates how much strength he has gained from reading Paul Gerhardt's hymns as well as the Psalms and even the book of Revelation. He remarks that he has read the Old Testament through two and a half times, and he has learned much.[205] On November 20, 1943, he asks, "Why does the Old Testament law never punish anyone by depriving him of his freedom?"[206] He makes no reference to the New Testament in this letter.

In his November 21, 1943 letter Bonhoeffer makes a comment about religion: "Don't be alarmed; I shall not come out of here a *homo religiosus*! On the contrary, my fear and distrust of 'religiosity' have become greater than ever here."[207] He states that he has been reading the

---

[201] Bonhoeffer, *Letters and Papers from Prison*, 53.
[202] Ibid.
[203] Ibid., 71.
[204] Bonhoeffer, *Letters and Papers from Prison*, 71-72.
[205] Ibid., 129.
[206] Ibid., 134.
[207] Ibid., 135.

early church fathers and believes that they are more relevant to his particular period of time than are the Reformers. His November 23, 1943 letter is written to Eberhard Bethge, and he writes of the possibility of his own death. But Bonhoeffer's December 5 correspondence to Bethge contains well-known sentences, "My thoughts and feelings seem to be getting more and more like those of the Old Testament, and in recent months I have been reading the Old Testament much more than the New. . . . In my opinion it is not Christian to want to take our thoughts and feelings too quickly from the New Testament."[208]

The letters from December 5, 1943, to March 9, 1944, contain minimal references to theology. There are many descriptions of air raids and Bonhoeffer's affection for many individuals. In his March 19, 1944 letter Bonhoeffer writes: "Once again I'm having weeks when I don't read the Bible much; I never know quite what to do about it. I have no feeling of obligation about it, and I know, too, that after some time I shall plunge into it again voraciously."[209] He closes this letter by asking if Bethge had enjoyed the reading Genesis 41:52 as much as he [Bonhoeffer] had. In this letter Bonhoeffer raises the possibility that there will not be a future meeting for the two of them. He writes that the years they spent in ministry together were "quite wonderful years."

In his April 11, 1944 letter Bonhoeffer writes that though the past few years have been difficult, he does not believe that they have been wasted years. He writes reflectingly:

> I heard someone say yesterday that the last years had been completely wasted as far as he was concerned. I'm very glad that I have never yet had that feeling, even for a moment. Nor have I ever regretted my decision in the summer of 1939, for I am firmly convinced—however strange it may seem—that my life has followed a straight and unbroken course, at any rate in its outward conduct. It has been an uninterrupted enrichment of experience, for which I can be thankful. If I were to end my life here in these conditions, that would have a meaning that I think I could understand.[210]

The consistent testimony of other prisons and even guards during his imprisonment is that he behaved in an exemplary manner, and even radiated peace and joy.

It is his April 30, 1944 letter addressed to Bethge which contains so much controversial material. He begins the letter remarking how quickly

---

[208] Bonhoeffer, *Letters and Papers from Prison,* 157.
[209] Ibid., 234.
[210] Ibid., 272.

time flys and that he wishes they could help each other through these difficult days. He also cites many biblical passages from I Peter, Psalms and Jeremiah. He writes that they both should repeat daily Jeremiah 45:5. He writes:

> You would be surprised, and perhaps even worried, by my theological thoughts and the conclusions that they lead to. . . . What is bothering me incessantly is the question what Christianity really is, or indeed who Christ really is, for us today. The time when people could be told everything by means of words, whether theological or pious, is over, and so is the time of inwardness and conscience—and that means the time of religion in general. We are moving towards a completely religionless time; people as they are now simply cannot be religious any more. Even those who honestly describe themselves as 'religious' do not in the least act up to it, and so they presumably mean something quite different from 'religious'. . . . How can Christ become the Lord of the religionless as well? Are there religionless Christians? If religion is only a garment of Christianity—and even this garment has looked very different at different times—then what is a religionless Christian?[211]

He continues in this letter asking such questions about Christ and His relationship to the world, the place of worship, the use of God in a *deus ex machina* sense, and that he would like to continue to explore the concept of the religionless Christianity. What Bonhoeffer means by the word "religion" has been debated.

Concerning his use of the phrase "religionless Christianity," there has been some discussion. In Germany, according to Bethge, there has been a debate over whether the phrase has its origins in Bultmann or Barth, and to which one is the phrase more similar.[212] This phrase is used by Bonhoeffer during the last year of his life, and he is re-examining during this period his theology. It is known that the books he read his first year at Tegel were concerned with the theme of "the past," especially the nineteenth century, but he eventually became dissatisfied with reading books pertaining to this subject. Bethge believes, "After his active "acceptance of guilt" in joining

---

[211] Bonhoeffer, *Letters and Papers from Prison,* 279-80. Cf. 871, Bethge explains that the phrase in English-speaking countries is "religionless Christianity," whereas in German-speaking countries the phrase is, "nonreligious interpretation."

[212] Bethge, *Dietrich Bonhoeffer,* 854. Cf. 856-57, 59, Bethge believes that Bonhoeffer's new theology has roots in his early Christology as well as his experiences with the Confessing church and the political conspiracy. Barth also notes that there is a definite change in Bonhoeffer's April, 1944 letter, but he considered previous works such as *The Cost of Discipleship* as worth reading while he believed the prison letters were not worth passing on.

the conspiracy Bonhoeffer became possessed by a new passion for theology. Even before they ended, his political duties had liberated him for a new theological beginning, opening the lonely man's eyes for the conditions and possible form of Christian belief in the future."[213]

Bethge admits that Bonhoeffer had endured much emotional pressure with his imprisonment, but this is not an explanation for the shift in his theological thinking. He apparently was working on a book which he never completed; he writes of this in his August 23, 1944 letter to Bethge. He refers to a chapter called, "A Stocktaking of Christianity," but all which survived is an outline. Bethge attempts to answer a common question if what Bonhoeffer writes are expressions of his earlier theology or if they represent a new turn in his theological thinking. He answers this inquiry by stating: "It seems to me that what we have is not the mature fruit of a new branch in Bonhoeffer's work, but it is also more than a vague, random attempt. Ultimately only the content of the brief fragments and their reception can decide this."[214] Bethge does believe, however, "What we have here is undoubtedly the essential basic ideas of Bonhoeffer."[215]

What is Bonhoeffer's understanding of religion? His understanding of the word is somewhat negative. He describes religion as comprising several elements such as the following: metaphysics, individualism, partiality, *deus ex machina*, privilege, guardianship, and dispensability.[216]

He mentions metaphysics in his May 5, 1944 letter: "What does it mean to 'interpret in a religious sense'? I think it means to speak on the one hand metaphysically, and on the other hand individualistically. Neither of these is relevant to the biblical message or to the man of today."[217] He is against a system of dogmatic abstract statements which are merely communicated by words, yet do not display how one can live out the message which is given. Though Bonhoeffer could argue well various difficult theological issues, he was not prone to do so. So much of his theology is christologically orientated, but yet he does not argue for example the issue of the hypostatic union.

He writes in this same letter about individualism, and we find this same theme in his April 30, 1944 letter by the use of such terms as

---

[213] Ibid., 856. Cf. 858, Bethge states that Bonhoeffer viewed Bultmann as an ally against Barth's "defined limits." He mentions Bultmann three times in his prison letters.
[214] Bethge, *Dietrich Bonhoeffer,* 862.
[215] Ibid., 863.
[216] Ibid., 873-78.
[217] Bonhoeffer, *Letters and Papers from Prison,* 285-86.

"inwardness," and "conscience." Bonhoeffer taught the importance of individual faith, but he always balanced this out with a working out of the Gospel into the social dimension. Bethge adds insight into this by writing:

> He never became so rigorous that he rejected intense personal declarations of faith, such as those in the hymns of Paul Gerhardt; but he was uncomfortable with the tendency to direct one's gaze to the private human sphere and cultivate the "salvation of one's own soul" at the cost of the world and the *familia Dei*. This sensitivity grew so strong that he never thought of leading those who had "come of age" back into the confinement of this kind of individualistic inwardness.[218]

Bethge makes an interesting observation concerning what he sees as a connection with Bultmann:

> The interest of the existential interpretation lies clearly with the individual, which encourages a sterility towards the kinds of questions that transcend the individual. Because of this it has been noted that there is a connection between Bultmann's theology and the pietistic world that Bonhoeffer termed "religious." Bonhoeffer suspected the same kind of connection when he extended his dislike of a pietistic or dogmatic pastoral care, which dwelled on the intimate sphere of human life or on the "inwardness" of human existence, to existential philosophy as well.[219]

We find at times a type of pietistic element in Bonhoeffer, and certainly his concept of community in Christ is deeply woven into his theology. On the other hand, it appears that he did not want to be overly sentimental or at least be seen in such a manner.

Bonhoeffer also speaks of religion as partiality, and this is found in his July 18, 1944 letter: "The 'religious act' is always something partial; 'faith' is something whole, involving the whole of one's life. Jesus calls men, not to a new religion, but to life."[220] To Bonhoeffer, many are in danger of relegating religion merely to one segment of life; thus, a person's religious life is not the controlling factor of one's decisions and even direction in life. A religious act to him is partial, whereas faith involves the totality of the person.

Bonhoeffer describes a religious conception of God as *deus ex machina* in the first verse of his poem entitled "Christians and Pagans."[221] He makes use of the phrase also in the following letters: April 30, 1944,

---

[218] Bethge, *Dietrich Bonhoeffer*, 874.
[219] Ibid., 875.
[220] Bonhoeffer, *Letters and Papers from Prison*, 362.
[221] Bonhoeffer, *Letters and Papers from Prison*, 348.

June 30, 1944, and July 16, 1944. He believes that all religion is based on this concept, that is, there is a all-powerful One who is totally sovereign and omnipotent. This supreme One is able to rescue and provide for those who call upon him. Bethge believes: "Bonhoeffer's concern here is to show that it is precisely religiosity, and even pietism, that can dangerously conceal humanity's real godlessness. Christ must not be made the "answer," the "solution," or the "medicine." Religion depends on the power of God."[222] "The Bible directs man to God's powerlessness and suffering."[223] He is speaking against any concept of God as a type of "errand boy" or someone to help a person get out of trouble or take care of a person's particular responsibility.

Bonhoeffer refers to the concept of privilege or favoritism in his April 30, 1944 letter, and though it is mentioned only once in his letters, Bethge believes that this is one of the most important concepts in Bonhoeffer's argument against religion. Religion he believes has become almost like a "status symbol," those who possess it are entitled to benefits and even social position. Bethge explains: "Bonhoeffer's life consisted of a constant fight to overcome the dangerously privileged character of the Christian religion: in his decision to take up theology, his move from teaching to pastoral work, and then to "becoming a man for his own times" in the conspiracy against Hitler. . . . Throughout its history the Christian religion has been continually perverted into a form of privilege."[224] Perhaps Bonhoeffer is more aware of this issue than many others since he indeed did come from a family of high social standing and privilege. His father was a respected psychiatrist in Berlin, and may have thought that his son may have chosen a route in life which displayed a life of privilege also. Bonhoeffer is ultimately speaking against a religion which divides people from one another, especially if this divisiveness is based on social class, or ethnicity.

Guardianship is another emphasis important to Bonhoeffer's critique of religion. Bethge explains:

> "Religious interpretation" is an exegesis of the Gospel of Christ's powerlessness that establishes priests (as the givers of life) or theologians (as custodians of truth) as the guardians and the rulers of the church's people, creating and perpetuating a situation of dependence. Nothing will be as difficult as overcoming the monarchial and patriarchal structures of hierarchies, theologies, and, indeed, dogmas. . . . on the other hand, he

---

[222] Bethge, *Dietrich Bonhoeffer*, 876.
[223] Bonhoeffer, *Letters and Papers from Prison*, 361.
[224] Bethge, *Dietrich Bonhoeffer*, 876.

[Bonhoeffer] can also urge us to accept responsibilities for others and make possible the mature cooperation and partnership of the world.[225]

He is arguing that the church must not dominate, but must attempt to share in the problems and concerns which are found in the world. To Bonhoeffer, this spirit of cooperation and helpfulness is extending Christ's community into a sphere which is desperately in need of redemption and encouragement.

His final definition of religion revolves around the concept of dispensability. In his letters he spoke of religion as passing away. Bethge clarifies this point: "Can faith ever escape becoming a religion, whether western, eastern, or African? But precisely in order to make faith possible, Bonhoeffer explains "religion" in its "Western form" as something we can do without and as a relic of past ages. His judgment here is so certain because he regards the age of Jesus as something different from the age of religion."[226] Bonhoeffer is essentially stating that religion does not extol Christ.

Concluding a discussion of Bonhoeffer's opinion of religion, Bethge writes:

> In summary: if "religion" has a tendency to be partial, we can speak of "nonpartial" interpretation instead of "nonreligious." Or, when Bonhoeffer says "worldly," we can speak of the "totality of interpretation, with all its relevance and claims." Here we see the reason for Bonhoeffer's love of Stifter's novel *Witiko*: The 'religious act' is always something partial, 'faith' is something whole, involving the whole of one's life. Jesus does not summon to a new religion, but to life . . . Young Witiko . . . set out into the world 'to do the whole thing.'"[227] The "whole thing" is other people, the revelation of one's own godlessness, the acceptance of common guilt, and the sharing of God's powerlessness in the world. In the fullest sense, Bonhoeffer's nonreligious interpretation is Christological interpretation.[228]

Bonhoffer's critique, then, of religion is negative. He understands that the essence of Christ is not conveyed with the use of the word.

---

[225] Ibid., 877.
[226] Bethge, *Dietrich Bonhoeffer*, 877.
[227] Bonhoeffer, *Letters and Papers from Prison*, 200, 362 in Bethge, *Dietrich Bonhoeffer*, 879.
[228] Bethge, *Dietrich Bonhoeffer*, 879. Cf. Dietrich Bonhoeffer, *A Testament to Freedom*, eds., Geffrey B. Kelly and F. Burton Nelson (San Francisco: Harper Collins Publishers, 1990), 42-44.

Bonhoeffer uses the term "world come of age" first in his June 8, 1944 letter:

> But first, a little more about the historical position. The question is: Christ and the world that has come of age. The weakness of liberal theology was that it conceded to the world the right to determine Christ's place in the world; in the conflict between the church and the world it accepted the comparatively easy terms of peace that the world dictated. Its strength was that it did not try to put the clock back, and that it genuinely accepted the battle (Troeltsch), even though this battle ended with its defeat. Defeat was followed by surrender, and by an attempt to make a completely fresh start based on the fundamentals of the Bible and the Reformation. Heim sought, along pietist and Methodist lines, to convince the individual man that he was faced with the alternative 'despair or Jesus'. He gained hearts. Althaus (carrying forward the modern and positive line with a strong confessional emphasis) tried to wring from the world a place for Lutheran teaching (ministry) and Lutheran worship, and otherwise left the world to its own devices.[229]

The theme of the "world come of age" is a resounding in Bonhoeffer's letters. Sometimes he uses similar phrases such as, "a world grown of age" or "a world coming of age." He apparently is not speaking about a postmillennial concept of the world becoming better and better morally. Bethge believes that Bonhoeffer is speaking about freeing oneself from a constricting relationship or guardianship. In his June 8 letter, Bonhoeffer does allude to becoming free from the "guardianship of 'God.'" God is in quotation marks here. But Bethge believes that Bonhoeffer is thinking of Kant's belief that the Enlightenment had freed humanity from enslavement to immaturity and ignorance.[230] Bethge writes: "But now Bonhoeffer took Kant's irrevocable description of maturity as an essential element of his *theologia crucis*."[231] Bonhoeffer, however, differs from other attempts to welcome modernity such as Tillich. Again Bethge gives insight by asserting:

> Bonhoeffer was not the first theologian who welcomed, instead of condemning, the evolution of secularization into a coming of age. If Bonhoeffer had been able to examine the material more thoroughly, he would have seen that . . . Paul Tillich had made similar breakthroughs earlier. The others, however, had been concerned with turning away from the Christology of the Reformation, whereas Bonhoeffer proclaimed the

---

[229] Bonhoeffer, *Letters and Papers from Prison,* 327.
[230] Bethge, *Dietrich Bonhoeffer,* 867.
[231] Ibid.

coming of age in the name of the crucified and risen Christ, and saw it as a necessary part of his Christology. For him it was the crucified Christ who enabled, judged, and renewed "true worldliness," "genuine this-worldliness," and "coming of age." This gave the category of "coming of age" a theological quality.[232]

Thus, it is apparent that even his concept of the world come of age has a strong christological element. This is a more positive interpretation of the relationship of the disciple, who is in community with Christ, and the world. The latter is seen as that which is worth rescuing and entering into dialogue.

Another significant phrase which Bonhoeffer uses is "arcane discipline." We find the phrase used in his April 30, 1944 and May 5, 1944 letters, and the word "secret" is used. There is a certain traditionalism about Bonhoeffer, though he has been interpreted by some to be the opposite! He uses the term in an attempt to describe, as much as can be, the mystery which surrounds worship. Bethge believes that this issue in Bonhoeffer's thinking has not been emphasized too much:

> In the general discussion of Bonhoeffer's ideas this arcane discipline has been considered the least; there has been the greatest uncertainty and also the greatest one-sidedness on this issue. Yet here the validity of the main theme is again immediately obvious, namely, the actual relationship to Christ as present, which can never be separated from the question: Who is Christ for us today? This is where we have statements about silence and invisibility, about the way in which the just man prays and acts, and about the difference between the ultimate and the penultimate.[233]

He is interested in protecting that which is sacred, that is, he believes it is important to imitate the early Christian practice of excluding the unbaptized and uninitiated from the second part of the worship service in which the sacrament of the Lord's Supper is celebrated. Bethge argues that this shows that Bonhoeffer does not want to include the world in the church:

> There is no doubt that Bonhoeffer regarded an arcane discipline as the indispensable counterpoint of nonreligious interpretation. Much to his own annoyance, he was not yet able to resolve the problem in a theologically satisfactory way. When he developed his new perspective he immediately raised the question of what was going to happen to the worship service, although not in the spirit of dismantling or even of getting rid of it. On the

---

[232] Ibid.
[233] Bethge, *Dietrich Bonhoeffer,* 880-81.

contrary, he was concerned to preserve—as he explicitly states—a "genuine worship."[234] This means that he has no intention of simply including the religionless world within the church or making the church and the world the same thing. Bonhoeffer would be completely misunderstood if the realization of his worldly interpretation were conceived to mean that there would no longer be any community gathered for worship, and that the word, sacrament, and the community could be simply replaced by *caritas*. In his non- religious interpretation the church's self-sacrifice that Bonhoeffer was thinking of, both for the church and for himself, cannot be equated at all with the loss of its identity. On the contrary, this is precisely what is to be re-won.[235]

Bonhoeffer still believes that prayer, fellowship and worship is essential, but he believes that if the church finds she is not able to relate to those who are considered outside, then the church should remain silent until she receives a call; her message will then be more compelling and stronger. He believes that ". . . a secret discipline must be restored whereby the *mysteries* of the Christian faith are protected against profanation."[236] Bonhoeffer believes that the dichotomy between world and church is not too accurate. There is no place that the Christian can go without Christ who himself is not interested in boundaries. Bonhoeffer wrote pertinent words years previous to his prison years:

> If one wishes to speak, then, of the space or sphere of the Church, one must bear in mind that the confines of this space are at every moment being overrun and broken down by the testimony of the Church to Jesus Christ. And this means that all mistaken thinking in terms of spheres must be excluded, since it is deleterious to the proper understanding of the Church. . . In the body of Jesus Christ God is united with humanity, the whole of humanity is accepted by God, and the world is reconciled with God. In the body of Jesus Christ God took upon himself the sin of the whole world and bore it. . . . Whoever sets eyes on the body of Jesus Christ in faith can never again speak of the world as though it were lost, as though it were separated from Christ; he can never again with clerical arrogance set himself apart from the world.[237]

---

[234] Bonhoeffer, *Letters and Papers from Prison, 328* in Bethge, *Dietrich Bonhoeffer, 881.*
[235] Bethge, *Dietrich Bonhoeffer,* 881-82.
[236] Bonhoeffer, *Letters and Papers from Prison,* 286.
[237] Dietrich Bonhoeffer, *Ethics,* ed., Eberhard Bethge (New York: Macmillan Publishing Co., 1978), 203, 205

The three phrases "world come of age," "nonreligious interpretation," and "arcane discipline," then, are three key paradigmatic statements which Bonhoeffer uses repeatedly in his *Letters and Papers from Prison*.

Another significant phrase that one finds in Bonhoeffer's writings is that of "this worldliness" (*Diesseitigkeit*). This phrase is found in his July 21, 1944 letter which was written to Eberhard Bethge. Bonhoeffer begins the letter by stating that he is always occupied with theological thoughts, and that he is enjoying reading; he again mentions how the hymns of Paul Gerhardt are so meaningful to him. He states that during the past year he has learned much about the "this-worldliness of Christianity." He says: "I don't mean the shallow and banal this-worldliness of the enlightened, the busy, the comfortable, or the lascivious, but the profound this-worldliness, characterized by discipline and constant knowledge of death and resurrection. I think Luther lived a this-worldly life in this sense."[238] He writes of a conversation which he had with a French pastor, Jean Lasserre, years before, and that this person had an impact upon his thinking; the book, *The Cost of Discipleship*, is an outgrowth of his personal friendship with Lasserre. Bonhoeffer remarks that he is:

> . . . still discovering right up to this moment, that is it only by living completely in this world that one learns to have faith. One must completely abandon any attempt to make something of oneself, whether it be a saint, or a converted sinner, or a churchman (a so-called priestly type!), a righteous man or an unrighteous one, a sick man or a healthy one. By this-worldliness I mean living unreservedly in life's duties, problems, successes and failures, experiences and perplexities. In so doing we throw ourselves completely into the arms of God, taking seriously, not our own sufferings, but those of God in the world—watching with Christ in Gethsemane. That I think is faith; that is *metanoia*; and that is how one becomes a man and a Christian (cf. Jer. 45!). How can success make us arrogant, or failure lead us astray, when we share in God's sufferings through a life of this kind?[239]

He closes this letter stating that he believes Bethge understands what he is attempting to convey, and that he, Bonhoeffer, has learned about "this-worldliness" on account of the path which he has traveled in life. In this letter, Bonhoeffer says that he is grateful for the past and the present; he does not mention the future. He again mentions Maria with affection in this letter.

---

[238] Bonhoeffer, *Letters and Papers from Prison*, 369.
[239] Bonhoeffer, *Letters and Papers from Prison*, 369-70.

In a sense, one can see that the theme of "this-worldliness" in *The Cost of Discipleship*. Bonhoeffer emphasizes following Christ, and though one is in the world, one is not of the world. A disciple performs his responsibilities, and lives as a Christian witness, but one's affections are not after the mindset of the world, but rather a disciple attempts to emulate Christ as much as possible. "This-worldliness" means a kind of relationship with Christ. In the community of other Christians, with Christ as the ultimate paradigm, one can live a life which is fulfilling and meaningful. It appears that in this final stage of Bonhoeffer's life, he is emphasizing less the discontinuity between the world and Church; Jesus Christ is Lord of both, and his disciples should not be overly concerned about making a distinction either. Godsey believes that there are four reasons why Bonhoeffer in his latter years took another look at the question of "this worldliness," and they are as follows: 1. his involvement with the resistance movement in which Bonhoeffer had contact with "secular" men who were willing to die for others; 2. his disappointment with the Confessing Church which was too concerned about its own needs and aspirations; 3. his contact with the "unchurched" during his prison years, and his awareness that Jesus died for them also; and 4. his study of the Old Testament where he saw God's blessing poured out on earthly life.[240]

---

[240] Godsey, *The Theology of Dietrich Bonhoeffer*, 263-64.

CHAPTER THREE

COMPARISON

A. Introduction

Both Rudolf Bultmann and Dietrich Bonhoeffer had a significant impact which continues into the twenty-first century. One interpreted the Gospel primarily in an academic setting while the other did so essentially without an official academic position. The religious world today, especially Christianity, has been impacted by the significant influence of both Bultmann and Bonhoeffer.

Bultmann saw clearly that one must have a personal relationship to the text in order for there to be any measure of credible interpretation. He wrote an astonishing amount of material which spanned a period of about sixty years. His influence is interdisciplinary in that though he was a New Testament scholar, he impacted theological, historical and philosophical studies. He brilliantly describes the fact that in the New Testament there is the Christian Gospel, but there is also the mythology of the first century. What is significant is the former and not the latter. The historical knowledge of the man Jesus is not relevant to the Christian faith as it is not possible to know with certainty anything about him. The essential story of Jesus has been somewhat distorted by the issue of the miraculous. Bultmann's many commentaries have enabled theologians to have a deeper understanding of the Scriptures. But he also proved himself to be a very effective communicator as is evidenced by the consistently compelling sermons which he preached especially in Marburg over many decades. His sermons are homiletical models as they display how one should proceed in order to communicate the Gospel to the modern person. One's personal involvement with the text enables the preacher to communicate in such a way that it is a meaningful experience to those who desire to hear the Word of God preached in such a manner that a decision must be made. His exegetical methodology leads to preaching which is scripturally based and relevant to those who heard his messages. He carefully explains the historical and cultural settings of a given passage and then effectively preaches the message, enabling his audience to make the application to their own lives.

After he had completed his academic qualifications, Bonhoeffer only had about fifteen years in which to devote himself to his scholarly pursuits. One wonders if he could not have accomplished more if he had obtained a professorship and given himself wholeheartedly to scholarship. Apparently, he was more attracted to the pulpit than to the professor's lectern, though he did teach for a short period of time in Berlin. He appears somewhat restless, moving from one interest to another. His experience at Union Theological Seminary in New York City had a significant impact upon the direction for the next several years of his life. He became acquainted with racism in America, and this experience gave to him a greater understanding of the intensity of racial issues in Germany during the 1930s, and like Bultmann, he was against National Socialism. Bonhoeffer was heavily involved in the Confessing Church and as the director of the Preachers' Seminary in Finkenwalde. His best-known work, *The Cost of Discipleship*, is not known especially as an academic work, but is more devotional in nature. Certainly he was capable of the best in theological scholarship as evidenced by his *Sanctorum Communio*. One wonders what would have been his future had he decided to stay in New York City and not return to Germany until after the war. But his sense of responsibility would not allow him to remain neutral. He believed that he would not have a right to have an authoritative voice in the new Germany if he did not return. His book on ethics was incomplete and some have claimed that his personal ethics were skewed in that he was involved in a plot to overthrow Hitler. Bonhoeffer was concerned about what it means to be a disciple of Christ and how to authentically implement that commitment. He does not seem to fit into any particular theological faction, and there continues to be an interest in his life and work in a variety of disciplines and from those involved in broader religious traditions. Bonhoeffer did not occupy an academic chair in a university, and his life situation was such that he did his research and writing in somewhat challenging circumstances. However, his preaching and busy schedule forced him into exegetical studies of the Scriptures.

B. Bultmann

Bultmann was a scientific theologian who took his insights from existentialist philosophy and enabled the modern person to have a clearer understanding of the Gospel. He saw himself as a reformer, somewhat like a modern-day Luther, who was concerned about a clear presentation of the Gospel. As a New Testament scholar, he implemented a new methodology for New Testament studies. He lived a long life, 1884-1976, and was a witness to the varied political upheavals as well as theological movements in Germany. From childhood, he was accustomed to the life of the Church as his father and several ancestors were pastors. His decision to study theology seems to be understandable in light of his early experiences and his family history. His ability was recognized early in his career, and he was recommended to succeed Wilhelm Heitmüller. For the next thirty years, 1921-1951, he served on the Theological Faculty at Marburg. Initially in his career, he was interested in comparing early Christianity in particular with ideologies and religious thought such as Hellenistic Gnosticism and Jewish Apocalypticism.

Bultmann is especially controversial among more conservative theologians in that some believe he has abandoned the Gospel by means of his program of demythologization. Some are unaware that he did not dekerygmatize. He was merely concerned that the Gospel be clearly proclaimed without what he believed were unnecessary encumbrances, i.e., the mythology as presented in the New Testament.

For Bultmann, the issue of method is of central importance. He desires that the biblical text be interpreted as correctly as possible. But he is aware that everyone has presuppositions (*Voraussetzungen*), and the interpreter always brings these into the task of interpretation. There is always some prior understanding which one has of a given topic, and this fact influences how one encounters the biblical text and to what conclusion he eventually comes. However, through an historical-critical methodology there is an attempt to understand a given text and to interpret it accurately.

Through the process of demythologization *(Entmythologisierung)*, the interpreter attempts to peel away the mythological elements which can be an encumbrance to the scientifically-orientated modern person. Such issues as angels, miracles and a bodily resurrection he believes are not essential to the Gospel message. He is reacting against the extreme liberal theology of the late nineteenth century with its heavy emphasis upon moralism. Also, he does not believe that it is possible to know anything definitive about the historical Jesus.

The interpreter must truly interact with the biblical text and not attempt to do so in a detached, merely objective manner. He does not advocate a simple historical, grammatical interpretation of the text; rather, one must be aware of the demands of the text upon his situation. Always the text calls for a decision to be made on the part of the interpreter. The interpretation is metaphysical in nature in that the issue of present reality and the interpreter's present stance is in question. Will one choose for authentic living or merely seek for the temporal and a god made in his own image? This is perhaps the most significant issue before the contemporary person. Always he finds himself between the crucible of choosing for authenticity or something else which can compensate.

It is possible to live an authentic life, in particular, for the person of faith who has seen Christ through faith. The person who has not experienced this relationship is still subject to angst and its grip upon his life. He realizes that death waits sometime for him in the future and there is virtually no hope for him. He attempts to compensate by using what the world has to offer him such as fame and fortune. But even these are not able to alleviate the dread which is at the core of his being. Sometimes he is able to achieve to a great extent and for a period he is able to calm the dread which possesses him; but eventually worldly accolades will not be able to compensate for the hollowness he experiences and the shallowness of the manner in which he views and lives his life. Bultmann certainly does have a high regard for philosophy which can help describe humankind's predicament; but only the New Testament message of the Christ which points to the transcendent, offers the final solution to the vicissitudes of life.

One always has a pre-understanding of an issue by which the interpreter is guided. But the best interpretation is when both the writer and the interpreter have the same experience of a given subject matter. The interpreter should endeavor to understand the original intent of the writer, but he must also be guided by his pre-understanding which acts as a guard to keep him from making unwarranted conclusions. Even though everyone has a particular worldview, one should not attempt to manipulate the results. The interpreter cannot go about the process in a simple objective manner, or the methodology of the natural sciences which is a subject and object relationship because he is involved with an *existentiell* encounter with the Scriptures.

Bultmann believes that philosophical Idealism, though a revered system, is not as effective in understanding and describing the human condition as is existentialism. Idealism is too impersonal, and this philosophical school does not take into account the issue of human freedom and choice. Man stands on the brink of eternity, and somehow he attempts to determine what the quality of the future will be which for the moment is not comprehensible. However, as he abandons his security and determines to live with authenticity as a goal, his future is promising. Death still waits, but the New Testament gives him the promise of a future filled with anticipation and hope.

Bultmann is critical of the liberal theology of the nineteenth century by which he believes the Gospel has been reduced to mere moralism and ethics. He claims that the kerygma has been deemphasized to such an extent that the Gospel message is no longer clear; he believes that mythology is not to be eliminated but demythologized. The Gospel is still retained with demythologization, but the nonessential and even confusing elements of the worldview of the first century are eliminated. To Bultmann, by means of his proposal, the modern person can more readily understand and accept the Gospel since he would not feel the need to sacrifice his intellect to accept a literal interpretation of the myth found therein. All concepts of the supernatural such as the virgin birth, miracles and bodily resurrections are not historical; thus, these stories must be existentially interpreted. To some scholars, especially those who are not in agreement with an existential interpretation, Bultmann's program of demythologization is an offense.

Bultmann was a prolific writer as testified by his impressive bibliography spanning his academic career and even into many years of retirement from his academic position. However several representative texts give insight into his exegetical methodology. In his "The Problem of a Theological Exegesis of the New Testament," Bultmann is critical of historical exegetical methodologies. In this essay, he is adamant that one must interpret the text according to an existential method. Through the influence of his colleague Martin Heidegger, Bultmann made use of existentialist philosophy in his own theological program.

The controversy caused by Bultmann's work, "New Testament and Mythology," was especially pronounced. In this work, he states that the cosmology of the New Testament is not what is significant. Rather, the important message to grasp is that living an authentic life is possible. He emphasizes that the event of the cross is a reality in one's life in the present. The cross becomes a *geschichtlich* event and is not merely one which is *historisch*.

In his "The Problem of Hermeneutics," Bultmann advocates that the exegete must have an understanding of the grammar of a given text, but he must also have an awareness of need for a psychological interpretation as well. There must be an attempt to understand the reason why an author wrote a particular work. As much as is possible, there must be a re-creation of the work in the mind of the interpreter. Though this is somewhat subjective, there is the real possibility that a coherent and precise interpretation can occur. One must be without presuppositions in regard to the results. The interpreter's pre-understanding of the subject matter will guide the quality of the questions which are asked of the text. But one is also questioned by the text during the process.

The material contained in "Jesus Christ and Mythology" is believed to be Bultmann's fullest expression of his views on mythology. His understanding of the kingdom is more eschatological in nature; that is, he believes that the issue of eschatology is a central theme in the New Testament. Eschatological preaching views the present in reference to the future. In this work he claims that he is not eliminating the mythological elements of the New Testament, but he desires to reinterpret them. Man is searching for God, and Bultmann believes that this fact is true since the question of God and the question about one's personal existence are the same. Bultmann believes that the human situation can only be correctly understood and appreciated by the existentialist method of interpretation. The Word of God meets one in his personal experience and must be actualized in his present experience. To Bultmann, demythologization is somewhat like Luther's doctrine of justification by faith, which removes all human merit from justification with God. Demythologization obliterates all attempts of objectifying knowledge and thus the attempts which humans make to assure security.

Bultmann's "Is Exegesis without Presuppositions Possible" emphasizes that the exegete's goal is objectivity. Rejecting an allegorical interpretation, he states that one must attempt to hear the text. The interpreter must understand the particular *Siz im Leben* of a particular text. He must also understand the rules of grammar, style and philology. The breaking in of the supernatural is ruled out as there is a closedness in history. However, it is possible for the past to come alive again during the process of interpretation.

Certainly Martin Heidegger's thought greatly impacted Bultmann. Man as a being realizes himself in the state of decision making. *Dasein* is a particular word which alludes to the fullness of human experience. Humans are unlike the animal world in that human beings are aware of the significance of their decisions and especially know that they are mortal. Human beings are thrown into the world, and they must choose how to be. The perennial question which man faces constantly is whether or not he will choose to live authentically. Bultmann believes that the beginning point for determining the meaning of a given text is an understanding of one's own existence. Unless this crucial issue is addressed, the exegete's attempt at interpretation is in vain. The subject of what it means to exist as a human being making decisions and living in the now is more important than the biblical milieu itself.

Bultmann is concerned that the kerygma not be demythologized; thus, he is critical of previous methods. There is always the possibility of a given historical text possessing an openness to the future as the interpreter lives in the moment of decision. He believes that Jesus encounters the contemporary person in the kerygma just as Paul himself was confronted, and this challenge forces one into a decision. It is not possible for one to go behind the kerygma according to Bultmann. He believes that the attempt to do so is attempting to find "Jesus Christ according to the flesh."

Bultmann was a master preacher; he knew the importance of presenting the sermon in such a manner that the recipient was compelled to make a decision. He attempts to preach in such a manner that the person will be moved to accept the kingdom of God and live with a determination to renounce self-sufficiency and concern for the future. His sermons encourage one to live life with an inner detachment from the seductions and cares of the world. He stresses that one must live in the present realizing that his future is ultimately in God's hands and that he is able to live victoriously in the present. Many of Bultmann's sermons are from the Gospels, and they are practical sermons aimed to enable the listener to understand the importance of making decisions which will lead to the living of life characterized by authenticity. The culture in which Christians find themselves is very seductive with promises of fame and fortune, but only God and finding His will for one's life can bring true fulfillment. It is imperative that the person's will be totally surrendered to God. There needs to be an inner detachment in one's life as he is not to be overly concerned about his exterior circumstances. The past or the future is not as significant as the present, and if one decides for such living, living in the present and making authentic decisions, he can live fully actualized and be characterized by peace. The promise is that as one responds to the Gospel, opening himself up to the claims of deliverance, he no longer will live life "according to the flesh."

As a scientific New Testament scholar, Bultmann is concerned about how people in the culture of his times view the Christian faith vis-à-vis science. Especially from the late nineteenth century and during the years leading up to World War II, people in Germany viewed science as a means to make this life better and also to explain many of the mysteries of life. To Bultmann, it is not necessary to force a worldview upon someone which may be contradictory and unnecessary. It is not worth seeing a person reject the Gospel because of a worldview which is certainly unscientific and illogical. Bultmann believes that it is possible to peel away that which obscures and even offends the one who is searching for the truth. To Bultmann, the method which he proposes avoids the pitfalls of classic liberalism and a more fundamentalist manner of interpretation.

Certainly there have been some who have disagreed with Bultmann's procedures and conclusions. Some have even argued that the result of his method is that the Gospel message has been obliterated. Bultmann never seems to have been overly concerned by the heated criticism which he received. Indeed he would be subjected to criticism during his lifetime and even posthumously. However, he had confidence in his method and his conclusions, and his work is considered by many to be ground breaking and initiatory of a new method in New Testament interpretation. He continued to hold in high regard the preaching of the Church as such preaching witnessed to the Christ event. Bultmann believes that it is not necessary to find "Christ after the flesh," since such an attempt is unwarranted and impossible. The cross and the resurrection must be interpreted according to *Daseinsanalyse*. The cross becomes a reality in the life of the Christian; thus, he realizes his co-crucifixion with Christ which enables the person to be a new creation in Christ and daily realizes his personal sanctification during his spiritual journey.

Bultmann believes that the interpreter must fully enter into the interpretation of the text. A non-participatory, strictly historico-grammatical analysis is not sufficient. The interpreter's personal experience is also significant in explicating a given passage of Scripture.

As a preacher of the Word, Bultmann encourages those to whom he preached to abandon every human security, to look to God and to realize the empowerment which is found in Jesus Christ. There is not only a consistency in his hermeneutical and exegetical methodology, but as one reads through his sermons, there is a remarkable consistency in the manner in which he delivered his messages. Always they are practical, but yet scholarly; they meet the person where he is in his life, encouraging him along the way of his spiritual adventure.

C. Bonhoeffer

Bonhoeffer is not known for hermeneutical and exegetical skills, though he was a competent interpreter of Scripture. He appears as one who was concerned about taking Jesus' message and applying it to everyday, practical concerns. He emphasizes the demands of the Gospel on the person who follows Christ and not with questions of demythologization. His message was literally that there is a cost for following the way of Christ. Some fault him for becoming so overly involved in the political life of his times, arguing that as a clergyman he should not have become entangled with politics but merely should have continued with his ministry as a clergyman ministering solely within the confines of the Church. Perhaps he would have had more time for ministry, for fifteen years after finishing his academic work, approximately two of those years he spent in prison, he was involved in ministry in a variety of roles. Indeed, his time was short for his life's calling. One has the impression that he believed that his first and highest calling was that of a pastor. His ministry of preaching and teaching forced him back into exegetical studies as he did not have the opportunity to hold a particular chair of theology and write and minister from such a position. But one is amazed at how remarkably well he did with the time allotted to him as well as in consideration of his resources and circumstances in which he found himself.

Bonhoeffer's major field of study was that of systematic theology, though one has the impression that he considered himself primarily a biblical scholar. He believed that both the Old and New Testaments contained the Word of God. However, it is obvious that he did not hold to a verbal view of inspiration. Though he wrote some works on the Old Testament, most would not view these treatises as his best work. For example, he was convinced that the Old Testament supported a christological interpretation. In particular, his Bible study which was entitled, "King David," contains many christological themes. Bonhoeffer understands that God speaks in both the Old and New Testaments, and one cannot exclude one from the other. However, he is not a literalist. For example, he believes that the early chapters of the book of Genesis are legend and are not to be taken literally.

Bonhoeffer loved the Old Testament and this affection would grow and become even more apparent during the time of his imprisonment. Some scholars, Woelfel for example, believe that the Old Testament dominated his thinking during the imprisonment years. During his imprisonment, his references pertaining to the Old Testament increases. He had studied some Hebrew while still a teenager, though there is no indication that he continued to study the language in a rigorous manner. He apparently did not view himself as an Old Testament scholar. For example, in defense of his study on Ezra and Nehemia, he claims that the work is more sermonic in nature rather than an academic treatise.

His letter of April 30, 1944, contains a reference to his perception that there is a movement toward a religionless time. He laments what he believes to be a deficiency in reading the New Testament with reference to the Old Testament. This emphasis of attempting to seek appropriate Old Testament passages to support various issues such as even baptism occupies his thinking until the end of his life. He preached on April 5, 1945, four days before his execution, from Isaiah 53:5. He believes that Christ fulfilled this particular passage. Bonhoeffer is not a detailed, exegetical preacher when studying and expounding on the Old Tetament. Again, one is impressed with the situation in which he found himself which setting was somewhat reversed compared to Bultmann. Bonhoeffer's situation in life especially before his time of imprisonment, followed the sequence of preaching and teaching leading him to conduct more exegetical work.

Bonhoeffer is more comfortable interpreting an Old Testament text theologically rather than performing exacting exegesis. An existentialist interpretation is seen in his Old Testament work, *Creation and Fall*. However, his christological interpretation is obvious in the work. His high regard for Scripture is evident as one reads through his exposition of the first three chapter of Genesis. Bonhoeffer refers to hearing God in the middle, that is, in our present situation. The Bible, according to Bonhoeffer, addresses humankind in the middle, and because of this offers hope with difficulties. Though Bonhoeffer is somewhat existentialist in his method of interpretation, one also senses a pietistic element in his thought, and this emphasis manifests itself in his christological interpretation of the first few chapters of the book of Genesis. There is an obvious existentialist interpretation in this work as he describes the theme of solitariness. As Christ experienced being alone, so in a sense every human being understands what to be alone means. Adam's story is about each one of us. We are alone but waiting for completion, which we find in the presence of another. Bonhoeffer does not offer any solution to the issue of theodicy, in particular the origin of evil and Genesis 3. He does state that Adam's sin is inexcusable; therefore, he is responsible, and Bonhoeffer insinuates that Adam made an inauthentic choice. The question, "Did God say?" is the godless question which is still before the individual today. For the question poses to the individual that perhaps God is not good and that the individual himself can find ultimate meaning in life. Again, we find Bonhoeffer's existentialist interpretation in this particular scenario.

Bonhoeffer's best-known work is that pertaining to the New Testament—*Nachfolge* or *The Cost of Discipleship*. Taking about four years to complete the work, he began with an outline in 1932 and completed the work in 1936, *The Cost of Discipleship* is almost synonymous with his name. It is not clear if his two former professors, Adolph Schlatter and Adolph Deissman, exercised much influence upon the writing of this work. Bethge believes that the themes found in *The Cost of Discipleship* proceeded from Bonhoeffer's personal study. This work is uniquely Bonhoeffer's, that is, he does not quote other theologians, but he gives what he believes to be an exposition of the Sermon on the Mount. To explore the text according to the methodology of critical scholarship is not the aim of Bonhoffer in *The Cost of Discipleship*. He is simply expressing what he believes it means to be a true follower of Jesus Christ. How should a person think and live who takes the call seriously to follow Christ today? This is his main theme in the work. Bethge correctly states that earthly community is at the heart of the work.

Bonhoeffer believes that, "only the believer is obedient, and only those who are obedient believe." With this statement, he is affirming Luther's belief in *sola fides* and *sola gratia*, with the added emphasis of their applicability to the believer and his life here on earth. He writes against not only individualism but in particular the concept of cheap grace, or the view that one can live as he wants even though he supposedly is in a relationship with Christ. He believes that cheap grace had characterized the Church in Germany for a long period of time.

Holding correct doctrine is not enough for the Christian; there must be a living out of that which the Christian understands. Bonhoeffer appears as an apostle of grace—he wants to establish clearly the fact that grace was and is costly. Grace is rooted in the incarnation and with the ultimate death of the Son. This grace is offered, but it will cost the Christian dearly also. Perhaps his dedication will not cost one his life, but certainly his life's ambitions, and this is especially difficult for those who are self-centered. At this point in his career, Bonhoeffer has a tendency to place the world and the Church at odds with one another; this emphasis will change especially during his time of imprisonment. But this change is characteristic of Bonhoeffer. Both Barth and Bethge state, somewhat humorously, that Bonhoeffer was always changing the venue of his theological interests and discussions.

Bonhoeffer's interest in the issue of ethics channeled into his discussion of the Sermon on the Mount, which he understands to be God's will for people today. He does not interpret the Sermon on the Mount as literal laws which are to be enforced, but what is possible for the Christian. He does believe that its demands are to be obeyed, but not in a slavish manner, but out of a spirit of love and obedience to Christ. The living out of the message of the Sermon of the Mount is the best defense against the false doctrine of cheap grace Bonhoeffer believes. He also believed that it was a good counter argument against the interpretation of the Sermon of the Mount as proposed by Bishop Ludwig Müller.

Having been taught higher critical methodologies at Tübingen and Berlin, Bonhoeffer was immersed in these theories. He does not hold to a verbal theory of the inspiration of the Scriptures. He does believe that the words of Scripture are fallible, but the Holy Spirit is still able to witness to the presence of Christ as contained therein. His exegesis is more theological rather than textual. Again, his christological interpretation is seen throughout his exposition of the Sermon on the Mount. He is not concerned with questions of philology, archaeology or giving the *Siz im*

Leben of the text. There is a measure of existentialist interpretation with the work *The Cost of Discipleship* in that Bonhoeffer presents the material in such a fashion that the reader must decide what he will do with the message which is presented. Deciding to apply the message of the Sermon on the Mount is the practical proof that one has understood the message! He even states that the purpose for Jesus' message is that people might be brought to the point of decision.

He places a heavy emphasis upon the character of the disciple, and it appears that Bonhoeffer is saying that a true disciple is one who is authentic. They are unlike those who are not disciples. Constantly they keep before them the goal of being a kingdom-bound pilgrim. He likens the German Christians to the masses, who have no ultimate loyalty to Christ, but are merely following a humanly contrived ideology. At times there appears to be some inconsistencies in Bonhoeffer's words and actions. Though he discusses Matthew 5:38-42 and speaks against revenge, he himself was involved in a plot against Hitler. It appears that portions of the Sermon on the Mount he does not interpret in an absolute manner, but he is interpreting the passage existentially, and the interpreter ultimately must decide on the specifics of the application.

Bonhoeffer approached the Scriptures in a meditative manner. Certainly he was familiar with the exegetical arguments, but his hermeneutical position used the historical critical method only minimally. Many of his writings completely lack any historical critical methodology, though he does express a positive attitude toward the method. He believes that Christ continues to confront one in the Scriptures. An interpreter of Bonhoeffer, Woelfel, believes that he was moving away from any particular system. He also suggests that Bonhoeffer held some Scripture to be more authoritative than others. Bonhoeffer wanted to write a book on the subject of hermeneutics, but he never did. Such a work would have been a most welcomed edition as it would have given more insight into his methodology.

He was not above accusing others of eisegesis. In his 1935 lecture entitled, "The Presentation of New Testament Texts," he thoroughly criticizes those who support Nazism. He claims that they twist the Scriptures and interpret them for their own purposes. He did not support any attempt to use the Scriptures without regard to its context, proper interpretation and application. He speaks harshly against the German Christians who claim the need for relevance of the Christian message. To Bonhoeffer, if one will read the Scriptures sincerely and opening, he will find Christ. Bonhoeffer also manifests a particular pietism in that he states his belief that Christ speaks through the Holy Spirit.

Bonhoeffer writes of the significance of exegesis in his "The Presentation of New Testament Texts." He writes of the exegesis of the Word moving from the present to the Scripture. This process can lead one into an awareness of the eternal. The exegete interprets Scripture according to his present personal stance and position. He does speak about the "presence of Christ" in the process of interpretation. Again, his christological interpretation is obvious. He even states that it is not the application of the sermon which is most importance, but that the Holy Spirit has been present in the sermon. For it is the Spirit which is able to create the present or the *concretissimum.* Some would say that Bonhoeffer's writings lack exegetical rigor and that he places too much of an emphasis upon pneumatology. He does not concern himself with any particular Scripture being more valid than another, rather, he believes that all witness to Christ. Interestingly, he does not rule out the possibility of an allegorical interpretation of Scripture. He strongly supports the study of Scripture in the Hebrew and Greek languages. His somewhat subjective method is seen in the belief that silence before the Word is needed. He does not give a methodology for achieving the results from this silence, nevertheless, he is convinced of its value. Bonhoeffer believes that Christ is found where Word and Sacrament occur.

Bonhoeffer's writings during the period of his imprisonment reflect new concerns and directions in his theological thinking. These new themes are somewhat mysterious, and some believe that they simply mirror the difficult circumstances in which he found himself toward the end of his life. Marle refers to Bonhoeffer's thinking during this period as "disturbing." Bethge also states that many of the terms which he uses are not fully understood. Whatever one's interpretation, it is apparent that Bonhoeffer has some new thoughts on subjects such as the Church, religion and the world.

More than a little after a year of his imprisonment, we find the tone of his letters takes a dramatic change. Up until this period, his letters had been somewhat positive. He even remarks, for example, in his April 11, 1944 letter, that he believes God has directed his life and that he does not regret his decision of 1939 to return again to Germany, even though it would have been possible for him to stay in New York City. He writes that he believes God has directed the events of his life up to this point, and that he can trust the providence of God. But it is his April 30, 1944 letter which contains controversial material. Bethge believes that this material does not represent his mature thought or a new line of thought. But he also argues that it is more than a random attempt to express his thinking.

Essentially, Bonhoeffer does not believe that the word "religion" is an apt one to describe the experience one can have with the living God and other human beings. The word is too abstract for him, and does not allow the person to see how it is possible to live out one's faith. Likewise, he is against any concept of individualism, for to Bonhoeffer the Church centers upon the idea of community. His interest in social issues also made him feel somewhat uncomfortable with the tendency of some to constantly be concerned about their inner subject experiences of grace. To Bonhoeffer the concern for *koinonia* and seeing that the Gospel would impact the social ills of his day are more important than perpetually wondering about the condition of one's soul, though of course, he did not ignore this subject. For Bonhoeffer, the decisive issue is that the Gospel be truly preached in a practical manner, that is, when the recipient hears the message, there will be no confusion in his mind of what the Gospel demands of him in his present situation. The Gospel transfers itself into the actual presence of humankind. This is not merely a message of religion, which actually to Bonhoeffer is not a positive word, but is a message of justification and places demands on the individual, who must indeed follow Christ and renounce all claims to self.

Bonhoeffer believes that one's faith in Christ involves the totality of his being. He speaks of a significant danger of religion is that it can be understood as partial; thus, the result could be that the person is deceived into thinking he is secure in his faith when the fact is that he has only given a portion of himself and his aspirations to God. Bonhoeffer believes that a life which is truly characterized by faith will overwhelm all desires to keep something back from total dedication to Christ. However, this commitment is no excuse for viewing God as the One who can rescue man; thus, relegating God to a human level of being one who does the Christian's errands.

Religion also connotes the idea of favoritism to Bonhoeffer, and certainly this is a perceived quality of Christianity from which Bonhoeffer revolted. This spirit of favoritism in religion he sees as divisive and thwarting to the unity which must characterize the Body of Christ. Bonhoeffer became intimately familiar with the concept of favoritism in America when he experienced the divisive nature of racism during his time in New York City. To Bonhoeffer, being a follower of Christ is the antithesis of any idea of possessing a favored position; the pilgrim who takes up his cross daily will experience rejection at times and difficulties in the spiritual journey of continuing to be a disciple of Christ.

Actually to Bonhoeffer, religion is characterized by dispensability, that is, religion as a concept is ephemeral—somewhat like an antique from the past with no relevance to contemporary humans and their issues in life. The call of Jesus to total surrender is essentially something different than simply what is implied by the generic term religion. The total surrender to the life of which Jesus speaks has a quality of the eternal inherent within it. All remnants of the flesh and self are obliterated, and the pilgrim is characterized by purity of motive as much as is possible in this earthly life.

Bonhoeffer according to Bethge was concerned about the concreteness of revelation. Christology is certainly a key theme in Bonhoeffer's thought and writings. Toward the end of his life he emphasizes more the lordship of Christ over the realm of the world. Bonhoeffer was not advocating atheism, an acceptance of the profane at the expense of the sacred, or an acquisition of a worldly ethos over the sovereignty of Christ. Rather, he sees the world as redeemable and as a sphere where the grace of God and ultimate redemption can reach and redeem.

His thought is a reminder that God is obviously concerned about the world and that as the Christian lives in and encounters those who are dominated by this sphere of influence, he must minister with the awareness and grace of God upon his thinking and actions. The Gospel and its claims must be brought into this arena as well. The Church has a tendency to isolate herself from the world, but Bonhoeffer is advocating that the Christian must be concerned with his responsibility in this realm as well. The preaching of the Gospel, backed up with a life of righteousness, has the authority of Christ supporting and buttressing the person who is actively involved in presenting Christ and the Gospel in the world. Certainly Bonhoeffer poses the burning question for the twenty-first century person of the relationship of one's individual faith to the world at large.

With the use of the term, *Diesseitigkeit*, this worldliness, he says that he is alluding to the person living fully in the world—living wholeheartedly and doing his best, even though he is ultimately a stranger in such a setting. He believes that by living in such a manner, one is completely dependent upon God and never independent. The Christian will need even more of God's grace when living with such a mindset. In man's daily struggle, in the context of penultimate matters, the grace of God in Christ is present. Jesus Christ is not only sovereign over the Church, according to Bonhoeffer, but He is also the Lord over the world. Ultimately the latter does obeisance to Him. If this is the case, then the Christian does not need to view the world as something threatening in whose presence he must constantly be fearful and expectant of some sinister plot against his person and faith.

D. Bultmann and Bonhoeffer: Summary

Both Bultmann and Bonhoeffer were concerned about communicating the Gospel effectively to their generation. For Bultmann the process began with exegesis and then proceeded to homiletics. For Bonhoeffer, the process was reversed in that his situation in life was such that his preaching led him to exegesis of the text.

Born in Wiefelstede on August 20, 1984, Bultmann lived until July 30, 1976. His career centered primarily in Marburg, Germany. Bultmann grew up in the home of a pastor of the German Evangelical Church, and it seems that Bultmann throughout his life viewed himself as a servant of the Church. His maternal grandfather and paternal great-grandfather had also been Lutheran pastors. From childhood he understood ministry from the perspective of one who was familiar with the Church. In the 1950s, he did considerable lecturing at various American universities. Bultmann appears to have been more comfortable around people and gregarious than was Bonhoeffer. When convinced that his conclusions were correct, it was highly improbable that he would change his mind and accept the alternate argument. The same can be said of Bonhoeffer.

Conversely, while Bonhoeffer was not raised in a secular home, religion and church attendance were not emphasized. His family apparently had not envisioned that he would study theology and be a pastor. Bonhoeffer was born on February 4, 1906, in Breslau (now Wroclaw, Poland), and he died on April 9, 1945, in the Flossenbürg camp. He enjoyed traveling and especially appreciated his time in the United States.

Bultmann appears as more intellectually orientated and concerned with the interpretation of Scripture for theologians and pastors as well as for the lay people. He is especially interested in communicating the Gospel to the contemporary person in such a manner that it is understandable and acceptable. Bultmann is a scientific theologian, and his thought conveys his interest in metaphysical issues as well as logic and analyses. He desires that people truly hear the Gospel and not something which is a substitute or that which can obscure the essence of the true message.

Through his method, he enabled especially those who studied theology academically to see the importance of approaching the Scriptures by means of the medium of an existentialist method of interpretation. An historical-grammatical approach is not sufficient to Bultmann as this method essentially does not address the issue of a personal decision on the part of the interpreter and subsequently the recipient of the message, i.e., those who hear the message preached. He emphasizes that the human being must decide for authenticity. He cannot live either in denial of the ultimate issues or seek after that which is ephemeral and lacking of eternal value. Bultmann is more interested in eschatological themes rather than the historical Jesus. He believed that people are tempted to follow the deductions of culture and somehow believe that what is offered in this realm is able to meet their essential needs. Over against this view, Bultmann advocates that God as revealed in the New Testament stands at odds with such a selfish and naïve worldview.

Though he was scholarly and recognized as a theologian who possessed great capacity for academic work by his mentors and other theologians, Bonhoeffer perhaps by virtue of the lifestyle he was forced to live after he finished his academic credentialing, did not produced works on the same academic level as Bultmann. *The Cost of Discipleship*, his best-known work, is more expositional in character. Bonhoeffer's life situation which consisted of teaching, leading seminarians and involvement in ecclesiastical matters, forced him back into the biblical text, whereas for Bultmann, his academic studies found a welcomed expression for him in the many sermons which he gave throughout his life. Bonhoeffer's theology is somewhat fragmentary as he apparently had a variety of interests. But the overarching theme of Christology was a lifelong concern for him.

There is something which is appealing about Bultmann's methodology with its emphasis that the questions about God and about the human being are essentially the same. The significant influence from existentialism is very obvious with his hermeneutical procedures. Being overly concerned about the future and attempting to manipulate events in one's life to assure a secure future to Bultmann is not to be a person whose life exhibits that he has been justified by faith. Any attempt to seek out something in place of God or to attempt to control one's existence, Bultmann believes is sin which results in subsequent existential estrangement. God's judgment is upon the one who attempts to live as if he is self-sufficient and master of his future. The person, who casts himself upon God in the present, making authentic decisions, can be assured of receiving a benediction of blessing from God. Theology is cold and dry without the existentialist method of interpretation.

Bultmann uses the analogy of friendship. One can study in an academic way what friendship is, but it is only when one experiences the concept in a personal manner that the person understands fully what the term is. Perhaps the layperson is not in need of a more sophisticated approach to the study of the Scriptures as is the theologian since the latter is more of a specialist and must be able to interpret as deeply and concisely as possible. Such a method allows the interpreter to move away from a cold, merely objective interpretation to a lively, personal and interactive interpretation of the Scriptures. One cannot approach the study of God by means of merely attempting to make him an object as if He is an object of our reason. God's Word and its interpretation occur in the eschatological moment. But of course, the interpreter must still make an authentic decision upon the insights which he has gained.

Bonhoeffer is interested in maintaining that the revelation of Jesus Christ is concrete, that is, this revelation is not merely a theological concept but is tangible and is best portrayed in the community of believers living out their faith purposefully, lovingly and courageously. There must be risk in the Christian's life if the Gospel is to be concrete and practical. One should obviously be aware of the various interpretations of a particular text, but it is the living out of the demands of the message by a life of obedience that is essential. He eventually came to believe that the Christian must embrace the world, of course not allowing his affections to be controlled by the ethos of the world, but to realize that it too is redeemable and is worthy of the attention of the Christian. After all, Jesus Christ is Lord both over the Church and the world.

There has been an attempt to display the historical relationship between Bultmann and Bonhoeffer. While some minimize the interplay between the two, there is a significant connection between Bultmann and Bonhoeffer.

We have seen that Bultmann is actually a very scientific theologian who has a strong Lutheran sentiment in that he endeavors to resurrect the doctrine of *sola fides*. In contrast Bonhoeffer lacks the strong unity and cohesiveness that Bultmann possesses. However, he too is greatly indebted to Luther.

Both Bultmann and Bonhoeffer are intensely concerned with the communication of the Gospel to modern humanity; thus, Bultmann believes demythologizing would aid the contemporary person. Likewise, Bonhoeffer believes that "dereligionizing" is the method to be imposed. Bultmann advoctes the historico-critico method, whereas Bonhoeffer finds such a procedure somewhat cumbersome. Bonhoeffer actually believes that Bultmann's method is too "religious" since it does not alleviate the problem of introspection and individualism. One difference is Bonhoeffer operates within a Hegelian system whereas Bultmann accepts a Kantian structure.

Bonhoeffer stresses a christological theme in the Old Testament whereas Bultmann feels uncomfortable with the Old Testament. Both Bultmann and Bonhoeffer see the indispensability of the Christ event in the New Testament.

Both Bultmann and Bonhoeffer believe that the message preached is God's Word. Bonhoeffer's concept of preaching, however, is not limited to just the *ekklesia*, but the message must be proclaimed to the world.

Bonhoeffer is not concened with making the Scripture relevant; there are no mythological elements which need to be peeled away before the message can be proclaimed. Bonhoeffer stresses that the preacher must only proclaim the Word.

Though Bultmann was born twenty-two, the younger of the two died thirty-one years before the elder. However, their lives have some similarities and intersections. Both were members of a students' association, the Hedgehogs (*Igel*); Bultmann joined in 1905 while Bonhoeffer in 1923. Both were impressed with the teachings of Heitmüller. The two were concerned that the New Testament be interpreted to enable the modern person to understand the true message.[1] Like Bonhoeffer, Bultmann reacted to the liberalism of the late nineteenth and early twentieth centuries. He states:

> The subject of theology is *God*, and the chief charge to be brought against liberal theology is that it has dealt not with God but with man. God represents the radical negation and sublimation of man. Theology whose subject is God can therefore have as its content only the 'word of the cross' (λογοσ του σταυρου). But that word is a 'stumbling block' (σκανδαλοτσ) to men. Hence the charge against liberal theology is that it has sought to remove this stumbling-block or to minimize it.[2]

Bonhoeffer wrote two works which qualified him for a professorship in a German university. His doctoral dissertation was *Sanctorum Communio*, which was written under the direction of Reinhold Seeberg. The dissertation pertains primarily to ecclesiology and the work attempts to unite sociology with a theology of revelation. His Habilitation, *Act and Being*, was accepted on July 18, 1930. Bultmann also wrote two works which qualified him as a university professor. His doctoral dissertation was entitled: *The Style of Pauline Preaching and the Cynic-Stoic Diatribe*, and his Habilitation was *The Exegesis of Theodore of Mopsuestia*.

---

[1] Bethge, *Dietrich Bonhoeffer: A Biography*, 879. Bethge claims that Bultmann and Bonhoeffer are similar in that both admit they are driven to the beginnings of their understanding. They formulated their views independently of one another, yet they overlap in that Bonhoeffer's inquiry revolves around hermenetuics and Bultmann's on the basis of philology and philosophical presuppositions.
[2] Rudolf Bultmann, "Liberal Theology and the Latest Theological Movement," in *Faith and Understanding,* ed., Robert W. Funk, trans. Louise Pettibone Smith (New York: Harper and Row Publishers, 1969), 29.

Interestingly, though Bonhoeffer's academic credentials are techinically in systematic theology, he is perceived more as a New Testament scholar, and while Bultmann's two qualifying works are in New Testament, he is seen by many as a systematic theologian.

Like Bonhoeffer, Bultmann was a strong opponent of the Nazis. Along with several members of the theological faculty of Marburg, he argued that the decision of the General Synod to exclude those of non-Aryan descent was unacceptable. Bultmann held that Jewish and Gentile Christians both were equally fitted for the office in the Church. Bultmann wrote critically of Nazism in *The Task of Theology in the Present Situation* (1933), and *The Meaning of Christian Faith in Creation* (1936).[3] However, Bultmann repeatedly stated that he was not a politician and he kept his involvement at a minimum, whereas in Bonhoeffer's brief life, much of his time and ministry were involved in political matters.

Both Bultmann and Bonhoeffer held Martin Luther and his understanding of Scripture in high esteem. Bultmann especially is fond of the Reformers; he also quotes Philip Melanchthon's well-known saying, '*christum cognoscere id est beneficia eius cognoscere*'[4] Bonhoeffer would cite Luther's famous dictum, *simul justus et peccator*. Bonhoeffer knew this saying was open to abuse; thus, he distinguished between "cheap grace," or the idea that there are not many demands upon the Christian, and "costly grace," which emphasizes the demands of discipleship and obedience.

Certainly, there were many areas theologically in which Bultmann and Bonhoeffer were not in agreement. But there appears to have been a mutual respect. Years after the death of Bonhoeffer, Bultmann quoted his younger colleague's words 'God is the beyond in the midst of our life' or 'The transcendent is not the infinitely remote but the nearest at hand'.[5]

---

[3]Ian Henderson, *Rudolf Bultmann* (Richmond: John Knox Press, 1967), 3. Cf. Bethge, *Dietrich Bonhoeffer* (Minneapolis: Fortress Press, 2000), 318-19. Bethge refers to the "Marburg expert opinion" in which various members of the Theological Faculty opposed the Aryan clause.

[4] Rudolf Bultmann, "Die Frage der dialektischen Theologie," *Zwischen den Zeiten*, 4 (1926): 40-56. Melanchthon's work, *Loci Communes,* appeared in 1521. This Latin work is considered to be the first theological treatise of the Reformation which began in Wittenberg. The work went through many editions during the time of Melanchthon, and it established him as the theologian of the Lutheran movement. Cf. Bethge, *Dietrich Bonhoeffer: A Biography* Minneapolis: Fortress Press, 2000), 70, 86. Bethge alludes to the high regard Bonhoeffer had for both Luther and Melanchthon.

[5] Rudolf Bultmann, "Der Gottesgedanke und der moderne Mensch." *Zeitschrift für Theologie und Kirche*, 60 (1963), 335-48.

Bultmann and Bonhoeffer both exerted a most significant influence upon the theological thinking of their times. The impact of these two theologians continues.

SELECTED BIBLIOGRAPHY

Primary Sources

Bonhoeffer, Dietrich. *Act and Being.* Translated by Bernard Noble. New York: Harper and Row Publishers, 1961.
—. *Christ the Center.* Translated by John Bowden. New York: Harper and Row Publishers, 1966.
—. *The Communion of Saints.* Translated by William Collins and Sons. New York: Harper and Row Publishers, 1960.
—. *The Cost of Discipleship.* Translated by R. H. Fuller. New York: Simon & Schuster, 1995.
—. *Creation and Fall.* Translated by John C. Fletcher. New York: Macmillan Publishing Co., 1978.
—. *Ethics.* Edited by Eberhard Bethge. Translated by Neville H. Smith. New York: Macmillan Publishing Co., 1978.
—. *Letters and Papers from Prison.* Edited by Eberhard Bethge. New York: Macmillan Publishing Co., 1978.
—. *Life Together.* Translated by John W. Doberstein. San Francisco: Harper and Row Publishers, 2003.
—. *No Rusty Swords.* Edited by E. H. Robertson. New York: William Collins Sons & Co., 1977.
—. *Psalms: The Prayer Book of the Bible.* Translated by James Burtness. Minneapolis: Augsburg Publishing House, 1970.
—. *True Patriotism.* Translated by E. H. Robertson and John Bowden. New York: Harper and Row Publishers, 1973.
—. *The Way to Freedom.* Edited by E. H. Robertson. Translated by E. H. Robertson and John Bowden. New York: Harper and Row Publishers, 1977.
Bultmann, Rudolf. "Bultmann Replies to His Critics," in *Kerygma and Myth.* Edited by Hans Werner Bartsch. New York: Harper and Row Publishers, 1961.
—. "The Concept of the Word of God in the New Testament," in *Faith and Understanding.* Edited by Robert W. Funk. Translated by Louise Pettibone Smith. New York: Harper and Row Publishers, 1966.
—. *Die Geschichte der synoptischen Tradition.* Göttingen: Vandenhoeck & Ruprecht, 1921.

—. *Essays Philosophical and Theological.* Translated by James C. Grieg. New York: The Macmillan Co., 1955.

—. *Existence and Faith.* Translated by Schubert Ogden. London: Hodder and Stoughton, 1960.

—. "The Gospel of Revelation in the New Testament," in *Existence and Faith.* New York: The World Publishing Co., 1963.

—. "The Historicity of Man and Faith," in *Existence and Faith.* Edited and introduced by Schubert Ogden. New York: The World Publishing Co., 1964.

—. *History and Eschatology.* New York: Harper and Row Publishers, 1962.

—. "Does God Speak to Us through the Bible?" in *Existence and Faith.* New York: The World Publishing Co., 1963.

—. "Is Exegesis without Presuppositions Possible?" in *Existence and Faith.* New York: The World Publishing Co., 1963.

—. *Jesus and the Word.* Translated by Louise Pettibone Smith and Erminie Huntress Lantero. New York: Charles Scribner's Sons, 1958.

—. *Jesus Christ and Mythology.* New York: Charles Scribners's Sons, 1958.

—. "New Testament and Mythology," in *Kerygma and Myth,* ed. H. W. Bartsch, Translasted by R. H. Fuller. New York: Harper and Row Publishers, 1961.

—. "The Problem of Hermeneutics," in *Rudolf Bultmann: Interpreting the Faith for the Modern Era.* San Francisco: Collins Publishers, 1987.

—. "The Significance of the Historical Jesus for the Theology of Paul," in *Faith and Existence.* Edited by Robert W. Funk. Translated by Louise Pettibone Smith. New York: Harper and Row Publishers, 1966.

—. "The Significance of the Old Testament for the Christian Faith." in *The Old Testament and Christian Faith: Essays by Rudolf Bultmann and Others.* Edited and translated by B. W. Anderson. New York: Harper and Row Publishers, 1963.

—. *Theology of the New Testament.* Vol. 1. Translated by Kendrick Grobel. New York: Charles Scribner's Sons, 1951.

—. *This World and the Beyond: Marburg Sermons.* Translated by Harold Knight. New York: Charles Scribner's Sons, 1960.

Secondary Sources

Books

Ashcraft, Morris. *Rudolf Bultmann.* Peabody, NA: Hendrickson Publishers, 1991.
Barrett, William. *What is Existentialism?* New York: Grove Press, 1964.
Bethge, Eberhard. *Dietrich Bonhoeffer: A Biography.* Minneapolis: Fortress Press, 2000.
Bornhamm, Günther. "The Theology of Rudolf Bultmann," in *The Theology of Rudolf Bultmann.* Edited by C. W. Kegley. New York: Harper and Row Publishers, 1966
Braaten, Carl E. "A Critical Introduction," in *Kerygma and History.* Editors and Translators, Carl E. Braaten and Roy A. Harrisville,. Nashville: Abingdon Press, 1962.
Carson, D. A., Douglas J. Moo, and Leon Morris. *An Introduction to the New Testament.* Grand Rapids: Zondervan Publishing House, 1992.
Conn, Harvey. *Contemporary World Theology.* Phillipsburg, NJ: P & R Publishing Co., 1974.
Corley, Bruce and Steve Lemke, Editors. *Biblical Hermeneutics: A Comprhensive Guide to Interpreting Scripture.* Nashville: Broadman and Holman, 1996.
De Gruchy, John. *Introduction to Dietrich Bonhoeffer: Witness to Jesus Christ.* Minneapolis: Fortress Press, 1988.
Dumas, Andre. *Dietrich Bonhoeffer: Theologian of Reality.* Translated by Robert McAfee Brown. New York: Macmillan Co., 1968.
Erickson, Millard J. *Christian Theology.* Grand Rapids: Baker Book House, 1985.
Evang, Martin. *Rudolf Bultmann in seiner Frühzeit.* Tübingen: J.C.B. Mohr, Paul Siebeck, 1988.
Feil, Ernst. *The Theology of Dietrich Bonhoeffer.* Philadelphia: Fortress Press, 1985.
Frame, John. *Apologetics to Glory of God.* Phillipsburg, NJ: P & R Publishing Co., 1994.
—. *The Doctrine of the Knowledge of God.* Phillipsburg, NJ: P & R Publishing Co., 1987.
Funk, Robert. *Language, Hermeneutic, and the Word of God.* New York: Harper and Row Publishers, 1966.
Geisler, Norman. *Inerrancy.* Grand Rapids: Zondervan Publishing Co., 1980.
Godsey, John. *The Theology of Dietrich Bonhoeffer.* Philadelphia: Westminster Press, 1958.

Good, Edwin M. "The Meaning of Demythologization," in *The Theology of Rudol Bultmann.* Edited by C. W. Kegley. New York: Harper and Row Publishers, 1966.
Greidanus, Sidney. *The Modern Preacher and the Ancient Text.* Grand Rapids: William B. Eerdmans Publishing Co., 1996.
Haynes, Steve. *The Bonhoeffer Phenomenon.* Minneapolis: Augsburg Fortress Publishers, 2004.
Harrelson, Walter. "Bonhoeffer and the Bible," in *The Place of Bonhoeffer.* Edited by Martin Marty. New York: Association Press, 1964.
Heidegger, Martin. "The Wayn Back into a Ground of Metaphysics," in *Existentialism form Dostoevsky to Sartre.* Edited by Walter Kaufmann. New York: The World Publishing Co., 1956.
Henry, Carl F. H. *Frontiers in Modern Theology.* Chicago: Moody Press, 1964.
Johnson, Roger A. *Introduction to Rudolf Bultmann: Interpreting Faith for the Modern Era.* Minneapolis: Fortress Press, 1991.
—. *The Origins of Demythologization.* Leiden: E. J. Brill, 1974.
Kaiser, Walter. *Toward an Exegetical Theology.* Grand Rapids: Baker Book House, 1985.
Kuske, Martin. *The Old Testament as the Book of Christ.* Philadelphia: Westminster Press, 1976.
Ladd, George Elden. *A Theology of the New Testament.* Grand Rapids: William B. Eerdmans Publishing Co., 1993.
Lange, Frits. *Waiting for the Word.* Grand Rapids: Eerdmans Publishing Company, 1995.
Macquarrie, John. *An Existentialist Theolgy.* New York: Harper and Row Publishers 1963.
—. "Philosophy and Theology in Bultmann's Thought," in *The Theology of Rudolf Bultmann.* Edited by Charles W. Kegley. New York: Harper and Row Publishers, 1966
—. *Principles of Christian Theology.* New York: Charles Scribner's Sons, 1977.
Malet, Andre. *The Thought of Rudolf Bultmann.* Translated by Richard Stracham. New York: Doubleday & Co., 1971.
Marle, Rene. *Bultmann ande Christian Faith.* New York: Newman Press, 1968.
Miller, Ed., and Stanley J. Grenz. *Introduction to Contemporary Theologies.* Minneapolis: Fortress Press, 1998.
Oden, Thomas C. *Radical Obedience.* Philadelphia: Westminster Press, 1964.

Ott, Heinrich. "Rudolf Bultmann's Philosophy of History," in *The Theology of Rudolf Bultmann.* Edited by C. W. Kegley. New York: Harper and Row Publishers, 1966.

Ogden, Schubert. *Christ without Myth.* New York: Harper and Brothers Publishers, 1961.

—. "Rudolf Bultmann for Contemporary Theology." in *The Theology of Rudolf Bultmann.* Charles W. Kegldy, ed. New York:: Harper and Row Publishers, 1966.

—. "The Significance of Bultmann for Contemporary Theology," in *The Theology of Rudolf Bultmann.* Edited by Charles Kegley. New York: Harper and Row Publishers, 1966.

Perrin, Norman. *The Promise of Bultmann.* Philadelphia: J. B. Lippincott Co., 1969.

Phillips, John A. *Christ for Us in the Theology of Dietrich Bonhoeffer.* New York: Harper and Row Publishers, 1967.

Pinnock, Clark. *Tracking the Maze.* San Francisco: Harper and Row Publishers, 1990.

Roark, Dallas M. *Dietrich Bonhoeffer.* Waco: Word Books, 1972.

Roberts, Robert C. *Rudolf Bultmann's Theology: A Critical Interpretation.* New York: Harper and Row Publishers, 1976.

Robinson, James M. "The German Discussion," in *The later Heidegger and Theology.* Vol. I: *New Frontiers in Theology.* Edited by James M. Robinson and John B. Cobb. New York: Harper and Row Publishers, 1962.

—. "Hermeneutics since Barth," in *New Frontiers in Theology.* Edited by James M. Robinson and John B. Cobb, Jr. New York: Harper and Row Publishers, 1964.

—. *A Quest of the Historical Jesus.* London: SCM Press, 1963.

Rott, Wilhelm. "Something Always Occurred to Him," in *I Knew Dietrich Bonhoeffer.* Edited by Wolf-Dieter Zimmermann and Ronald Gregor Smith. New York: Harper and Row, 1966.

Schmithals, Walter. *An Introduction to the Theology of Rudolf Bultmann.* Minneapolis: Augsburg Publishing House, 1968.

Smart, James D. *The Divided Mind of Modern Theology.* Philadelphia: Westminster Press, 1967.

Smith, David. *A Handbook of Contemporary Theology.* Grand Rapids: Baker Book House, 1998.

Sproul, R. C., John Gerstner, and Arthur Lindsley. *Classical Apologetics.* Grand Rapids: Zondervan Publishing Co., 1984.

Stumpf, Samuel Enoch. *Socrates to Sartre.* New York: McGraw-Hill, Inc. 1993.

Thiselton, Anthony C. "New Testament Interpretation in Historical Perspective," in *Hearing the New Testament*. Edited by Joel B. Green. Grand Rapids: Willia B. Eerdmans Publishing Co., 1995.

Toon, Peter. *The End of the Liberal Era*. Wheaton, IL: Crossway Books, 1995.

Wendel, E.G. *Studien zur Homiletik Dietrich Bonhoeffers*. J.C.B. Mohr, 1985.

Woelfel, James W. *Bonhoeffer's Theology*. Nashville: Abingdon Press, 1970.

Wüstenberg, Ralf K. *A Theology of Life*. Grand Rapids: Eerdmans Publishing Company, 1998.

Periodicals

Ballard, Paul. "Worship in a Secular World: Bonhoeffer's Secret Discipline," *Princeton Seminary Bulletin* 68 (Autumn 1975): 28.

Bultmann, Rudolf. "Ist Voraussetzunglose Exegese möglich?" *Theologische Zeitschrift*. 13 (1957): 409-17.

Dinkler, Erick. "Existentialist Interpretation of the New Testament," *The Journal of Religion*. XXXII, No. 2 (April 1952): 90-99.

Jeske, Richard L. "Rudolf Bultmann: 1884-1976." *Dialog*. 17 (Winter 1978): 22-25.

Fennell, William O. "Dietrich Bonhoeffer: The Man of Faith in a World Come of Age," *Canadian Journal of Theology*. 4 (July 1962): 172-80.

Ladd, George E. "What Does Bultmann Understand by the Acts of God?" *Journal of the Evangelical Theological Society*. 5 (Summer 1962): 91-94.

Martin, Marty. Review of *Dietrich Bonhoeffer* by Eberhard Bethge. *Commonweal*. 93 (October 2, 1970): 27-28.

Ott, Heinrich. "Theology and Understanding." *Union Seminary Review* No. 3 (March 1966): 279-89.

Palmer, Russell W. "Demythologization and Non-Religious Interpretation: A Comparison of Bultmann and Bonhoeffer," *The Iliff Review* 31 (Spring 1974): 3-15.

INDEX

Advent, 79, 80, 81, 84, 93, 94, 112, 202
Africa, 3, 189
Amillennialist, 157
Angels, 10, 28, 32, 35, 102, 197
Aristotle, 41
Ascension, 178
Augustine, 56, 64

Barmen Declaration, 68
Barth, Karl, 1, 7, 15, 19, 36, 43, 49-50, 51, 59-60, 68, 108, 122, 125, 132, 132, 136, 147, 152, 155, 186, 205, 221
Baptism, 40, 130, 144, 149, 176, 177, 203
Beatitude, 92, 93, 157, 158, 160, 161
Bell, G.H.A., 125
Berlin 2, 6, 58, 84, 125, 127, 144, 155, 166, 188, 196, 205
Bethge, Eberhard, 1, 2, 3, 4, 7, 10, 13, 14, 16, 20-21, 22, 121, 122, 124, 126-132, 143, 144, 145, 147, 148, 150, 152, 153, 154, 155, 165-167, 172, 182-193, 204, 205, 207, 209, 213, 214, 217, 219, 222
Body of Christ, 24, 148, 149, 177, 178, 179, 180, 208

Carson, D.A., 27, 219
Church, 5, 6, 7, 14, 15, 16, 21, 22, 24, 27, 34, 61, 62, 67, 68, 73, 77, 84, 86, 87, 101, 103, 104, 112, 113, 121, 124, 125, 127, 134, 140, 141, 142, 145, 147, 148, 149, 150, 152, 153, 154, 155, 156, 157, 158, 159, 160, 163, 164, 167, 171, 172, 173, 174, 175, 176, 178, 179, 180, 181, 182, 184, 185, 188, 189, 190, 191, 192, 193, 194, 196, 197, 202, 205, 207, 208, 209, 210, 212, 214
Christ the Center, 16, 24, 165, 166, 217
Christmas, 81
Christocentric, 17, 146, 167, 172
Confessing Church, 68, 73, 124, 154, 155, 159, 167, 185, 194, 196
Conn, Harvie, 2, 4, 8, 11, 15, 28, 29, 30, 35, 37, 40, 52, 63, 73, 81, 85, 106, 107, 114, 115, 117, 137, 146, 147, 148, 151, 160, 176, 178, 179, 187, 208, 212, 220
Coventry Cathedral, 14
Cullmann, Oscar, 35

Demythologization, 5, 6, 8, 10, 13, 18, 20, 29, 31, 35-36, 38, 40-41, 43, 44, 47, 61, 100, 102, 104, 117, 118, 197, 199, 200, 202, 220, 222
Dilthey, Wilhelm, 11, 41-42, 45, 55
Discipleship, 2, 17, 23, 75, 82, 124, 126, 127, 143, 144, 147, 148, 149, 150, 151, 152, 153, 154, 156, 157, 158, 159, 160, 161, 162, 163, 164, 169, 172, 175, 176, 177, 178, 179, 180, 185, 193, 194, 196, 204, 206, 211, 214, 217
Dumas, Andre, 5, 14, 15, 16, 19, 219

Easter, 21, 56, 59, 99, 108, 109, 182, 189
Ebeling, Gerhard, 2, 4, 20
Ecology, 119
Enlightenment, 33, 41, 190
Eschatology, 11, 12, 44, 51, 63, 115, 135, 200, 218
Exegesis, 2, 9, 12, 16, 17, 18, 19, 23, 24, 25, 27, 30, 33, 36, 37, 38, 40, 43, 47, 48, 63, 64, 72, 117, 121, 126, 127, 128, 131, 132, 133, 147, 155, 156, 164, 167, 168, 169, 170, 171, 188, 199, 200, 204, 205, 207, 210, 213, 218
Existence, 5, 10, 11, 13, 26, 29, 31, 35, 36, 37, 38, 41, 43, 44, 45, 46, 51, 52, 53, 54, 55, 56, 57, 58, 60, 61, 63, 64, 65, 66, 70, 72, 73, 76, 77, 79, 94, 95, 99, 101, 102, 104, 105, 106, 111, 112, 116, 117, 119, 120, 132, 148, 160, 178, 187, 200, 211
Existentielle, 11-12, 27, 35, 48, 64, 117-118, 198

Faith, 3, 15, 17, 19, 21, 22, 24, 26, 28, 30, 35, 38, 39, 40, 41, 46, 47, 55, 57, 66, 68, 69, 71, 72, 73, 79, 81, 83, 87, 88, 89, 90, 94, 95, 98, 99, 101, 102, 103, 104, 107, 108, 109, 111, 112, 113, 114, 115, 116, 118, 119, 125, 140, 145, 146, 147, 148, 150, 151, 153, 161, 162, 166, 167, 168, 169, 173, 175, 177, 179, 181, 187, 189, 192, 193, 195, 198, 200, 201
Finkenwalde, 22, 144, 150, 153, 154, 172, 196
Form criticism, 10, 27, 32, 58
Frame, John, 28, 220
Fruit of the Spirit, 39

Geisler, Norman, 28, 219

German Christians, 73, 149, 150, 154, 155, 167, 168, 206
German National Church, 157
Gerstner, John, 28, 221
Gifford Lectures, 2
Godsey, John, 5, 7, 8, 14, 18, 175, 194, 219
Goethe, 73
Gospel, 4, 8, 10, 14, 16, 22, 27, 28, 32, 33, 34, 61, 65, 77, 80, 86, 98, 99, 100, 101, 109, 111, 112, 113, 114, 115, 117, 119, 127, 136, 138, 143, 146, 147, 149, 150, 153, 155, 168, 175, 187, 188, 195, 196, 197, 198, 199, 201, 202, 208, 209, 210, 212, 218
Grace, 17, 40, 74, 79, 89, 90, 91, 93, 94, 95, 96, 97, 98, 111, 113, 114, 115, 124, 136, 140, 149, 150, 151, 153, 154, 155, 162, 163, 164, 172, 178, 205, 208, 209, 214
Greek Gnosticism, 33
Greidanus, Sidney, 28, 220
Grenz, Stanley, 4, 9
Gunkel, Hermann, 51, 58

Harnack, Adolph Von, 1, 6, 33, 51, 58, 59, 62
Hegel, Georg, 5, 11, 15, 19, 37, 56, 135, 212
Heidegger, Martin, 1, 2, 3, 5, 37, 39, 41, 50-57, 58, 61, 63, 71, 102, 117, 122, 199, 200, 220, 221
Heitmüller, Wilhelm, 51, 59, 60, 197, 213
Hermeneutics, 1, 4, 5, 17, 20, 24, 25, 26, 30, 31, 32, 33, 36, 40, 41, 43, 44, 45, 50, 56, 58, 62, 63, 115, 116, 121, 165, 167, 199, 206, 218, 219, 221
Herrmann, Wilhelm, 3, 51, 59, 60
Historical criticism, 108, 166
History of Religions School, 25, 37, 59, 62, 117

Hitler, Adolf, 67, 69, 75, 81, 82, 84, 121, 123, 124, 188, 196, 206
Holl, Karl, 6, 134, 181, 198
Holy Spirit, 23, 45, 75, 111, 138, 155, 164, 168, 169, 170, 174, 178, 205, 206, 207
Homiletics, 1, 4, 17, 20, 22, 24, 210
Hope, 5, 40, 45, 73, 74, 79, 89, 94, 95, 112, 115, 118, 130, 131, 136, 169, 198, 204

Idealism, 25, 27, 33, 46, 51, 62, 68, 198
Incarnation, 5, 19, 23, 36, 99, 146, 151, 157, 178, 205
"Is Exegesis without Presuppositions Possible?" 27, 30, 36, 47, 48, 63, 64, 218
Israel, 83, 133, 156

Jesus, 2, 4, 5, 9, 13, 14, 16, 17, 20, 22, 26, 27, 29, 33, 35, 36, 38, 43, 44, 45, 50, 58, 59, 62, 64, 65, 66, 67, 68, 71, 72, 74, 75, 76, 77, 78, 79, 80, 81, 82, 83, 84, 86, 87, 89, 90, 91, 92, 96, 99, 101, 102, 104, 105, 106, 107, 108, 111, 113, 114, 115, 116, 117, 125, 127, 128, 131, 132, 136, 137, 139, 142, 144, 145, 146, 147, 149, 151, 152, 153, 156, 157, 158, 159, 160, 161, 162, 163, 164, 165, 170, 172, 173, 175, 176, 177, 178, 179, 181, 187, 189, 190, 192, 194, 195, 197, 199, 200, 201, 202, 204, 206, 209, 211, 212, 218, 219, 221
Jewish apocalypticism, 26, 33, 59, 116, 197
Joy, 71, 73, 75, 81, 86, 89, 91, 92, 94, 99, 100, 114, 159, 172, 180, 183, 184
Jülicher, Adolf, 51, 59
Justification, 20, 47, 110, 114, 118, 148, 149, 150, 151, 200, 208

Kaiser, 27, 220
Kant, 5, 9, 13, 19, 50, 137, 190, 212
Kerygma, 10, 13, 21, 29, 32, 33, 34, 35, 38, 39, 49, 57, 58, 61, 62, 65, 66, 93, 97, 100, 101, 102, 103, 104, 106, 107, 108, 109, 117, 118, 197, 198, 200, 201, 218, 219
Kierkegaard, Soren, 5, 19
Kingdom of God, 26, 33, 43, 59, 66, 92, 110, 116, 137, 201
Kristallnacht, 79
Koinonia, 24, 208

Ladd, George, 21, 35, 36, 220, 222
Lasserre, Jean, 147, 193
Letters and Papers from Prison, 2, 10, 13, 15, 123, 129-131, 144-145, 180, 183-194, 217
London, 9, 50, 153, 218, 221
Lord's Supper, 15, 40, 78, 107, 139, 177, 191
Love, 22, 44, 45, 46, 57, 59, 61, 69, 78, 79, 80, 82, 84, 89, 90, 97, 98, 99, 103, 104, 112, 113, 115, 119, 120, 127, 130, 141, 158, 160, 161, 162, 175, 179, 182, 205, 208
Luther, Martin, 3, 6, 7, 13, 37, 39, 46, 47, 50, 51, 87, 88, 90, 91, 93, 113, 114, 118, 122, 141, 148, 150, 151, 153, 164, 166, 168, 171, 176, 190, 193, 196, 200, 205, 210, 212, 214
Lutz, Erwin, 153, 154

Marburg, 2, 3, 13, 36-37, 50-51, 59-60, 67, 69, 71, 84, 90, 96, 118, 119, 195, 197, 210, 214, 218
Marle, Rene, 220
Marty, Martin, 16-17, 124, 125, 127, 220, 222
Melanchthon, Philipp, 214
Miller, Ed, 29, 30, 59, 220

Miracles, 5, 10, 36, 46, 48, 73, 80, 88, 96, 98, 99, 100, 102, 104, 109, 113, 114, 146, 197, 199
Myth, 3, 4, 5, 6, 8, 9, 10, 13, 16, 18, 19, 20, 21, 26, 27, 29, 31, 32, 33, 34, 35, 36, 38, 39, 40, 41, 43, 44, 45, 47, 49, 57, 58, 60, 61, 62, 64, 65, 67, 77, 100, 101, 102, 103, 104, 106, 107, 108, 114, 116, 117, 118, 129, 136, 144, 145, 146, 169, 170, 184, 185, 195, 197, 199, 200, 202, 212, 213, 217, 218, 220, 221, 222
Moo, Douglas J., 27, 37, 49, 82, 219, 220
Morris, Leon, 27, 59, 219

National Socialism, 1, 73, 95, 99, 121, 150, 196
Nature, 9, 34, 37, 44, 46, 53, 54, 55, 69, 72, 73, 74, 77, 86, 97, 98, 111, 119, 142
Naturalism, 25, 37, 117
Neo-Kantianism, 9, 13
New Testament, 2, 3, 4, 9, 10, 13, 21, 25, 26, 27, 28, 29, 31, 32, 33, 34, 35, 36, 38, 39, 40, 43, 44, 45, 46, 47, 50, 51, 55, 56, 57, 58, 59, 60, 61, 62, 65, 66, 77, 79, 88, 99, 100, 101, 102, 103, 104, 105, 106, 107, 108, 113, 114, 116, 117, 126, 127, 130, 131, 139, 143, 144, 145, 146, 147, 153, 155, 164, 167, 168, 169, 170, 171, 174, 179, 183, 184, 195, 196, 197, 198, 199, 200, 201, 202, 203, 204, 206, 207, 211, 212, 213, 214, 217, 218, 219, 220, 222
"New Testament and Mythology," 10, 13, 21, 26, 32, 34, 35, 36, 38, 57, 61, 101, 103, 104, 106, 107, 108, 199, 218
New York City, 153, 196, 207, 208
Niebuhr, Reinhold, 125, 126

Niemoeller, Martin, 73

Oden, Thomas, 8, 14, 21, 73, 82, 84, 139, 220
Old Testament, 17, 19, 72, 99, 102, 119, 126, 127, 128, 129, 130, 131, 132, 134, 135, 143, 144, 145, 146, 155, 157, 160, 170, 183, 184, 194, 203, 204, 212, 218, 220

Parousia, George, 35
Patmos, 182
Pentecost, 35, 99
Peter the Apostle, 29, 88, 89, 114, 175, 185, 222
Pinnock, Clark, 29, 221

Rationalism, 33, 167
Reformation, 7, 8, 22, 48, 122, 126, 144, 172, 174, 190, 214
Reformers, 148, 173, 184, 196, 214
Religion, 1, 4, 5, 7, 13, 14, 15, 18, 20, 25, 32, 33, 37, 48, 58, 59, 60, 62, 67, 70, 95, 117, 128, 129, 130, 140, 145, 148, 183, 185, 186, 187, 188, 189, 192, 203, 207, 208, 209, 210, 212, 222
Renaissance, 33
Resurrection, 18, 26, 29, 36, 38, 40, 43, 99, 100, 101, 106, 107, 108, 109, 111, 112, 115, 117, 136, 139, 145, 146, 157, 193, 197, 199, 202
Revelation, 8, 15, 22, 28, 34, 38, 45, 64, 65, 68, 73, 84, 85, 100, 103, 104, 113, 119, 125, 145, 169, 175, 183, 189, 209, 212, 213, 218
Romanticism, 33
Russia, 84, 86

Sacraments, 15, 40, 176, 177
Sanctification, 107, 111, 148, 177, 180, 202

Schlatter, Adolph, , 2, 6, 143, 144, 168, 183, 204
Schleiermacher, Friedrich, 7, 41, 45
Second Coming, 99, 102
Seeberg, Reinhold, 1, 6, 7, 213
Sermon on the Mount, 146, 152, 153, 154, 155, 156, 158, 160, 163, 166, 204, 205, 206
Society of Evangelical Theology, 38
Sola fides, 3, 6, 205, 212
Spirit, 5, 23, 37, 38, 39, 42, 43, 45, 62, 65, 67, 68, 69, 71, 75, 76, 77, 80, 82, 83, 86, 87, 89, 91, 92, 93, 94, 95, 98, 99, 111, 112, 115, 117, 138, 139, 143, 144, 148, 149, 150, 153, 155, 164, 168, 169, 170, 174, 176, 178, 180, 189, 191, 202, 205, 206, 207, 208
Sproul, R.C., 28, 221

Tegel, 144, 182, 185
Tertullian, 56
The Cost of Discipleship, 17, 23, 127, 143, 144, 147, 148, 149, 150, 151, 152, 153, 156, 157, 158, 159, 160, 161, 162, 163, 164, 172, 175, 176, 177, 178, 179, 180, 185, 193, 194, 196, 204, 206, 211, 217

"The Problem of a Theological Exegesis of the New Testament," 25, 36, 199
"The Problem of Hermeneutics," 26, 30, 31, 36, 40, 43, 50, 199, 218
Theodicy, 141, 204
Tillich, Paul, 122, 190
Troelsch, Ernst, 2
Tübingen 2, 37, 60, 126, 143, 155, 205, 219

Verbal-plenary inspiration, 19
Virgin Birth, 36, 39, 101, 102, 104, 167, 199
Vorverständnis, 11-12, 30, 45, 116

Wedemeyer, Maria von 182
Weiss, Johannes, 43, 51, 59
Weltanschauung, 10, 32, 71, 81, 104, 117
Woelfel, James, 4, 5, 6, 20, 128, 144, 152, 166, 167, 181, 182, 203, 206, 222
World War I, 3, 7
Word War II, 1, 13-20, 69, 76, 79, 81, 82, 84, 88, 89, 90, 91, 93, 94, 95, 114, 118, 129, 196, 201